Teaching English Worldwide

Paul Lindsay

A Practical Guide to Teaching English

Acquisitions Editor: **Aaron Berman**
Content Editor: **Jean Zukowski Faust**
Production Editor: **Jamie Ann Cross**
Cover Art: **Bruce Marion Design**
Interior Art: **Bruce Marion Design**
Interior Design: **Martie Sautter**

© 2000 Alta Book Center Publishers

Alta Book Center Publishers
14 Adrian Court
Burlingame, California 94010 USA
Phone: 800 ALTA/ESL • 650.692.1285—*Int'l*
Fax: 800 ALTA/FAX • 650.692.4654—*Int'l*
Email: info@altaesl.com • Website: www.altaesl.com

ISBN-13: 978-1-882483-77-8
ISBN-10: 1-882483-77-4
Library of Congress Number: 00-100923

To Diana, sine qua non.

CONTENTS

PREFACE

SO YOU WANT TO TEACH ENGLISH? You've made a good choice! Teaching English as a second or foreign language has been a growing profession for more than forty years and shows no sign of declining. More non-English-speaking countries than ever need teachers to meet the enormous demand for courses in English.

Teaching English Worldwide was designed to get you started in the field. It is intended to give you a general picture of the field of teaching English as a second or foreign language and provide the practical knowledge, ideas, and activities you need for teaching all aspects of the English language. It introduces you to the *teaching* of English to speakers of other languages and to the *learning needs* of the students. The information in *Teaching English Worldwide* can be applied "worldwide," just as the title indicates; its variety of techniques and procedures work well in classrooms across the world. Wherever your teaching takes you, this resource provides the basic "musts" to get you started.

Teaching English Worldwide is designed to help you if:

- ◆ You are thinking about teaching English but haven't had any training.
- ◆ You are planning to take a pre-service training course in TESOL (TEFL/TESL).
- ◆ You have just started work in an English language school.

If you are just beginning to teach, I recommend you read this book from cover to cover. Once you've started teaching, you may review sections of the book that you need to give you extra help. However you choose to use this practical guide, I hope it proves to be an invaluable companion in your teaching days.

A NOTE FROM THE AUTHOR

THIS BOOK IS ABOUT TEACHING THE ENGLISH LANGUAGE. You might reasonably expect to find a method or one approach underpinning all the ideas and techniques that I recommend. I wish there were some simple package with all the solutions to learning a language; it would certainly make life easier for the language teacher and the students.

I have tried many methods and approaches as a teacher and as a teacher trainer but I haven't found the all-purpose method and I don't believe there is one. And in spite of the claims, you can't learn a language subliminally in your sleep or in three and a half weeks with multimedia!

There's been a lot of research into language learning in the past few decades but we still don't fully understand how people learn a second language. What we do know is that we must keep trying to find good ways of teaching and better materials to help the diverse needs of learners as individuals and as members of a learning group. I hope we've discovered that language *teaching* is less important than language *learning*.

I believe that the best language teachers study their learners, analyze their needs, choose suitable materials, and adapt their teaching to the students. We should be less concerned with methods and think more about the content of the language course. Above all, the language teacher is there to serve the learner. The success of the learner should be the aim of teaching and the ultimate test of good teaching.

In the last fifty years, language teaching has seen a number of 'revolutions' in methods and in technology. (There have been a bewildering number of changes to keep up with!) This book has put together what I believe are the most practical techniques—the basic tools for the teacher and the knowledge that you need to prepare yourself for teaching English. When you have mastered the basics, keep an open mind on new ideas about teaching and learning. Try interesting new ways but don't get hooked on one method.

Learning a language is challenging and the learners need our sympathy and our help. Be a flexible and sensitive helper and you'll be a good language teacher. It's a fascinating job with many rewards.

Paul Lindsay

Paul Lindsay

ACKNOWLEDGMENTS

I WISH TO THANK MY COLLEAGUES on the teacher training teams at St Giles Highgate, London and at St Giles, San Francisco for their practical help and their ideas and suggestions. In particular, I acknowledge the help given by John Bevan and Chris Macrae.

The editor, Jean Zukowski-Faust, was invaluable and her keen professional eye was a great help. I would like to thank Jamie Cross at Alta Books for her cheerful and consistent care and attention to the author's needs. Moreover, Jamie contributed many ideas and ways to making the book user-friendly.

A special "thank you" to my publisher, Aaron Berman, for his belief and confidence in the book.

We are grateful to the following for their generous permission to reproduce copyright material:

Extract from *Modern English Teacher,* Volume 13, No. 2, Winter 1985-86. Reprinted by permission of Modern English Teacher (MET). Extract from *Junior Files 2* by Elite Olshtain et al. Copyright 1993 by Alta Book Center Publishers. Extract from *Look Who's Talking!* by Mary Ann Christison and Sharron Bassano. Copyright 1995 by Alta Book Center Publishers. From *The Little Girl and the Wolf,* by James Thurber. Copyright 1940 by James Thurber and renewed 1968 by Helen Thurber and Rosemary A. Thurber. Reprinted by arrangement with Rosemary A. Thurber and the Barbara Hogenson Agency. Extract from *Rebecca,* by Daphne du Maurier (retold by Margaret Tarner). Copyright 1938 by Daphne du Maurier. Reprinted by permission of Curtis Brown Ltd., London, on behalf of the Chichester Partnership. Extract from *1000 Pictures for Teachers to Copy,* by Andrew Wright. Copyright 1984 by Andrew Wright. Reprinted by permission of Addison Wesley Longman. Extract from *Elementary Communication Games* by Jill Hatfield. Copyright 1984 by Jill Hatfield. Reprinted by permission of Addison Wesley Longman. The lyrics of the song, *My Way,* by Paul Anka, Jacques Revaux, and Claude Francois. Copyright 1967 by Societe des Nouvelles Editions Eddie Barclay, Paris, France. Copyright renewed. Copyright

BASIC QUESTIONS

BASIC QUESTIONS

WHAT DO YOU NEED TO DO to become a successful teacher of English? The obvious answer is that you must become aware of the language. Without some conscious knowledge of the structure, form and meaning of the spoken and written language, you cannot begin to understand the special features of English and how it differs from other languages. We need this language awareness so that we can help students with their learning problems.

However, teachers need to know *how* as well as *what* to teach. Before you launch into the sections on language awareness, take a moment to think about how you can become a good teacher. This introduction attempts to answer some basic questions about language teaching and gives you an overview of what makes a good teacher and a good learner.

As a beginning teacher of English, you probably feel overwhelmed with questions. Following are some common, basic questions about language teaching. Reading and understanding them will be the first step in helping you become a good language teacher.

What is the role of the teacher? The traditional role of the teacher has been that of explainer. To fulfill this role, the teacher is expected to know the language, to explain how it works, and explain its meanings. If you accept this view of the teacher, you will take up your position in front of the class as if you were a lecturer at a university, expecting your students to listen and take notes (see diagram A on page 22 and compare with the diagrams B-1, B-2, and B-3 on page 23).

Today the role of the teacher has changed. It has moved from explainer/knower to helper/counselor. We are much more aware of the distinction between teaching and learning. We know we cannot assume that when we are teaching, our students are learning. We can control our input and put a lot of energy and effort into our teaching, but we can never be sure that the students are learning. Indeed, teachers could be doing very little, and their students could be learning a lot. People learn by doing; they often do not learn much from listening to others—no matter how expert the others may be.

Consider two other roles of the language teacher apart from explaining: the role of organizing and the role of enabling.

The organizing role of the teacher

This approach to teaching involves using a variety of techniques and materials that help students to learn actively. For example, solving problems (see *Information gap activities,* Chapter 8, page 149) is part of this approach. The teacher who adopts the organizer approach explains when explanations are needed, but doesn't rely solely on explaining. Essentially, this kind of teaching aims at getting the learners actively involved in using the language. The teacher is in control but seeks opportunities for the learners to practice and develop their language skills.

The counseling/enabling role of the teacher

This is a development of the role of the teacher as organizer, but its aim is to enable the student to become independent of the teacher. Therefore, there is less control and overt organizing. These days, most language schools are equipped with self-access centers where students can use language laboratories, computers, videos, and a wide variety of reading and writing materials (see Chapter 16, *Learning with Self-Access).* The teacher plays a counseling/enabling role in these centers by advising students about the most suitable learning materials available for self-teaching or independent learning. Even the best-equipped student resource centers, however, are not the answer to a realistic use of language skills to communicate with other people. In the classroom, teachers can provide many real and realistic opportunities for communication by using drama and simulation (such as role-play), information gap exercises with students in pairs, and everyday situations (shopping, using the telephone, etc.). Using these techniques helps students become independent of the teacher.

The counseling/enabling role of a teacher is vital to the learning process because students in groups have different needs at different stages of learning. Students also have individual needs and problems with learning. To enable students to learn, teachers must address these various needs. A good teacher constantly reviews his or her results in terms of what is effective for the learner. The techniques and ideas in this book will help you to become the kind of teacher who enables students to learn.

What do we know about how people learn to speak languages?

We know that there is a continuum from natural to deliberate intake of language. On one end is the natural acquisition of language (what children do), and on the other end is the artificial learning of language (what learners in a classroom do). The development in language teaching and learning circles for the past several decades has been towards making classroom language learning as much like natural language acquisition as possible. This goal of language teaching strives to make students competent in all kinds of communication, with ability in all language skills.

What are the basic language skills?

The four major language skills are:
- **listening** with understanding,
- **speaking** and being understood,
- **reading** with understanding,
- **writing** and being understood by the reader.

These four basic skills are not simple. They comprise other sub-skills that are analyzed and described in detail in the chapters on listening, speaking, reading, and writing.

Receptive versus productive skills

The four basic (*macro-*) skills are divided into *receptive* and *productive* skills. The receptive skills, listening and reading, have sometimes been described as *passive;* the productive skills, speaking and writing, are described as *active.* This division is misleading. There is nothing passive about listening unless one is not listening (such as hearing a speech without paying any attention to what is actually being said). Reading also actively engages the mind. If students are simply looking at the words and not trying to understand the text, they are not reading.

Each macro-skill, whether receptive or productive, needs to be broken down into various *micro-* or *sub-skills.* For each skill, students need specific training with different kinds of texts that require different kinds of practice. By highlighting one skill at a time, this book helps you learn how to teach and integrate the basic language skills.

How do I teach and integrate the basic language skills?

Although it is helpful to examine the four basic language skills one at a time, it is important to bear in mind that language skills are not normally used separately. For example, students need practice in listening to the sounds and utterances in English, but in the real world of communication, listening and speaking are interdependent and need to be developed together. Obviously, if you want your students to participate in a conversation or discussion, they cannot respond without listening to one another. Therefore, good lessons contain some practice in all four skills.

This practice (activities and exercises that use all four language skills) is referred to as *integrated skills practice.* You will find that many of the activities suggested in *Teaching English Worldwide* integrate the four language skills, even though their main focus may be on one of them. For example, in Chapter 8, *Teaching Speaking,* the activities require students to integrate what they say with what they hear; in Chapter 9, *Teaching Reading,* the activities involve a discussion of the reading topic, vocabulary review, pronunciation practice, and oral comprehension checks. Furthermore, many of the tasks that follow reading exercises include free or guided writing, and many of the writing tasks involve reading.

What are the different levels of students, and how are they graded?

Students are usually assessed on entry to a school and placed into one of four levels (four is usually the minimum) or into a six-to-nine level grading system. In a small school, there may only be classes at beginning, high-beginning/low-intermediate, intermediate, and advanced levels. In a large language school, classes may be more finely graded to include pre-intermediate, intermediate, and high-intermediate levels. Similarly, the advanced level could be sub-divided. For a general description of these levels and what the student can express and understand at each level, refer to the nine-point scale given in Appendix 1.

Will I be expected to teach any level?

A newly-trained teacher would normally be expected to teach only the lower levels (beginning and low-intermediate). Teaching at beginning levels is easier in the sense that at these levels the needs of the learner are obvious—the learner needs to be able to ask questions or to make statements with simple everyday vocabulary and needs to know how to change statements into the negative. A beginner's motivation tends to be high, and the student quickly perceives whether progress is being made or not. Starting from zero and gaining a little knowledge is greatly rewarding. At the intermediate or advanced levels, however, it is more difficult to see one's development. For this reason, students at higher levels are easily frustrated by a sense of not making progress and the job of reviewing your teaching results can be much more difficult.

What does a student need to learn and to be taught at the different levels?

To answer this question, you should refer to the graded textbooks that are prescribed in most professionally organized language schools. Teachers naturally expect to use a textbook appropriate to the level of the class and to rely on the book to provide suitable, graded language in meaningful contexts for teaching and easy learning. Textbooks are useful guides if they are well designed and suitable for your students. Textbooks, however, cannot provide for all of the needs of each group, nor can they cater to each individual learner. The teacher is the only person who can adapt the learning materials to the real needs of the students. That is one of the language teacher's essential jobs. You should select what is useful from a textbook or other learning material and reject what is not (see Chapter 18, *Using Textbooks*).

It is much more common these days to find textbooks based on language functions. The aim in these textbooks is to enable the learner to express basic communicative purposes. The first units of the course are built around how to do things with language, such as how to greet people, how to introduce oneself, how to ask for directions, and how to express likes and dislikes. The grammar, structures, and vocabulary are limited to what is needed to realize the functions. Teachers who are new to the functional syllabus should not assume that grammar has been swept aside or neglected. Generally, you will be expected to adopt a mixed or eclectic approach and teach grammar or structure as required by the communicative needs of your students. Grammar has been put in its proper place as the means to express meaning and communicative purpose.

Another way of defining what is to be taught is by specifying performance objectives for students at different levels. Many language-teaching centers present their teachers with specific objectives for the students at the different levels. These teaching programs indicate to the teacher what the student should be able to do by the end of a course at their level. The advantage of a list of performance objectives is that it clearly includes the need to teach not only language functions and grammar, but also the need to teach the kind of vocabulary that is required for the specific objectives (see Appendix 2).

Will I need to design a syllabus?

A syllabus is a list of everything that will be included in the course. Although you will probably not be expected to design the syllabus for the level you are teaching, it is important to have some idea of how a syllabus is designed. The traditional approach is based on grammar and a structural analysis of the language. Simple sentence patterns and structures are to be introduced before the complex. For example, the structures *This is a _____, Is this a _____?* and *This isn't a _____* are to be taught before the structure *If I had a _____, I'd be able to _____*. In this traditional approach, new language forms are presented in realistic situations or with visual aids, but the order of teaching them is based on grammatical forms and structures.

A much more common syllabus today is the functional syllabus, as outlined in the previous question (for more information see *Functional approach,* Chapter 21, page 341).

Should I use English all the time or should I translate into the language of the students?

It is highly desirable for teaching and learning to be conducted through the medium of English so that the process of learning and the product (attaining a higher level of competence in English) go hand in hand. If you are teaching English in an English-speaking country, your class will probably be multilingual and multicultural, and you will have to teach in English all the time. Translation will hardly be possible. In such a situation, there is the advantage that English is spoken outside the classroom as well as inside, and therefore the students will be obliged to use English as a means of communication with one another. However, students in a multilingual learning situation who have difficulty understanding may become dependent on the bilingual dictionary. This dependence can be very unsatisfactory. Such bilingual dictionaries are often too small to give a range of meanings or contexts for an accurate translation. Students who depend on dictionaries do not tend to become fluent and are slow to develop their communicative skills. In such cases, you should be aware of the difficulties of the slower student and provide extra help with his or her understanding. This help should not be dependent on words to explain words. Often a simple gesture or a visual aid, such as a drawing, will help. If the new word is important for the context (and it may not be), then you may have to offer controlled use of an adequate bilingual dictionary.

If you are teaching English in a monolingual setting in a country where English is not widely spoken, it is more difficult to teach in English all the time. Your students will tend to use their own language whenever they cannot understand your instructions or your explanations. It is of great importance, especially with beginners and elementary learners, to be very careful in planning all stages of presenting new vocabulary and new grammatical structure so that the situations or contexts in which the new items occur are helpful in conveying the meaning of the items. For example, if you are presenting new vocabulary and new verbs that refer to an office, your students will not need translation if they can see what these words refer to in a photograph of an office.

Teaching English Worldwide provides practical suggestions to help you avoid the need for translation, especially in teaching vocabulary, using contexts, presenting meaning, simplifying classroom language, and giving instructions. As it is crucial to teach English through English from the beginning, new teachers should look at the lesson plan in Appendix 3 for help in creating the first lesson with a class of students who do not know English at all.

Although you should avoid translation, there is no need to go to tortuous lengths to use English 100 percent of the time. If you are able to convey meaning quickly and accurately by means of a translation, then it is common sense to do so. If there is a one-to-one equivalent word in the students' mother language, convey the meaning through the translation and then get back into English as quickly as possible. It is better to translate occasionally and sparingly to help students who would otherwise become discouraged. The bilingual teacher has the great advantage of being able to check understanding through translation when it becomes necessary. You should be assured, however, that you do not have to be bilingual to be a teacher of English to monolingual classes (see Chapter 20, *Teaching Monolingual Classes)*.

What should I always keep in mind when teaching?

Though there are many things to remember when teaching, always keep the following three basic steps first and foremost in your mind:
1. Keep your language short, simple, and direct.
2. Present new language in context through visual or role-play situations (for example: *We're in a restaurant. This is the menu. What do you want to eat?)*.
3. Don't ask questions unless you've taught the students how to answer them (for example, give the names of jobs or professions before you ask, "What's his job?").

What makes a good teacher?

In an effort to define what makes a good teacher, I compiled some answers to this question from both students and teachers. Together, their comments paint a somewhat "picture-perfect" model of a good language teacher.

The students' views

I asked groups of students from Europe, Japan, and South America what they expect of a language teacher. Following are the results of two surveys (taken in 1997 and 1998) of approximately 100 students each. The students were enrolled in language schools in San Francisco, California and London, England.

Students have the following expectations of their teachers:

◆ **Patience.** Students do not want to feel stupid if they don't grasp the meaning immediately. Teachers should be willing to explain the point as many times as necessary.

◆ **Sincerity.** Students want teachers to show genuine interest in their needs. Students expressed a strong dislike of teachers who put on a false show of friendliness.

◆ **Organization.** Students expect teachers to have well-prepared lessons and to have a sense of purpose and direction for the course as a whole.

◆ **Punctuality.** Students expect lessons to start on time even if other members of the class are not punctual.

◆ **Awareness of needs.** Students expect teachers to be aware of their difficulties and problems. They want teachers to deal with questions as they arise rather than keeping rigidly to the lesson plan. They also want teachers to monitor their progress or lack of progress and to give equal attention to all the individuals in a class.

◆ **Flexibility and imagination.** Students do not want a book-bound teacher. They want teachers to use textbooks with discrimination and to bring other materials to supplement or replace unsuitable or uninteresting textbooks.

◆ **Variety and balance.** Students want teachers who provide a varied "language diet" of grammar, vocabulary, listening, and speaking practice. They don't want an overload of fun and games, or the reverse (too much grammar and sourcebook material).

◆ **Approachability.** Students want teachers who can be like counselors—someone they feel at ease with when they need to discuss their learning problems.

◆ **Professionalism.** Students expect teachers to be professionals who are committed to their progress and satisfaction. Teachers who are too easy-going or lacking in purpose are not usually respected.

◆ **Control.** Students expect teachers to have control of a lesson through planning and staging. Teachers must be able to direct the learning.

◆ **Knowledge.** Students expect teachers to have knowledge of the language, especially a competent grasp of the grammar. Teachers should be able to explain or demonstrate concepts clearly and concisely.

◆ **Stimulation.** Students want teachers to be stimulating, motivating, and able to create a cooperative classroom atmosphere. Students expressed a strong desire for teachers who show genuine interest in the lessons and in them.

◆ **Security.** Underlying many of these expectations, there is a deep need for security. Students generally need and want a teacher they can rely on: a person who takes responsibility, can direct their learning, and is committed to helping them with their learning problems.

The teachers' views

I also asked experienced teachers what defines a good language teacher. Following is a compilation of their views; you will notice that many of these characteristics overlap with what the students expressed.

- **Interest.** A good teacher is truly interested in language learning and enjoys the challenges that language learning poses.
- **Cultural awareness.** A good teacher is aware of the cultures of his or her students and avoids stereotyping them.
- **Knowledge.** A good teacher has knowledge of the language and of language learning and is able to use this knowledge.
- **Reflection.** A good teacher is a person who reflects on his or her performance, can be self-critical, and seeks to develop and try new ways of teaching.
- **Patience.** A good teacher is patient and open with students. The teacher is a person who is sensitive when correcting and never causes students to lose their self-esteem.
- **Encouragement and praise.** A good teacher monitors and appraises the students so that the learner is made aware of progress or lack of it, giving praise when it is earned and encouragement when it is needed.
- **Clarity.** A good teacher is clear in conveying meaning and concepts—he or she presents language that is graded to help learning.
- **Control.** A good teacher doesn't dominate the lesson nor allow students to take over without any direction.
- **Encourage independence.** A good teacher has the overall aim of helping the students to become independent. He or she encourages students to make full use of facilities and opportunities to learn outside of the classroom.
- **Open mind.** A good teacher should be open to new ideas and new ways of learning and teaching; he or she should be able and willing to learn from colleagues.

What makes a good learner?

Teachers should play an active role in developing good learners. This role, referred to as learner training, involves raising students' awareness of their learning strategies and questioning whether they are effective. Teachers need to find out how students use their spare time and study time outside of class. Good learners don't depend on the lessons as their sole source of exposure to the language, especially if they are studying English in their own countries.

A common question is "Should teachers teach learning as well as teach the language?" The humanistic answer is that teachers aren't just teaching a language; they're teaching people. And people (students) need help with learning and how to learn. The following tips address learner training and help answer the question, "What makes a good learner?"

- ◆ **Good study skills.** The learner must practice study skills. The section on *Using a dictionary* (Chapter 4, page 54) explains how to train students to be effective users of a dictionary. Notebooks on vocabulary and grammar are helpful as long as the learner keeps it organized (see *Remembering words,* Chapter 4, page 51).

- ◆ **Self-access centers.** The learner must be familiar with and use self-access centers. Teachers cannot be oblivious to the advantages offered by new electronic learning aids, especially if the teacher is to accept the responsibility of learner training. Students depend on teachers to show them how to use the latest technology in language learning. Furthermore, teachers need to have positive attitudes towards electronic learning aids. In turn, students, will welcome the opportunity to use such aids (see Chapter 16, *Teaching with Self-Access*).

- ◆ **Reflection.** The learner needs to reflect on the process of learning. You can have interesting and useful discussions with students about learning processes and approaches to studying the language. These discussions encourage learners to think about and refine their language learning. Following is a list of useful questions to ask:
  1. What kind of learner are you?
  2. Are you dependent on your eyes (do you need to see words written on the board)?
  3. Do you believe your ears? That is, can you accept the new sounds you are hearing?
  4. What helps you the most to remember things?

5. What are your priorities in learning a language? Do they match up with the aims and objectives of this course?

6. Do you agree with and/or like the methods and materials used in the lessons? If you disagree and/or don't like them, why?

Such questions raise important aspects of both teaching and learning and, if discussed in a positive atmosphere, help students change or modify their learning strategies. It is difficult to discuss these matters with beginners, unless you speak their language. It is wise to wait until you have gained the confidence and trust of the students before bringing up questions about your teaching methods and materials.

◆ **Awareness of teaching ways.** The learner should know why teachers teach in certain ways. Even if a student doesn't agree with your methods, he or she should become aware that you have reasons for using such different teaching strategies. Understanding how you organize material for learning can be very helpful to a learner who is trying to develop his or her own language skills. Reflect on your own teaching style and raise awareness of your teaching strategies by asking your students some questions:

1. Why did I start the lesson with a task or a problem to be solved? Why didn't I start with the rules, for example, about using the past tense ending?

2. Do you learn more by doing and using the language or by listening to the explanations?

3. I often encourage you to speak as well as you can and I seem to ignore your mistakes. What reasons do I have? Would you prefer me to correct you more often? Do I seem to be neglecting grammar and the accurate use of language?

These questions raise important issues about teaching methods and strategies and can be helpful to students who come from societies and cultures where teachers use different methods. Such students suffer from educational culture shock and may be afraid to ask questions (in some cultures, a teacher is a person who must not be questioned!).

Remember that good learners go hand in hand with good teachers. As a teacher, you need to integrate learner training into your lessons, though it need not be raised consciously or obviously. The training that students get through your lessons will equip them to learn more efficiently on their own.

Looking ahead   The information in this introduction is intended to give you signposts, not detailed maps on your journey to becoming a good English language teacher. The following chapters will provide you with more detailed help and advice. The chapters also include tasks for you to try so that you can check your understanding and your language awareness.

Let's begin the journey to *Teaching English Worldwide!*

Further reading   Campbell, C. and Kryszewska, H. *Learner-Based Teaching.* Oxford University Press, 1992.

Krashen, S. *Second Language Acquisition and Second Language Learning.* Prentice Hall, 1988.

Nunan, D. and Clarice, L. *The Self-Directed Teacher: Managing the Learning Process.* Cambridge University Press, 1996.

MANAGING YOUR CLASSROOM

MANAGING YOUR CLASSROOM

A N EFFECTIVE TEACHER HAS TO BE A GOOD CLASSROOM MANAGER and organizer. Time and resources are always limited, and teachers need to create lessons in an economical and efficient way. To make the most out of your classroom time, concentrate on the basic components of a lesson:

◆ the learning environment (the classroom),
◆ giving instructions,
◆ organizing the learning relationships and activities.

Do not forget that classroom management involves dealing sensitively and sympathetically with people. A class of students is a group of individuals who cannot simply be instructed and organized in a mechanical manner. A good manager tries to ensure that the lesson starts in a friendly atmosphere (warmed-up!) and proceeds smoothly and purposefully. Attention to the needs and feelings of the individual students is a powerful part of good classroom management. If you're new to the class and students don't know one another, then start with getting to know the students' names and introduce yourself to the students. Knowing your students' names, their background, and some of their interests is always an important first step.

Creating a learning environment

Think about the furniture and the seating arrangement in your classroom. Before starting a lesson, decide whether the chairs, tables, or desks (including the teacher's desk) are suitably arranged for the purpose and activities of the lesson. Tables can get in the way and hinder easy interaction and communication between students and may prevent you from moving around to monitor pairwork or to help individual students. A teacher who usually sits or stands behind a table puts a barrier between himself or herself and the students. Move around the classroom; go and sit with your students; give instructions, and then get out of the normal teaching position (at the board in front of the class) and be unobtrusive.

If the seats are in a semi-circle, the arrangement is much better and more suitable for communication between students and teacher than in rows. Desks or tables in rows hinder communication and are most unsuitable for adults, especially for language learning. Such traditional classroom seating is not conducive to good learning or teaching with any age group, though it may be unavoidable in large classes for children or young learners.

Giving instructions

Clear and concise instructions are crucial to managing your class. Instructions need to be given to the whole class before starting any activity. Tell the students what they are going to do, how the activity is to be organized, and why they are going to do it (unless the purpose is obvious). Especially with games, the language learning aim may not be clear or obvious. When students realize that the game or task has a learning purpose, their motivation to do it increases. If the students are asked to do a problem-solving exercise that is completely new to them, try giving a short demonstration of how to do it.

Remember that learners are dealing with a dual problem: understanding what you say and understanding what they are supposed to do. Keep your language simple and easy to understand. Of course, the instructions must be in a language adapted to the level of the students. Show rather than tell. Use gestures or quick sketches rather than words whenever possible. You can train your students to recognize certain gestures or signals for common concepts (for example: pointing behind you can indicate that the students should use the past tense, pointing down can indicate use of the present, and pointing forward can indicate use of the future).

Following are tips on how to keep your instructions simple, clear, and direct:

◆ **Don't be too formal.** Try to avoid formal use that may cause confusion. Imperative forms work well because they utilize the base or root form of the verb and are more readily understood. For example:

"Ask the student next to you."

"Tell her your name or your job."

"Listen carefully."

"Write this sentence down."

"Please repeat what I said."

◆ **Mind your language!** Apart from the evident need to restrict your vocabulary, avoid using idioms and phrasal verbs that are unknown to your students and hard to guess. "Do this exercise" is simpler than "Tackle this exercise." However, don't go to great lengths to avoid natural ways of expressing yourself. It's better for beginners to get used to hearing and saying "I can't" or "it's" than to listen to the teacher saying "I cannot" or "it is." As another example, if you want your students to look up a word in a dictionary, you don't have to avoid saying "look the word up" because "find the word" is less idiomatic.

◆ **Keep it short.** If you need to give lengthy detailed instructions, break them down into short steps or stages. Let the students do the exercise one step at a time. Use situations and examples that are known and easy to relate to. If you want the students to practice conditional forms (If you were somebody, what would you do?), give examples that are easy to imagine and within their cultural knowledge and experience.

Task 1: Giving instructions

A. Write down simple ways of asking the following questions to students. If possible, compare your re-phrased questions with someone else's (preferably a native-speaker).

1. What do you think this object is called?
2. If your friend suggested eating at a restaurant and you agreed, what would you reply?
3. Let's imagine that you have purchased a damaged article from a store and have to return it. What would you say at the store?
4. I wonder if you can remember the destination of the man in the story.
5. Could you please write a similar dialogue in pairs, substituting your own ideas wherever possible?

B. For each group of instructions on the next page, number the sentences in order of how easy they are to understand. Put the easiest sentences first.

1. __ a. Could you say that again, please?
   __ b. Say the same thing as Mario has just said.
   __ c. Repeat, please.
   __ d. Again.

2. __ a. Practice with a partner.
   __ b. Together.
   __ c. You two, you two . . .
   __ d. Practice with the person sitting beside you.

3. __ a. During the dialogue, listen up for the answers to these questions.
   __ b. While you are listening, find the answers to these questions.
   __ c. Listen and answer the questions.
   __ d. Answer the questions as you listen.

Organizing learning relationships and activities

The role of the teacher as manager changes according to the teaching aim of each phase of the lesson and to the learners' activities. Variety and flexibility are the key ingredients—no one fixed pattern of teaching suits all aims or all learning activities. The traditional pattern in which the teacher tries to teach all the students the same thing at the same time is called *lockstep*, as if all the students were marching together. Lockstep is used, for example, when the teacher is presenting new sounds and wants everyone in the class to practice the sound confidently in a chorus. The teacher thus announces, "Okay, let's say it together." This interaction style is represented in the diagram A1 (teacher ➡ students) and its reverse pattern, A2 (students ➡ teacher).

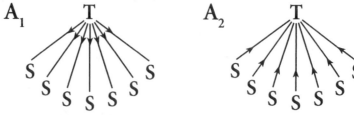

Arranging students into pairs and/or small groups maximizes student participation (see diagrams B1, B2, and B3). Students in pairs get much more listening time, speaking time, and active practice than when working with the whole class. However, the teacher must pay careful attention to the "pairing up" of students. A confident, talkative student is likely to take over if his or her partner is reserved and quiet. Pairs must not be fixed for too long; a teacher with good management skills makes the needed changes to increase the amount of time each student is actively using the language. For some activities, groups of three or four work well. Group tasks are often more stimulating than dealing with problems in pairs. Putting students into groups fosters creative work and is potentially very helpful to weak students. Like pairs, make sure that the more confident students in a group don't take over and dominate the quieter students. A wise manager will try to ensure that there is one strong student to act as a kind of leader in each group. It may not be democratic, but it's effective to encourage the quick learner (the strong one) to become a group organizer and, in fact, a teacher in his or her group.

B_1

$$S \longleftrightarrow S \quad S \longleftrightarrow S$$
$$S \longleftrightarrow S \quad S \longleftrightarrow S$$

B_2

B_3

Putting students into pairs or small groups has become a very common feature of English language teaching; it is almost a "knee-jerk" reaction for the trained teacher. However, like all good things, it can be overdone. In considering pair and small groupwork, we must also realize the possible disadvantages. As was pointed out earlier, no fixed pattern of classroom teaching suits all learning activities. The role of the teacher in managing pairwork and small group activities is to adapt and change the arrangements according to the teaching aims or activities. Three classroom activities that the teacher almost always has to orchestrate are:

- presenting a new listening comprehension task on tape,
- practicing a structure presented in context,
- free speaking in role-play situations.

Management of the above activities can be guided by the following questions:

- Are any of these activities appropriate for the teacher to present to the whole class?
- For which of these activities should students work in pairs?
- For which of these activities should students work in groups?
- At what phase of a lesson is pairwork or groupwork most useful and appropriate?

You need to find out whether your students gain from working in pairs or groups. Some students are slow learners or have special difficulties; others are quick and find learning comparatively easy. Do both types of learners benefit from being in pairs? In small groups? It would seem sensible to put a slow learner with a quick learner, but is it fair to the latter? Should students work together in the same pairs or groups throughout the lesson, or should the teacher make students change partners and groups for each activity? The advantage of frequent change is that it brings variety and fresh stimulus. It may also answer the question of whether it is beneficial to pair slow learners with quick learners.

Task 2:
Organizing
learning
relationships

Think about the advantages and disadvantages of arranging learners into pairs and small groups. With these in mind, read the following learning activities. Write down the seating arrangement or interaction pattern that you think would work best for each activity. Use the diagrams on page 23.

1.   Interview practice (graduate school, jobs) _____

2. Role-play (policeman/driver, doctor/patients, bank manager/
    clients asking for loans) _____

3. Information gap activities (see Chapter 8, page 149) _____

4. Dialogue practice (see Chapter 3, page 32) _____

5. Question and answer games (see Twenty questions and its
    variations, Chapter 14, pages 237–238) _____

Student interaction

There are two kinds of student interaction: cooperation and competition. Both are desirable, but should be used for different kinds of learning activities. Working together in pairs usually fosters cooperation and helps students to get to know the others in the class. It's easier to get useful pair cooperation in a multilingual class than in a monolingual group where there is a strong tendency for the students to translate and cooperate by using their native language. The teacher has to anticipate this native language-interpreting and translating and "prohibit" it in his or her instructions, prior to pairing up the students (see Chapter 20, Teaching Monolingual Classes).

There is certainly a place for competition within cooperative pair or groupwork. For example, after the initial problem-solving or information gap task has been done, you can act as quiz-master and award points for the best results achieved by the pairs or groups.

Review questions

1. Name three things you should focus on to be a good classroom manager.

2. How can you keep instructions to students as simple as possible?

3. What is the teaching technique known as *lockstep?* When is it appropriate to use this technique?

4. What is the main advantage of putting students into pairs or small groups? For what kind of learning activities is pairwork more suitable?

5. Think of some activities that foster cooperation and/or competition. How have these two types of interaction affected your classroom learning?

Further reading

Greenwood, J. *Classroom Dynamics.* Oxford University Press, 1992.

Underwood, M. *Effective Class Management.* Addison Wesley Longman, 1987.

PRESENTING MEANING AND CONTEXT

Meaning

Context

Presenting meaning through drama and dialogue

Presenting meaning through songs

Concept checking

      - Checking lexical concepts

      - Checking structural concepts

      - Checking functional concepts

Review questions

Further reading

PRESENTING MEANING AND CONTEXT

THE FIRST NECESSITY IN TEACHING A LANGUAGE is to make sure that students understand new language (vocabulary or structures learners are not likely to understand or be able to use). When presenting new language, you need to employ a variety of techniques and aids to understanding. These techniques and aids should make the meaning and context of the new language clear and easy to understand.

Meaning

When teaching the meaning of new words or new uses of known vocabulary, keep in mind the following points:

- Show rather than tell—examples are better than definitions.
- Use as few words as possible.
- Try to use known words to introduce unknown words.
- Elicit meaning from the students whenever you can. Even if they don't get it quite right, give the students a chance to show what they know.
- Be prepared to demonstrate meaning in more than one way (for example, if mime and gesture don't work, use drawing or more examples).
- Don't hammer the point if students still don't understand. Change the activity, and come back to the point later.

There are many ways to teach meaning. Some of the following suggestions may seem obvious, but it's useful to be simple and clear when presenting meaning. If these techniques are not a clear and natural means for you to present meaning, take the time to develop them with your students.

- **Use mime and gesture.** Use gestures like saluting, waving, or motioning (such as to "stop"). Check that the gesture means the same in the various cultures of your students.
- **Use facial expressions.** Use your own face to show emotions like *happy, sad,* and *surprised.*

♦ **Draw.** Stick figures are easy to draw and often the quickest way to get across meaning (see Using the board, Chapter 12, page 215).

♦ **Use pictures or photographs.** When using visual aids, make sure the graphics are large enough to be seen by everyone in the class. They must also be clear and unambiguous.

♦ **Use objects (realia).** Bring in objects from outside the classroom. Household utensils, clothing, fruit and vegetables, and toys are just a few of the items you may have around your house that can be of great help in communicating meaning.

♦ **Use things in the classroom.** Look around! The word you are trying to define might be right there—from a lamp to a map.

♦ **Involve yourself and your students.** Parts of the body, clothes, shades of color, and adjectives (tall, short) can often be defined by pointing them out on ourselves!

♦ **Mimic sounds.** We aren't all naturals at imitating sounds, but we can certainly create a few if need be (bark like a dog, whistle, chime like a clock). There are plenty of sound recordings (available at music stores). One can also use instruments, etc. to make the needed sounds.

♦ **Use a text.** A text that is both short and comprehensible encourages students to guess the meanings of new words. Note that context must be understood before guessing is possible.

♦ **Translate.** Use this option sparingly and with care! In monolingual classes, if you can translate accurately, do so quickly and get back into English. If all else fails, translation is an economical way of conveying meaning.

Task I: Teaching meaning

Below is a list of words and phrases. How would you teach each one? Using the list above, decide which technique would be most suitable for getting the meaning of each item across to a group of students.

to stroll	a can opener	miserable
weary	a truck	gaze
a duck	a disaster	to creep
in front of	elbow	a mountain

Context   The meaning of a word or a lexical item is highly dependent on context, or the situation in which the language item occurs. New language can usually be understood in one of the following contexts:

- ◆ the context of a *situation* which can be real or simulated
- ◆ the context of different types or examples of texts which can be real or imagined, such as narratives, dialogue (made-up or authentic), texts on audio tape, texts on video, or texts in books
- ◆ the context taken from newspapers, magazines, or other authentic materials

A question often asked is whether new language should be presented to students in authentic contexts or in specially written texts and dialogues. Real contexts and authentic language are preferable only if the students can cope with the complexities and subtleties of the text. It is wise to start with easier and more manageable contexts like specially written and graded texts (these can still be realistic and lifelike). As students advance, they can be introduced to authentic texts.

Choosing a suitable context is the key to helping students learn and remember new material. The following questions should be considered when deciding on the context:

- ◆ Is the context likely to be *interesting* to the students?
- ◆ Is the topic *relevant* to their interests and purposes?
- ◆ Is the topic full of abstract concepts and vocabulary, or is it specific and concrete in its references? For example, a discussion on the environment and pollution could be general and universal, or it could be specific (such as the impact of the automobile in particular cities or rural areas). Most people, and therefore most students, can relate to and understand the specific more easily than the general and abstract.
- ◆ Is the context dramatic? Is it funny or sad? If it's dramatic and emotional, it's more likely to be remembered.
- ◆ Does the language of the context help the learner to understand the new language? If the text uses simple structures and known vocabulary, it eases the problem of guessing the meaning of new language.
- ◆ Is the context going to help the teaching and learning of a particular structure, communicative function, a lexical set, or

some other goal in the course? For example, if the aim is to demonstrate that in scientific texts passive forms are often used, then the context must have plenty of examples that the students can easily grasp. Such texts, if authentic, may contain too wide a range of passive structures, which results in confusing rather than helping the learners.

Task 2: Choosing contexts

Think of suitable contexts, including situations, that would help you present the following functions and structures:

1. Warning someone not to do something, using conditional forms like *If I were you … I wouldn't do that …*
2. Giving advice, using *Why don't you … ?* and *You should …*
3. Inviting other people to go out and eat or drink, using *How about … ?, Would you like to have … ?,* and *Have you ever been … ?*
4. Future plans or intentions, using *… be going to …*
5. Giving permission, asking for permission, and refusing permission, using *can, could, must,* and *mustn't*

Presenting meaning through drama and dialogue

A dramatic situation presented through dialogue can set the scene quickly and give the language a lively context. Conflict situations, like a police officer bullying a driver, "road rage" situations, or a dissatisfied customer in a store, are easy to exploit for drama and for meaning. Consider the following example:

Target structures: Imperatives and conditional form (*If you do/ don't, I'll …*)

Vocabulary: thief, bank manager, wallet, briefcase

Instructions: Play the following roles and describe the situation.

Student A: You are a thief. You want to take this man's money.

Student B: You are a bank manager. You have just come out of the bank into the street.

Situation: It is a dark evening. The bank manager (Student B) is holding a briefcase full of dollar bills.

The Dialogue

Thief:	Excuse me sir, can you give me a dollar? I need a cup of coffee.
Bank Manager:	I'm sorry, I don't have any change.
Thief:	Give me your brief case! I'll see if you have any money.
Bank Manager:	I can't give it to you. The case is locked.
Thief:	Open the case, or I'll shoot!
Bank Manager:	_____

(What does the Bank Manager say next, or what does he do?)

Intermediate and advanced students can be asked to contribute to the dialogue and change it. This activity can be done in pairs or groups. Make sure that all the students get a chance to play the roles. (For other uses of drama techniques, see Chapter 14, *Teaching with Drama*.)

Presenting meaning through songs

Using songs is a great way to increase students' motivation and their enjoyment of learning through listening. Be aware that your song choices may not be the students' choices. For this reason, it's better to let the students choose a song whenever possible. If you do this, the lesson becomes more learner-centered and students are more willing to learn the meaning of the words and message. Your role in such a situation may change to that of resource person and facilitator. This change may be advantageous, though there are some learning and teaching problems to consider when choosing songs.

Students may choose a song that is authentic, but not be suitable for their level. Moreover, the song they've chosen may have a singer who uses a non-standard American or British accent or dialect. These points and others need to be considered when using songs to present meaning (for more advice and tips on using songs, see Chapter 15, *Teaching with Songs*).

Concept checking

After you have presented the meaning of new language, it's essential to check that the learners have understood the concepts. Asking a general question like "Have you understood?" is useless. Even if your students say "Yes," you still don't know whether they have understood the new concepts nor do you know *what* they might have misunderstood. Following are examples of ways to check lexical concepts, structural concepts, and functional concepts.

Checking lexical concepts

Consider this simple example: you need to present the words *watch* and *clock* to beginning-level students. First you point to a clock on the wall and then to a watch on a student's wrist and elicit the correct responses, asking, "What's this? What's that?" If you want more active verbal responses, you could ask, "How can we know what time it is?" Then ask the following questions to give students the opportunity to manipulate and differentiate between the words:

Can you wear a watch?
Can you wear a clock?
Where do you see a clock?
Where do you see a watch?
Which is larger, a clock or a watch?

These questions will not only tell you whether the students have understood the different uses of the words, but also help students who are not absolutely sure of the difference between new words (and are reluctant or afraid to ask).

With more difficult or subtle lexical concepts, you may need to ask more questions in more stages. For example, after explaining the words *stranger* and *foreigner,* you need to check that the overlapping concepts can be distinguished and used appropriately by your students. The following questions should be asked:

Stranger
Do you know this person?
Do you know the person's name?
Could this person be someone from the same country that you
    come from?
Could this person be from another country?
Foreigner
You are at home in your own country, and you are introduced to a
    person from another country. Is that person a foreigner or a
    stranger?
Where do you come from?

You are studying here in the USA. Are you a foreigner or a stranger?

If you wanted to check if students can differentiate between verbs that are often confused, you could once again use questions. For example, how can you make sure that students have understood and can differentiate between *to own, to rent,* and the noun *rent* in the expression *to pay rent?* You could present the verbs using the words *house, apartment* and *car:*

You live in a house. You have bought this house.

Do you own the house? Do you have to pay rent?

You live in an apartment. You own the apartment.

Do you have to pay rent?

When you need a car for the weekend, what can you do?

Do you have to buy a car?

Checking structural concepts

When checking *structural* concepts, don't use the target structure in your concept questions. Using a question that includes the structure does not show you that its meaning has been understood. In the concept questions, use structures that the students know well and already understand. For example, if you presented *should've* as the target structure with the model sentence, "Steve *should've* gone to the dentist," you would want to check that the students have understood that there was some kind of obligation for Steve to have gone to the dentist (perhaps he had an appointment) and that Steve didn't fulfill the obligation (or, to put it simply, Steve was told or arranged to go to the dentist, *but he didn't go).* You can check whether the students understand *should've gone* by using the following questions:

1. Did someone tell Steve to go to the dentist, or did Steve have an appointment with the dentist?
2. Did Steve go to the dentist?

Here is another example using the present perfect tense as the target structure:

"She has lived in Los Angeles for three years."

This sentence has two inherent meanings:

She started living in Los Angeles three years ago.

She still lives in Los Angeles.

The concept questions should be:

When did she start living in Los Angeles?

Does she still live there?

Checking functional concepts

The *functional* meaning of utterances must also be checked. If necessary, you must check the relationship between the speakers and other factors relevant to the context as well. For example, the communicative meaning of a polite expression like *Do you/Would you mind … ?* needs to be checked after it has been introduced and contextualized. In a dialogue, a man asks a woman:

"Do you mind if I use your phone?"

To check the understanding of the function *Do you mind … ?*, ask the following questions:

Who wants to use the phone?

Whose phone is it?

Why does he ask her? Is he being polite?

Could there have been a problem if he hadn't asked to use her phone?

Could he have asked the question in another way?

Task 3: Checking lexical concepts

This vocabulary check can be done as a game—sometimes known as *Odd Man Out, Category,* or *Spot the Odd Word.* First, write out groups of semantically related words. In each group, write one word that doesn't belong. Ask students to work in pairs or small groups. They must pick out the "odd word" and explain why it doesn't fit.

Example: movie   play   film   novel   musical

The word novel doesn't fit. All the others use live actresses and actors to carry out their story.

Think of other semantic sets with an odd item. Write them below and explain why the "odd word" doesn't belong.

1. _____

_____

2. _____

_____

3. _____

_____

Task 4: Checking structural concepts

Write concept questions for the following language structures. Assume that they have already been presented.

1. I wish she had come.

    _____

    _____

2. They must have gone out.

    _____

    _____

3. I didn't mean to hurt you.

    _____

    _____

4. You should stop smoking.

    _____

    _____

5. We wouldn't have missed the plane if we'd caught the taxi.

    _____

    _____

Task 5: Checking functional concepts

Write concept questions to check understanding of the communicative purpose of the following:

1. How are you doing today?

    _____

    _____

2. Why don't you see a doctor?

    _____

    _____

3. Are you kidding?

_____

_____

4. I have to go now. Why don't you call me some time?

_____

_____

5. I wouldn't do that if I were you.

_____

_____

Review questions

1. Name some techniques you could use to present the meaning of new language items.

2. When presenting the meaning of a new word, is it better to give a definition of its meaning or an example of its use in a context? Why?

3. In choosing contexts for new language items, should you use authentic texts or texts specially written for classroom use (textbooks, etc.)? Why?

4. Think of a dramatic dialogue or a song. How could you use it to present meaning?

5. You have presented some new lexical items in a text. In order to check that the items have been understood, which of the following would you do? Why?
   - Ask the students, "Have you understood these words?"
   - Elicit responses to show that the students can use the items appropriately.

Further reading

Doff, A. *Teach English: A Training Course for Teachers* (trainer's handbook). Cambridge University Press, 1988.

Kramsch, C. *Context and Culture in Language Teaching*. Oxford University Press, 1993.

TEACHING VOCABULARY

Knowing a word

Limiting new vocabulary

Lexical sets and semantic fields

Using synonyms

Using antonyms

Guessing

Word formation

Remembering words

- Vocabulary notebooks

- Advertising/selling techniques

Teaching vocabulary: *do's* and *don'ts*

Using a dictionary

- A dictionary quiz

Review questions

Recommended English-to-English dictionaries

Further reading

TEACHING VOCABULARY

THE TEACHING OF VOCABULARY is essentially the teaching of the meaning of words in situations or in context. Teaching vocabulary is not primarily a matter of teaching *single* words, however. A lexical item or unit of meaning may be one word or may consist of two or more words. For example, the word *dictionary* is one lexical item but the phrasal verb *to get (something) over with*, as in "He wanted *to get* the exam *over with*," is one unit of meaning comprising four words. On the other hand, one word can have several meanings. Words like *hand* or *get* have many entries in the dictionary, each one a different lexical item. You cannot, therefore, teach the meaning of a verb like *get* apart from a particular context, nor can students learn the meanings of *get* unless each meaning is presented in context.

This introduction to teaching vocabulary is intended to prepare you for practical work in the classroom. It includes memorization techniques and a special section on dictionaries to help build vocabulary awareness for both you and your students.

Knowing a word   We know much more about the words of our native language than we realize. Non-native speakers of English can only be expected to cope with the essential aspects of new vocabulary in the early stages of learning the language. It is worth briefly analyzing how you know the words in your vocabulary:

♦ **Recognition.** You know the word in the sense that you recognize it in its spoken or written form.

♦ **Denotation.** You know what the word or lexical item refers to (for example, the word *cat* refers to an animal). Dictionaries usually give the *denotational* meaning first.

♦ **Connotation.** You know the emotional associations, including attitude, expressed in the word. An item of vocabulary can have positive or negative connotation. For example, *He's a pig!* has a strongly negative connotation, and *She's naïve!* is generally not complimentary. The term *spinster* is rarely used to describe an unmarried woman because of its uncomplimentary connotative meaning, whereas *bachelor* doesn't have the negative associations for an unmarried man.

◆ **Collocation.** You know the word and words that frequently, or always, occur with the item. Lions roar, they don't bellow; dogs bark, they don't shout. There are also fixed idiomatic collocations like *red herrings* and *white elephants.* Other collocations are less fixed: *handsome* usually describes *man,* though it can be used to describe *woman. Pretty* usually describes *girl* or *woman,* though it can be used with *boy* (but not usually with *man*).

◆ **Grammar.** You know how to place the item in a phrase or sentence, and you know the correct or acceptable form of the word or item.

◆ **Sound/Pronunciation.** You know how the item is pronounced and can say it so that it can be understood.

◆ **Register.** You know how to use the item appropriately at a suitable level of formality or informality according to the situation or context.

Learners cannot be expected to learn or know all these aspects of new vocabulary at once, nor do they need to know words in such depth for everyday purposes. Teachers must prioritize the aspects. Some basic guidelines about presenting texts in which new words occur are given in this section and in Chapter 3, *Presenting Meaning and Context.*

Limiting new vocabulary

How many new lexical items can your students learn in one lesson? Ten, twenty, thirty? Most people can learn and memorize seven digits for twenty to thirty seconds without any practice and for a longer period with rehearsal and practice. New words with visual meaning and non-verbal associations are easier to remember than half-understood new items of vocabulary with no visual or non-verbal associations. You should limit the number of new lexical items to a manageable number between seven and fourteen. Much depends, however, on how the words are presented and on the learners' needs and interests. A group of Swiss, German, or Japanese bank employees may not be greatly interested in the vocabulary of wild flowers in the New England meadows! If you have a class of nurses or medical students, they are likely to be interested in the names of the parts of the body. What seems relevant to students' needs or interests is likely to be learned and remembered. How much of the new vocabulary becomes part of the learners' vocabulary will depend on how *actively* it is used and practiced.

Even in our native language we can recognize and understand many more words than we can use to express meanings. Students who are learning a foreign language can ignore many words because they will not need them in order to achieve everyday communication and to express basic needs. Teachers similarly should distinguish between the vocabulary that their students need for *active* use and the vocabulary they need for *passive,* receptive purposes (for understanding the gist of a text). Students do not need to know every word in order to understand a story. It is reassuring to the learner to realize that a limited aim can achieve comprehension. Moreover, the teacher will achieve more in vocabulary comprehension by choosing to teach fewer words. A teacher should select new words that students will need for active purposes and spend more time and effort on the meaning and *sound* (pronunciation and syllable stress) of these words than on words that are needed for receptive purposes.

Lexical sets and semantic fields

Semantic field theory is based on the assumption that a native speaker's vocabulary is not a random collection of words but rather is organized into networks or inter-related sets of semantically similar words. The adult student has to acquire and learn *lexical sets* (for example, kinship words like *brother/sister)* and develop semantic networks. Words that are semantically related tend to occur together in a context. A teacher may reasonably decide to teach a number of related items in one learning unit. This strategy works well if each lexical item refers to something that can be clearly differentiated (for example, parts of the head or body). However, experience shows that presenting verbs of similar meaning together often leads to confusion. It may not be wise, therefore, to introduce a group of elementary students to the verbs *begin* and *start* in one lesson as if they were interchangeable (you can *start* a car, but you can't *begin* it). In summary, one item that is clearly presented (if possible through a visual context or an action) is more likely to be understood and remembered than a pair or group of so called "synonyms."

Lexical sets help in learning and checking on learning when there is active involvement in a task, as in the following example:

Which of the following is not a member of the family?

   mother   father   sister   godfather   uncle   cousin

Other tasks may be carried out after seeing pictures or handling real objects. For example, the teacher may ask students to write words under the pictures or write the names of objects in their appropriate category:

Arrange the words below under the following two headings:

FRUIT   VEGETABLE

_____   _____

_____   _____

_____   _____

_____   _____

_____   _____

_____   _____

apple	banana	bean
tomato	orange	onion
peach	potato	pear
carrot	cabbage	pineapple

Note: Cultural differences can cause confusion even within common categories like fruits and vegetables. The avocado is a kind of pear, but in some countries and cultures, *avocado* would not be included in the list of fruits. Always be aware of cultural interference as well as native language interference in learning (see Chapter 20, *Teaching Monolingual Classes*).

Another category task is to organize a *branching diagram*. In this task, the teacher chooses a general category like *The Arts* and helps the learners to write down the main subjects in this category. The teacher then leaves gaps for the students to suggest, discuss, and fill in on the diagram. This type of exercise is most suitable for intermediate to advanced students.

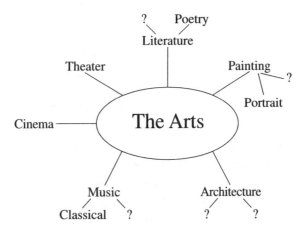

Using synonyms

Using synonyms is often the quickest, though not always the best, route to teaching the meaning of an unknown word. For example, students encounter the word *rival* in a book they are reading. One of the students asks for the meaning. The teacher gives a synonym, *competitor,* and quickly checks that the student understands the words *compete* and *competition*. The teacher does not expand upon his or her explanation because it would take too long to illustrate the difference or think of a suitable example for *rival* in a sentence.

It is not easy to avoid using synonyms when learners ask for the meaning of an unknown word. Students want a simple, quick explanation—the teacher doesn't always have the time or the resources (such as visuals) to illustrate the meaning, hence the meaning is explained in a "synonym" format:

"What does *x* mean?"

"Oh, it means *y*."

This use of a synonym does work, provided that the students understand *y* more than *x*. It's not much use introducing another word if that word needs explaining as well. For beginning to intermediate students, an example of the word's use or a phrase of similar meaning often is more helpful than a synonym. For the word *rival*, the teacher would say "A *rival* is someone who wants the same thing that you want," or "Germany's biggest *rival* for the World Cup is Brazil." These examples take more time and need preparation—if you can't think of a good, clear illustration quickly, use a synonym. However, for more advanced students, it's important that they understand the different uses of apparently synonymous words. Consider the following:

"What does *idle* mean?"

"It means *lazy.*"

This example may be true in some contexts (such as cases where the teacher wouldn't need to point out that workers may be idle because of a lack of jobs, not because they are lazy or unwilling to work). The advanced student, however, needs to know that *idle* is a more ambiguous term than *lazy.* In such situations, the advanced student should be given the task of using a dictionary to discover other uses of the word.

Generally, teachers need synonyms of words to help learners get a quick idea of the meaning of the unknown item, even if using synonyms is a rough and ready tool. Always keep in mind the problems which the use of synonyms could create; a clear example is usually more helpful than a definition. Good dictionaries give examples in sentences, hence showing how the word is used in context.

Using antonyms

Words of opposite meaning, known as *antonyms,* can also be used in learning new vocabulary. There seems to be a strong connection in our memories (in our native language) between words that are opposites. If you play a word association game like, "Say the first word that comes to mind when I say *hot*," the most common response is *cold* (not *warm*). In helping beginners and low-intermediate learners to build their vocabulary, you may find it useful to teach basic adjectives by pairing them with their opposites. It also helps to establish the meaning in many pairs of words like *true/false, dead/alive,* and *same/different.*

Care must be taken when using the notion of "oppositeness." With many pairs of closely associated words (kinship words, for example) there is a reciprocal relationship called *converseness* rather than oppositeness. It could therefore be misleading to ask students, "What's the opposite of *wife?*" It would be better to give the names of a man and a woman, show that they are married, and then introduce the terms *husband* and *wife*: "Jill is Jack's *wife;* Jack is Jill's *husband."* Then check that the students can use the terms appropriately by asking questions like "Who is Jack's wife?"

Similarly, with verbs that express the reciprocal of converse actions (examples of these verbs are *buying* and *selling* or *lending* and *borrowing),* you have to establish clearly who is doing what or what the relationship is between the persons involved. You should present the words in situations and then check that students understand the words by eliciting active use. Transforming sentences is a good task for accomplishing this goal. For example:

Mary Lou is Tom's sister.

Tom is Mary Lou's brother.

Note that verbs like *lending* and *borrowing* can be easily confused by students whose native languages do not have two different verbs for these actions. Also, students from some cultures will be confused by the lack of correspondence between certain terms in English that refer to family relationships. The converse terms may, therefore, not be easily transferred. For example, in Spanish, brother is called *hermano,* and *brothers and sisters* are called *hermanos.* In both Spanish and French, *cousin* has a masculine and feminine form.

There are other types of antonyms called *gradable opposites.* In gradable opposites, there are a number of terms on a scale and the appropriate opposite depends on the speaker's opinion or other social factors. The opposite of *big* is usually *small,* but other words could be used on a sliding scale from the polar extremes of *enormous* to *tiny.* To extend students' vocabulary, the teacher could draw a scale showing the very big to the very small and elicit suitable examples:

huge, large, big, medium, average, small, tiny, miniscule

Another useful exercise is to give students the polar extremes and then ask them to construct a scale for each set of terms (make sure to check that they can use the words appropriately). For example:

hot/cold (to describe the temperature of water)
interesting/boring (to describe a movie)
love/hate (to describe chores)
beautiful/ugly (to describe paintings or buildings)

Task 1: Using antonyms

Transform the following sentences using the verbs in parantheses:

1.   The automobile salesman sold John a sporty convertible.

John _____. (buy)

2.   He borrowed $10,000 from the bank.

The bank _____. (lend)

3.   Bill is Margaret's nephew.

Margaret is _____. (aunt)

Guessing

Although it's good to encourage your students to develop the skill of guessing the meaning of unknown words, don't expect them to be able to do it unless they really understand the context. It's difficult to guess the meaning of a word without contextual clues. The following are tips on helping learners to guess word meanings:

◆   Ask if the learners can tell you the grammatical category of the word. (Whether it's likely to be a noun, adjective, or adverb.) This is an important part of understanding the meaning. For example, in the sentence, "Sandra was wearing a *gaudy* dress because she liked bright, cheap clothes," is *gaudy* a noun or an adjective?

◆   Ask learners if there are any clues in the sentence. In the example sentence above, the second clause tells what kind of dress Sandra likes (bright and cheap).

◆   Ask learners to look at the structure of the unknown word. Is there a prefix or suffix that they recognize? If the unknown item was the verb *misled*, learners may know that *mis-* is a negative prefix. Do they know the verb *lead* and its past tense, *led*? If learners understand the meaning of the suffix or prefix, they are on their way to guessing the meaning of the word!

Generally speaking, guessing is appropriate for students above the intermediate level. The more vocabulary one knows, the more he or she can understand the context and therefore be in a position to guess the meaning of new words.

Word formation

Knowledge of word structure and word building is essential for at least two reasons: it helps in the extension of the learner's vocabulary, and it helps in inferring or guessing the meaning of words. There are two main processes of word formation:

◆ **Affixation.** Forming words by means of adding prefixes and/or suffixes to the base word form: *happy/unhappy/happiness/unhappiness*.

◆ **Compounding.** Forming words from two or more separate words *(good + looking = good-looking; hard + working = hard-working; business + man = businessman)*.

In teaching new words generated by affixation, it's important to point out any changes in the pronunciation of the derived words. For example:

democrat /ˈde mo crat/
democratic /ˌde mo ˈcra tic/
democracy /de ˈmo cra cy/

When adding prefixes or suffixes, there may also be spelling changes that cause difficulties. The rules for these changes should be pointed out (for example, *y* becomes *i* in words ending in *y*: *happy = happiness; lively = liveliness*).

It is difficult to generalize about affixation in English. English is a Germanic language profoundly influenced by French and Latin. Its vocabulary is a rich mixture of words from French and Latin sources, as well as others (such as Greek). In the formation of English words, the learner is faced by a bewildering variety of prefixes and suffixes. This variety often causes problems in learning. Attempts have been made to categorize words according to the origin of their base form (the so-called "root"): whether it derives from Nordic/Anglo-Saxon,

Latin, or French. These classifications are of little practical value. In fact, they can increase the problem for students who do not know which words are of Germanic, Latin, or French origin.

It is more useful to approach affixation through *meaning*. For example, you could group together the negative prefixes *(un-, in-, non-, dis-)* with examples of their meaning. You could also combine the practice of using dictionaries with work on common prefixes/suffixes and how they change meaning.

Task 2:
Understanding
word meanings
through
affixation

A. The prefix *mis-* usually changes the word to mean *badly* or *wrongly*. Work out the meaning of the underlined words and check your answers with a good English-English dictionary.
1. I didn't mean that. You <u>misunderstood</u> what I said.
2. He's sincere, but his opinions are very <u>misguided</u>.
3. I haven't lost my passport. I've <u>mislaid</u> it.
4. He was not allowed to practice as a doctor because he was accused of professional <u>misconduct</u>.
5. He's not really friendly. Don't be <u>misled</u> by his smile.

B. The prefix *dis-* is similar to the negative prefix *un-*. It usually means *not* or *the opposite of*. Work out the meaning of the underlined words:
1. The small raise in pay left the staff feeling <u>discontented</u>.
2. Many veteran soldiers were <u>disabled</u> in the Vietnam War.
3. The main <u>disadvantage</u> of the job is the long hours.
4. Her parents strongly <u>disapproved</u> of her leaving college before she had finished the course.
5. Before the heating could be repaired, the main electricity had to be <u>disconnected</u>.

Task 3:
Forming
words

The following task is a word formation awareness exercise for teachers. It might also be appropriate for advanced classes.
A. Complete the boxes in the chart :

	Adjective	Adverb	Noun	Verb	Negative
a.	happy	happily	happiness	(no verb)	unhappy
b.	different			differentiate	
c.	equal			equalize	
d.	visible			(no verb)	
e.			emphasis		
f.	sweet				
g.			economy		
h.			obedience		
i.	false				(no negative)
j.		attractively			

Note: The meaning of the negative form *indifferent* does not mean *not different*. The meaning will have to be explained or looked up in the students' dictionaries. The word *economy* refers to a country-wide financial situation. *Economical* and *economize* are related to saving money or spending it wisely.

B. Now look at the variety of suffixes in the chart. Answer the following questions:
  1. Which class of words has a regular pattern of endings?
  2. Are there any common endings for verbs? What are they?
  3. Which class of words has the greatest variety or lack of pattern?

Remembering words

A lot of time and effort is wasted if new words are not remembered. This section outlines two ways to make learning new vocabulary an easy memorization process: keeping notebooks and using advertising techniques.

Vocabulary notebooks

Have students keep notebooks in which they record the new words they learn (sometimes this can be together with a translation into their own languages). Use of these notebooks allows you to check on students' attempts to build their own vocabulary. You should suggest ways in which the notebooks can be better organized to help understanding and memorization. Very often, students write down a random list of words with translated equivalents. It's worth pointing out that words that are not connected meaningfully (into lexical sets) are difficult to remember. Practical tips could include the following:

♦ **Categories.** Students should categorize their notebook pages. They can do this by writing new words under topic or subject headings; for example, the heading *Sports and Leisure* creates a category for words like *running, jumping, swimming, jogging,* and *vaulting*.

♦ **Pronunciation.** Students should mark the stressed syllable when they write down words. For example, they should write: (attorney /a ˈttor ney/)

♦ **Grammatical classification.** Students should write down what the new word is grammatically (a noun, adjective, adverb, etc.).

♦ **Mnemonics.** Can the word be associated or linked to a visual image, a rhyming word, or a sound in the student's own language? Even nonsense links can be a great help, especially if they're funny mnemonics. For example, the Japanese phrase which is used to respond politely to "thank you," written in English, looks like *Do I ta shi ma shi te,* which is much easier to remember when it is said because it sounds like "Don't touch mustache!"

♦ **Common use.** Students should indicate beside each word whether it is common and useful, a colloquial item, or a literary and possibly archaic word.

♦ **Register.** Advanced students should make a note about the word's register (whether it is formal or informal).

Without realizing it, students are helping their memory processes by making these extra notes in the above ways. Active learning is always more effective than just receiving knowledge; merely translating a new word, although it's better than being totally passive, is not much help to the memory. The process of noting the pronunciation, the grammar, the semantic field, and other associations is a powerful aid to the memory.

Advertising/selling techniques

Advertising and selling techniques provide numerous ideas for you to help students memorize vocabulary words. Consider the following presentation principles, based on advertising and selling methods:

◆ **Exaggerate!** Images need to be large or sound very clear to make an impact. If the new word is *obese* and your students know the word *fat*, then draw a caricature of a grossly fat animal.

◆ **Make it absurd!** Make them laugh! Link new words to absurd images whenever you can, or get students to be imaginative and produce their own linked images, preferably into a short narrative that also helps the memory. The mental picture of an overheated dachshund puppy with a long bun connected to the meaning of *hot dog* helps some students.

◆ **Make it sexy!** If you have to teach comparative and superlative forms of adjectives and extend vocabulary at the same time, it's more fun to make ridiculous comparisons. For example, the scientist Einstein and the singer/movie star Madonna could be used to explain *smart* and *sexy*. Who's smarter? Who's sexier?

◆ **Use color!** Use vivid colors whenever you can. Underline key new words in red. Use colored pictures rather than black and white.

◆ **Use all the senses!** It's not just the visual association that helps the memory—a memorable image, formed by using as many of the basic bodily senses as you can, also helps. If the learner can see it, hear it, smell it, touch it, and if possible, taste it, you will have formed an unforgettable memory of the word! For example, teach *pepper* by bringing in the peppercorns and a pepper mill; then teach *grind, ground, mill,* and *flakes.*

◆ **Use music and song!** If the new words can be introduced in a song, they are often easy to remember. Music is another powerful aid to memory (see Chapter 15, *Teaching with Songs).*

Teaching vocabulary: *do's* and *don'ts*

◆ Do keep explanations short and simple, using words that are known.

◆ Do use visuals whenever possible.

◆ Do check understanding after illustrating or explaining the meaning of a new word (see *Concept checking*, Chapter 3, page 33).

- Don't rely on words to explain other new words.
- Don't ask the question, "Have you understood the word?" It's a waste of time. Instead, follow up your explanation with questions that will elicit evidence of understanding.
- Don't ask students to define the meaning of words (even advanced students find defining difficult). You want to know if the students can *use* the new word or recognize its meaning.
- Don't check by asking "What is a *prison?*" or "What does *prison* mean?" Instead, ask questions like "What do we call the building in which convicted criminals are kept?"
- Do ask if someone in the class knows the word before explaining it.
- Do allow the students to show their knowledge even if it isn't correct or accurate. It may be nearly right, at which time you can approve of the attempt and then put the word right and in context.
- Do anticipate problem words or phrases and the new items that may block understanding. Be prepared with graphics, and use clear examples that show how the new words are used.

Using a dictionary

In order for students to learn and understand vocabulary on their own, they need training in the use of dictionaries. As a teacher, you are in a position to advise students which English-English dictionary to buy according to their level of understanding. Once students have dictionaries, help them to recognize the phonetic symbols, grammatical symbols, and other abbreviations used. Emphasize to students that their dictionary is a valuable self-help and self-study tool. The following quiz is an in-class task that provides useful introductions to good dictionary use and helps refresh your familiarity with a dictionary as well!

A dictionary quiz

Give students the following quiz. Tell them to look up the italicized words if they are not sure of the meaning, the grammar, or the register.

1. General meaning
   What is *taffy* made of?
   Who would wear a *diaper*?
   What does a *janitor* do?

2. Synonyms/Antonyms
   Find a word similar in meaning to *wicked.*
   Find a word similar to *allow.*
   What's the opposite of *sane?*

3. Style or register
   "You couldn't see the *backside* of the house from the drive."
   In the above sentence, *backside* is not suitable. Which of the
   following words would be a better choice?
   behind   rear   bottom
   "What time does the lesson *terminate?*"
   Is *terminate* an appropriate word to use in an informal situation?
   What word would be more suitable?

4. Grammar
   Is the word *cowardly* a noun, a verb, an adverb, or an adjective?
   What's the past tense of *dive?*
   Is the word *news* countable or uncountable?

5. Spelling
   How do you spell the plural of *story?*

6. Pronunciation
   Which syllable is stressed in the word *photographer?*
   Which letter is silent in the word *plumber?*

7. Abbreviations
   What do the letters *SCUBA* mean?
   What do the letters *NATO* stand for?

8. Information
   What do you call a person who comes from *Peru?*
   How large is an *acre?*

Task 4: Teaching vocabulary

A. Place the following words in pairs according to their similar meanings. One word of each pair is more formal than the other word. Put the formal word first. Example: man—guy. Think of how you would explain or illustrate the differences between each word in the pair.

the john	toilet
employer	taxi
home	residence
boss	policeman
cop	cab

B. How would you explain or illustrate the difference in meaning between the pairs of words below? For intermediate and advanced students, how would you convey that the pairs of words have something in common? (Think of a sentence framework such as *Both are (describe)_____ but the first (is used) _____, and the second _____. Or use a framework like The difference between _____ and _____ is that _____).*

a. handsome/beautiful
b. large/great
c. tall/high
d. famous/notorious
e. teacher/professor

C. How would you illustrate the different meanings or uses of the following words?

march	hike
crawl	stroll
strut	stagger
limp	wander

D. Which word includes all the others? Think about how this type of activity can be helpful when teaching vocabulary.

bus	vehicle	jeep
truck	car	camper

E. If you buy something and sell it for a higher price, the extra money is your _____.
    a. income
    b. winnings
    c. profit
    d. salary
    e. investment
        Think of sentences you could use to illustrate the uses of the other words in the above list.

F. What is the relationship between the following pairs of word groups? Are they synonyms, antonyms, collocations, inclusive terms with examples, or derivative forms?
    a. lender—borrower
    b. male—female
    c. often—frequently
    d. flock—sheep
    e. photograph—photographic—photographer
    f. shirt—clothes—skirts
    g. teacher—learner

Review questions

1. What is a *lexical item?* Is it the same as a word? Give an example of a lexical item consisting of two or three words.

2. What is a *lexical set?* Give an example. How can lexical sets be used in teaching vocabulary?

3. What are the disadvantages of using synonyms or antonyms to convey the meaning of unknown words? Give an example.

4. What are the two main processes of word formation? Give examples.

5. How can you help students remember words?

6. How would you go about training students to use a dictionary? Give two kinds of dictionary exercises that would be useful.

Recommended English-to-English dictionaries

There's a wealth of dictionaries on the market today. Here are some that I recommend, including their appropriate levels:

Oxford Elementary Learner's Dictionary
Elementary and pre-intermediate levels

Oxford Wordpower Dictionary
Intermediate levels up to Cambridge First Certificate level

Longman Dictionary of Contemporary English
Advanced levels

The Longman Dictionary of English Language and Culture
Advanced levels

Further reading

Suggestions for teaching vocabulary can also be found in Chapter 3, *Presenting Meaning and Context;* Chapter 7, *Teaching Speaking;* Chapter 11, *Teaching with Visual Aids;* and Chapter 13, *Teaching with Games* (see *Vocabulary games,* page 233).

Other reading suggestions are:

Buzan, T. *Use Your Head.* BBC, 1979. (Useful for ideas on remembering words.)

French, Allen V. *Techniques in Teaching Vocabulary.* Oxford University Press, 1983.

Gairns, R. and Redman, S. *Working with Words.* Cambridge University Press, 1986.

Morgan, J. and Rinvolucri, M. *Vocabulary.* Oxford University Press, 1986.

Nation, P. *New Ways in Teaching Vocabulary.* TESOL Publications, 1994.

Wallace, M. *Teaching Vocabulary.* Heinemann, 1982.

UNDERSTANDING BASIC GRAMMAR

UNDERSTANDING BASIC GRAMMAR

WHAT DO LEARNERS MEAN WHEN THEY SAY they want to be taught the "grammar" of English? Mostly, they want to learn how to speak and write English according to the rules. Learners assume that teachers (whether native or non-native speakers) know the rules of grammar. Teachers who are native speakers have the advantage of *native speaker intuition,* the unconscious knowledge of what is acceptable or grammatically unacceptable. The learner, of course, doesn't have this knowledge and needs guidance and clear indications as to which *forms* of English are correct (or at least acceptable) and which forms are not.

Grammar doesn't only deal with word forms. It also deals with word order and structural patterns that dictate how one puts words into phrases, clauses, and sentences. *Structure* in this sense refers to a sequence of words that makes a grammatical unit. For example, sequences include a verb phrase structure like "he/she *was sleeping*" or "they *would have been* late." Some sequences include a noun phrase structure like *article + adjective + noun* as in *"the beautiful picture."*

One of the main purposes of this chapter is to make you aware of the meanings and uses of verb forms. The tasks and exercises are designed to draw attention to the problems of the learner. This is not an attempt to cover systematically the meanings and uses of all the verb tenses in English. Rather, it is intended to build your awareness and understanding of verb forms that cause the most difficulty and confusion to students.

Structural and lexical words

Words can be divided broadly into two classes:
1. *Structure* words (also known as *function* words)
2. *Lexical* words

Structure words include words like *the, some, any,* and *but;* prepositions like *to* and *of;* and pronouns like *he, she,* and *it.* These grammatical items are essential to the structure of languages. They have little meaning on their own but are important in showing grammatical relationships between words, phrases, and sentences. In most languages, they belong to limited sets. For example, there are a fixed number of pronouns in any language.

Lexical words refer to things, notions, qualities, states, or actions and are usually classified as nouns, verbs, adjectives, and adverbs. Examples include *banana* (noun), *eat* (verb), *tasty* (adjective), and *hungrily* (adverb). Lexical words have meaning even in isolation (for example, *danger* or *walk)*, though the meaning is clearer in context. Lexical words belong to open sets; there's really no limit to the number of nouns, adjectives, adverbs, and verbs in a language. Dictionaries and lexicons have to be constantly updated because the list of lexical words changes and grows.

Language teachers must also be aware of the *relationship* between lexical and structural words and pronunciation. Sentences in spoken form have stresses on the lexical words but not on the structural words:

We'll be arriving **mid**day **Sun**day at the **down**town **bus ter**minal.

In fact, if you were expressing a message like this in written form and had to pay for every word (as we used to do in telegrams), you'd probably omit the structural words altogether. Your message might read: *Arriving midday Sunday downtown bus terminal.* Though there are no structural words, the series of lexical words conveys the meaning, provided the word order or syntax follows the normal pattern.

Task I: Understanding structural and lexical words

Even nonsense has to follow certain linguistic rules. Look at the famous first verse of Lewis Carroll's nonsense poem, *Jabberwocky,* and complete the tasks.

Twas brillig, and the slithy toves

Did gyre and gimble in the wabe:

All mimsy were the borogroves,

And the mome raths outgrabe.

1. Divide the words of the verse into two groups: *structural* and *lexical*. Do this separation by underlining the *lexical* words.
2. Which words or syllables of the lexical words are stressed? Mark them with a small box above the syllable.
3. Why did Carroll follow the normal syntactic (word order) patterns? Would it have been amusing or memorable if he hadn't? For example, what if he had written, *Toves the slithy and brillig twas?*

Word classes

Language teachers need to know some *metalanguage;* that is, language terms that refer to language. You are probably quite familiar with some of the basic terms that refer to language, such as *word classes* (nouns, verbs, and adjectives). There are other word classes that will help you in your teaching (especially in correcting students' errors). Try the following tasks to review the most common terms used to refer to word classes.

**Task 2:
Understanding
word classes**

A. Read the sentences *a* through *h* and the list of grammatical terms 1 through 12. Which grammatical term applies to each of the words or phrases underlined in the sentences? Write the number above the word. The first one has been done for you. If you do not know the grammatical term, look it up in an up-to-date grammar reference book or in a good dictionary (see *Further reading* at the end of this chapter).

1 9 1

a. They're sitting on the <u>grass</u> in <u>the</u> <u>park.</u>

b. He didn't <u>mean</u> <u>to hurt</u> you.

c. She was taken to <u>a</u> hospital in a <u>critical</u> <u>condition</u>.

d. Take <u>my</u> car, <u>but</u> drive <u>carefully</u>.

e. She works <u>hard</u> but doesn't earn <u>very</u> much.

f. There'll be dancing <u>in</u> the streets <u>and</u> singing <u>at</u> the bus stops!

g. <u>She</u> wanted to take a photograph of <u>him</u>.

h. They stopped <u>to have</u> <u>a</u> drink.

1. noun	8. possessive adjective
2. main verb	9. definite article
3. adjective	(determiner)
4. adverb	10. indefinite article
5. conjunction	11. infinitive
6. subject pronoun	12. preposition
7. object pronoun	

B. Using the *Jabberwocky* poem on page 62, decide which word class (noun, verb, adjective, etc.) the nonsense words belong to. For example, is *brillig* a noun? What clues lead you to decide whether these words belong to one class or another?

Function   Grammatical correctness is important, but learners need more than that in the real world of communication. Learners need to know how to use language appropriately according to the social context and, even more fundamentally, how to achieve their purposes with language. This is where language *function* comes into play. Language *function* deals with learning to use language for communication. A *function* is the reason for using language—its communicative purpose. Common examples of language functions are giving instructions, requesting other people to do something, persuading, warning, giving advice, and apologizing. Consider the following examples, which use the *imperative* form to communicate several different *functions:*

"Shut the door!" (functionally, an order)
"Push back the lid, and then bend it." (functionally, an instruction)
"Try the pickled cabbage." (functionally, a suggestion)
"Come to my place this evening." (functionally, an invitation)

Note: The function of a statement cannot be known by only studying the meaning of the words. For example, "You've left the door open" may not be a simple statement of fact. On a cold day, the statement is probably a *request,* similar in function to "Please close the door." In order to understand the *function* of language, we therefore need to know the context or situation in which the words are used.

Task 3:
Understanding
function

A. Read the following questions and write the function (communicative purpose) of each one.
1. Could you open the window?
2. Hi! How are you? (You say this to someone you know.)
3. Do you have a match?
4. Have you met my sister? (You are with your sister at a party.)
5. Is that really the time?
6. Is that right?
7. Would you like to sit down?
8. Can I help you?
9. Can I speak to Maria, please?
10. Oh, is that a problem?

B. Think of different structures that could be used to fulfill the function *giving advice* and write them below. For example, a question: "Why don't you _____?"

_____

_____

_____

Verb forms

As stated in the introduction, this section focuses on some of the verb forms, especially tenses, that cause confusion and difficulties for students learning English as a second or foreign language.

Auxiliary verbs

There are two kinds of *auxiliary verbs* in English:

◆ **Primary auxiliaries:** *am/is/are/was/were, have/has/had, do/does/did*

◆ **Modal auxiliaries:** *can/could, may/might, will/would, shall/should, must/ought to/used to/need (to)*

Use the chart below to compare primary auxiliaries and modal auxiliaries.

Primary auxiliaries	*Modal auxiliaries*
am	can
is	could
are	shall
was	should
were	will
have	would
has	may
had	might
do	must
does	ought to
did	used to

Primary auxiliaries are different from modal auxiliaries in the following ways:

◆ **Past tense forms.** The primary auxiliaries have past tense forms (*am/is/are* have the past forms *was/were*). The modal auxiliaries do not (is there a past form of *must* or *may?*).

- **Third person forms.** The primary auxiliaries have third person forms (he/she *is/has/does*). The modal auxiliaries do not change. They have no -*s* form.
- **Infinitives.** The primary auxiliaries are related to an infinitive: *to be, to have,* or *to do.* There is no infinitive form for the modal auxiliaries.

Note: Need doesn't fit into either category; it can be used as a full verb: *need, needs, needed,* and *needing;* and as a modal auxiliary verb:

We *need* milk from the store.

We *need* to get going.

We *didn't need* to hurry.

We *needn't* hurry.

We *didn't need* to go to the police.

We *needn't go* to the police.

Focusing on modal auxiliaries

Modal auxiliaries are used to express a variety of moods or attitudes towards actions and events in the past, present, or future. The main uses can be grouped as follows:

- To express probability, behavior inference, or a range of meanings from certainty to possibility:
  It *may/might/should* happen.
- To express the ability to do something:
  He *can* do it. (He knows how to or is physically capable.)
  The doctors *couldn't* do it. (The doctors have not succeeded in or managed to do something.)
- To express obligation, necessity, or the absence of choice:
  You *must* have a passport to enter a foreign country.
- To express correct behavior or moral duty *(should* or *ought to):*
  You *should* attend the wedding.
- To express permission, allow an action, or ask whether it's permitted *(can* or *could):*
  Can I change the radio station?

Note: It used to be considered more correct or polite to use *may* or *might* when asking for permission to do something. This sounds very formal now; *Can I?* or *Could I?* are more frequently used.

◆ To express the necessity; the notion that an action is or isn't necessary *(need, need to, or needn't):*
I *need* to take that test.

◆ To express condition *(would or should* in sentences with an *if* clause; see page 88 for more information):*
Tammy *would* drive there if the road wasn't closed.

**Task 4:
Understanding
modals and
their meanings**

A. Look at the following pairs of sentences. The underlined modals are used to express different meanings. How would you explain these different uses of the same modal?

1. a. You <u>should</u> see a doctor.
    b. She <u>should</u> be here soon.

2. a. <u>Can</u> I borrow your dictionary? Yes, you <u>can</u>.
    b. <u>Can</u> you swim? Yes, I <u>can</u>.

3. a. It <u>may</u> rain this evening.
    b. <u>May</u> I speak to the president now? Yes, you <u>may</u>. He's expecting you.

4. a. I <u>must</u> pay my electricity bill.
    b. My wallet has gone! Someone <u>must</u> have taken it.

5. a. <u>Could</u> I use your phone?
    b. When I was younger, I <u>could</u> run faster.

B. Each of the modal auxiliary verbs has a number of meanings. The modals can therefore be used to express different functions. Look at the list of modal forms below and think of a real example for each function. The first one is done for you.

Can

ability: <u>*Can you lift this bag, please? It's very heavy.*</u>

permission: _____

request (or polite order): _____

possibility: _____

prohibition (not allowed to): _____

Could

request: _____

suggestion: _____

possibility: _____

past ability: _____

permission (in the past): _____

Must/mustn't

obligation: _____

deduction (no other explanation): _____

prohibition: _____

Needn't

absence of obligation: _____

Ought to

advice: _____

probability: _____

May

probability/possibility (future): _____

permission (formal, very polite): _____

Might

permission (very polite): _____

possibility *(I don't think it will, but it might …)*: _____

_____

suggestion *(What can I do to stop smoking? You might try …)*: _____

_____

Should

advice: _____

moral obligation:_____

probability *(Is the plane going to be late? No, it should …):* _____

_____

attributing blame or criticism (in the past: *I should have done …):*

_____

Would

request: _____

habit/characteristic behavior (in the past: *When we were children, we*

would …): _____

complaining (after *I wish: I wish it would* _____ *raining):* _____

_____

conditional uses (see the section on conditional sentences, page 88):

_____

conditional uses (see the section on conditional sentences, page 88):

Expressing present time: the simple present and present continuous

In English, there are two types of verb tenses used to refer to the present time: the *simple present* and the *present continuous* (sometimes called *present progressive*). This is a problem for some learners, as many European languages only have one way to refer to present time.

The *simple present* is formed by a main verb without an auxiliary:
I *swim* in the lake on the weekends.
She *swims* at the local recreation center.
The *present continuous (present progressive)* is formed by the *be* verb *(am, is,* or *are)* plus the *-ing* form of the main verb:
Please don't disturb me! *I'm working!*
Note: There are some verbs that do not usually have a present

continuous form. Such verbs describe *states*, not actions. Examples of these verbs are:

- ◆ **Thinking verbs:** *think, know, understand, mean, remember*
- ◆ **Opinion verbs:** *believe, agree, realize, consider*
- ◆ **Emotion verbs:** *want (to), prefer to, intend to, wish to, love, hate, like, dislike*
- ◆ **Perception verbs:** *see, hear, smell, taste* (*Note:* If you want to express continuing states with these verbs, you use *can* or *could:* I *can taste* the garlic in the soup now.)

Task 5: Understanding the simple present

In the left-hand column below, there are eight sentences using the simple present. In the right-hand column, there are eight statements. In the blanks, write the letter of the statement that goes with each sentence.

___ 1. He watches the 8:00 a.m. news every day.

___ 2. Oil floats on water.

___ 3. The plane to Sydney leaves at 11:00 a.m.

___ 4. She smokes a lot.

___ 5. … and Pele scores a goal!

___ 6. He lives in Boston.

___ 7. I'll tell her when she comes back.

___ 8. Jumbo Jet Crashes in Thick Fog

a. present situation
b. habits
c. routine actions
d. general truths
e. schedules/timetables
f. in statements about the future after *when/if*
g. newspaper headlines on recent events
h. commentaries on sports or current events

Task 6: Understanding the present continuous

A. Study the following uses of the present continuous. What do they have in common?

1. Where is Bill?
   He's playing golf with Jim.

2. What are those art students doing?
   They're making sketches of the model.

3. Oh no! It's raining, and I forgot my umbrella.

B. Decide which form of the verb in parentheses is appropriate: the simple present or the present continuous. Write the correct form in the blank.

1. I usually _____ (enjoy) Italian food, but I _____

    _____ (not/enjoy) this meal.

2. "Can you swim?"

    "No, but I _____ (learn). A friend _____ (teach)

    me."

3. She _____ (smoke) 20 cigarettes a day, but she _____

    _____ (not/smoke) at the moment.

The present perfect and present perfect continuous

The *present perfect* is formed by *has* or *have* plus a past participle (such as *have done; done* is the past participle):

> They *have been* to India. (*They've* been to India.)
> It *has arrived* at the airport. (*It's* arrived at the airport.)

The present perfect has a number of different uses:

1. To talk about your experience, such as what you have done in your life up to now, often used with *ever* and *never*:
    > "Have you ever eaten caviar?"
    > "No, never." (I've never eaten it.)

    Note: The point is *whether* you have eaten caviar before now, not *when*. A question like, "Have you been to Paris?" finds out *if* you have visited Paris at any time up to now. The person asking the question does not want to know *when* you went there.

2. To talk about something that happened very recently:
    > "Have they arrived yet?"
    > "Yes, the plane has just landed."

3. To talk about recent events or actions, the results of which are still relevant or apparent:
    > She isn't here. She's gone away.
    > Have you heard the latest? Jack's been fired.

Note: The active form of the passive sentence is "Someone *has fired* Jack."

The *present perfect continuous* is formed by *has/have + been + verb -ing:*

> *I've been e-mailing* her every day.
>
> Jerry *has been training* for the Olympics.

If the action is *on-going* or *not completed,* we normally use the present perfect continuous.

> I have read that book. (The action is completed. I've finished it.)
>
> *I've been reading* that book. (The action is not completed. I'm still reading it.)
>
> In the children's story, *The Three Bears,* Papa Bear says, *"Who's been eating* my soup?" (Some soup had been left.)
>
> Baby Bear says, *"Who's eaten* my soup? It's all gone!"

Both the present perfect and the present perfect continuous can be used to express something that began in the past and has continued up to the present, often used with *since* or *for:*

> "How long have you been in the USA?"
>
> "I've been here for two years."
>
> "Have you been studying English?"
>
> "I've been studying it since I arrived."

Task 7: Understanding the present perfect and present perfect continuous

A. Study the following three examples. How would you explain the reason for choosing *for* or *since* in each one?
   1. I have lived in this city *for* five years.
   2. I've been working here *since* January.
   3. She's been taking classes *since* she arrived in America.

B. Explain the difference in meaning of the following sentence pairs. Why was the present perfect used? Why was the present perfect continuous used?
   1. a. Who's been eating my chocolates?
      b. Who's eaten my chocolates?
   2. a. It's been snowing for an hour.
      b. Look! It's been snowing.
   3. a. The boss has spoken to Pat.
      b. The boss has been speaking to Pat for an hour.

Task 8:
Adverbs and
the present
perfect
tenses

A. Certain adverbs or adverbial phrases *(ever, never, before, just, already, recently, for,* and *since)* usually go with the two present perfect tenses. Answer the following questions using adverbials.

1. Have you been to the theater recently?

   _____.

2. Have you ever been to Egypt?

   _____.

3. Have you just taken a bath?

   _____.

B. The adverbials *ago, yesterday,* and *last week* are not usually used with the present perfect. Which verb tense usually occurs with these adverbials? Write the appropriate tense for the following sentences.

1. We _____ (see) that film a month ago.

2. I _____ (go) to the beach last weekend.

The simple past
tense

The *simple past* is the past tense form that uses the main verb without an auxiliary. For most verbs in English, the simple past tense is formed with the ending *-ed. (Note:* in spoken form, there are three ways of pronouncing *-ed.* See page 104.)

The main use of the simple past is to describe an action or happening at a definite time in the past:

   I *saw* her yesterday.

The simple past is also used to describe something that is unlikely to happen in the present or the future:

   I wish I *had* a million dollars.

Task 9: Use of the simple past

Read the following sentences, all of which use examples of the simple past. Only some of them refer to past time. Which ones are they?

1. I <u>lived</u> in Sicily for a year.
2. They <u>met</u> a year ago.
3. I'd rather you <u>gave</u> it to me tomorrow.
4. We <u>visited</u> the Museum of Modern Art when we <u>were</u> in New York.
5. If you <u>loved</u> me, you wouldn't do such a thing!
6. I wish I <u>had</u> a new car.
7. <u>Did</u> he really <u>say</u> that?
8. When I <u>told</u> them about the fire, they <u>didn't</u> believe me.

Task 10: Simple past contrasted with present perfect

In each sentence pair below, one sentence uses the simple past tense and one sentence uses the present perfect. How would you explain the difference in the meaning between each pair of sentences?

1. a. We've known about the problem for ages.
   b. He knew about the problem for ages.

2. a. I've been waiting for you since half past four.
   b. I waited for you from half past four.

3. a. Have you seen the Monet exhibit?
   b. Did you see the Monet exhibit?

4. a. Have you ever been to Yosemite?
   b. Did you go to Yosemite?

The past continuous tense

The *past continuous* is formed with *was* or *were* followed by the *-ing* form of the verb:

He *was waiting* for the bus.

The past continuous shows that a state or action continued for a limited period in the past:

What were you doing at 9:00 p.m. yesterday evening?

I was watching TV.

The past continuous is also used to indicate that a continuous action was interrupted by some other action or event:

I *was having* a bath when the phone rang.

Be aware that learners often make the mistake of using the simple past for both actions, as in the following:

*I had a bath when the phone rang.

Task 11: Using the past continuous

Write down the question that is likely to prompt or elicit each of the following answers:

1. _____?

   I was eating.

2. _____?

   She was helping me.

3. _____?

   I was living in Canada at that time.

4. _____?

   Between 7:00 and 8:00 yesterday evening? I don't remember.

5. _____?

   I was studying at the university.

The past perfect tense

The past perfect is formed with the simple past of *have* + a past participle. For example: *had been, had gone, had done,* and *had lived.* The past perfect is used to show that an action or state happened or was completed before another event or action in the past:

It *had happened* before we arrived.

Note: There is also an "unreal" past perfect used for actions or states that didn't take place or were not possible (see the section on conditional sentences, page 88):

If you *had been* born in China, you would have known how to speak Chinese.

I wish I *had known* that before I came to the USA.

The past perfect continuous tense

The *past perfect continuous* is formed with *had + been* + verb + *-ing*:

> It *had been snowing* all night, so the driveway was blocked.

Use the past perfect continuous to indicate that something continued to happen for a period of time before another past action or event. Sometimes, as in the example above, the continuous action produced an effect that was noticed after it stopped. Here's another example:

> He went back to school. He *had been looking* for a job for a year. (Before he decided to go back to school, he had been looking for a job for a year.)

Task 12: Using the past perfect continuous

Make each set of statements below into one sentence using the adverbs in parentheses.

1. The firemen got there. The fire had been burning for two

    hours. (when) _____

    _____

2. She had been working there for ten years. They gave her a

    raise. (after) _____

    _____

3. The car broke down. They had been traveling for eight hours.

    (when or after) _____

    _____

4. The child star of *The Piano* won an Oscar. She had only been

    acting for six months. (although) _____

    _____

5. They had been dancing for hours. We got to the party.

    (when) _____

**. Using
past tenses**

Students have problems differentiating between the perfect and past tenses. Look at the following statements made by students. Some are acceptable, some are not, and some are only acceptable in a particular context. Decide which sentences are correct or acceptable and which are not. Think of a simple explanation why some sentences are not acceptable.

1. I wish I knew about it in time.
2. They have been here last week.
3. Giovanni was in America for several months when he took the TOEFL exam.
4. I was living in the country when I was a child.
5. She had been cutting her finger when I arrived.
6. He used to live here for four years.
7. I was going to my teacher yesterday, and he was satisfied with my work.
8. She was watching TV for half an hour when the phone rang.
9. Sharon had been going into the bar when I last saw her.
10. As I was driving to work, I was listening to the car radio.

The passive and phrasal verbs

The *passive* is formed by *be* + a past participle:

The spray *is used* in the bathroom.

She *was given* a dozen red roses.

All the jewelry *has been taken.*

Compare the location of the subject, verb and object between an active and passive statement:

Active: The man kissed the woman. (Subject, verb, object)

Passive: The woman *was kissed* by the man. (object, verb, subject)

Though the focus changes in passive sentences, the meaning usually does not.

The passive form allows the omission of the *subject (man* in the active sentence above) where the *subject* is unknown, not important, or can be assumed. In the question, "Why is the passive used?," we do not need to say, "Why do people use the passive?" nor "Why is the passive used by people?"

In fact, most passive constructions do not need the subject. If the subject is an important item of information, the passive allows us to introduce it at the end:

> This building is important and original. It was designed by Frank Lloyd Wright.

A problem for the learner is that some verbs can have two *objects:*

> Active: Someone offered Tina a job.
>
> Passive: Tina was offered the job. (*Tina* is the object.)
>
> Passive: The job was offered to Tina. (*The job* is the object.)

Note: In situations like the above, it is more usual to use the first object at the beginning of the passive sentence. The second object is most commonly used to begin the passive construction to answer the question:

> Who was the job offered to?
>
> It (the job) was offered to Tina.

Another tricky problem for learners is *phrasal/prepositional verbs.* In the following verbs, the verb and a preposition-like particle form a unit, such as *write to, hope for* and *talk about.* These verbs have objects and can therefore be expressed in the passive:

> His performance *was talked about* for years.
>
> A big improvement in the economy *can be hoped for*
> later in the year.

Note: The learner finds it strange to end a phrase or a sentence with a preposition so he/she tends to omit it, resulting in a common error like the following:

> *His performance was talked for years.

Task 14:
Understanding
the passive

A. 1. The following sentences mean the same as the first statement in English. In what way is the English sentence different from the French, Spanish, Italian, and German sentences?

> English spoken
>
> On parle anglais
>
> Se habla ingles
>
> Si parla inglese
>
> Man spricht englisch

2. Why do you think the passive is often used in scientific reports? In newspaper headlines? In official statements by

diplomats and politicians?

3. Why isn't the passive as common in ordinary colloquial speech?

B. Match the statements on the left with the contexts on the right:

1. Town Destroyed by Floods	a. notice in a hotel
2. Elementary particles are the basic units of which all matter is composed.	b. newspaper headline
	c. science textbook
3. Vehicles towed at owner's expense	d. notice in a private parking lot
4. Checks not accepted without I.D.	e. sign at the check-out in a store
5. Breakfast served from 7:00 to 10:00 a.m.	

C. Read the following exercise, which is an example of something you might find in an "old-fashioned" grammar textbook. Comment on whether the active sentences are well chosen for transformation into the passive. Then change the sentences into the passive. The first one has been done for you.

1. John wrote that letter.

   <u>That letter was written by John.</u>

2. They showed us the house.

   _____.

3. Somebody broke into our apartment last night.

   _____.

4. No one has ever climbed that mountain.

   _____.

5. We are looking forward to the vacation.

   _____.

6. The cow jumped over the moon.

   _____.

D. The following text was adapted from three different newspapers. Underline the passive verb phrases and identify the tenses. The first one has been done for you.

Malcolm X Widow Badly Burned in Fire 'Started by Grandson'

Dr. Betty Shabazz, the widow of civil rights leader, Malcolm X, was in critical condition in a hospital in the Bronx last night. Most of her skin <u>had been burned</u> *past perfect* in a fire at her apartment which police say was started by her grandson.

Shortly after the fire was reported, the twelve-year-old boy was found wandering the streets nearby in a daze, his clothes smelling strongly of gasoline. The boy, Malcolm, who had been in his grandmother's care, was missing from her apartment when the firefighters arrived. According to the police, the boy seemed angry because he had been forced to live with his grandmother.

Malcolm is the son of Qubilah, Malcolm X's daughter, who was indicted on charges of plotting to kill Louis Farrakhan, the leader of the Nation of Islam, in January, 1995. Farrakhan had been accused by Betty Shabazz of taking part in the assassination of Malcolm X in 1965. Qubilah saw her father being killed in a ballroom in Washington Heights when she was only four years old. When her indictment was dismissed last month, she moved to Texas, but her son, Malcolm, was sent to live with his grandmother in New York.

Detectives said yesterday that the boy had been taken into custody and will be tried as a juvenile in Family Court. According to police reports, Malcolm drenched the hallway of his grandmother's three-bedroom apartment with gasoline and waited until she arrived before setting fire to it. Firefighters found Dr. Shabazz lying outside her apartment on the hallway floor. "She had been severely burned, but was conscious enough to tell us that someone else had been in the apartment with her."

It was announced today that Betty Shabazz had died of her burns. The news left friends of the family shocked and unable to believe what has happened. President Clinton said, "Dr. Betty Shabazz devoted a long career to education and helping deprived women and children."

Verbs followed by the infinitive or the verb + -ing	In addition to the tenses outlined in this chapter, there are three types of verbs that may cause teaching and learning problems:
	1. Verbs that can only be followed by an *infinitive:*
	    I *hope* to see you next week.
	    Other verbs of this type include: *decide, agree, promise, refuse, wish, used to,* and the auxiliary verbs *be, have,* and *ought to.*
	2. Verbs that can only be followed by the *-ing* form:
	    She *enjoys* dancing.

Other common verbs of this type include: *dislike, (not) mind, deny, can't bear, can't help, look forward to.*

3. Verbs that can be followed by either an infinitive or by a verb + *-ing*. This is a problem area for the learner because the choice may involve a change of meaning (see the following task).

**Task 15:
Verbs followed
by an infinitive
or the
verb + *-ing***

A. Read the following pairs of sentences. Does each pair mean the same thing? If not, how would you explain the different meanings to a student?

1. Do you like dancing?
   Would you like to dance?

2. I stopped smoking cigarettes.
   I stopped to smoke a cigarette.

3. I remember leaving the key for you.
   I remembered to leave the key for you.

4. We love going to the movies.
   We love to go to the movies.

5. We regret to inform you that your application has been rejected.
   We regret informing you that your application was rejected.
   (It was an error on our part.)

B. Read the following sentences written by students. Correct and explain the errors.
   1. I'm not used to eat such a big breakfast.
   2. I'm looking forward to meet you.
   3. I enjoyed very much to see it.
   4. I'm not interested to go to baseball games.
   5. I object to have to work so late.

C. The following exercise is suitable for students after they have been taught and have practiced using verbs that are followed by an infinitive or the verb + *-ing*. It will help students if you introduce them to one rule that applies in this area: always use the verb + *-ing* when you need a verb after a preposition.

   She insisted <u>on going</u> with us.

Write the appropriate form of the verb (infinitive or *-ing* form) in the blanks:

1. If you want to be fit and healthy, what do you have to stop _____ (do)?

2. What do you remember _____ (do) as a child?

3. She criticized me for _____ (spend) so much money.

4. Let's go out tonight instead of _____ (watch) TV.

5. Have you ever forgotten _____ (meet) someone for a date?

6. Do you always remember _____ (send) birthday greetings to your parents?

7. We're looking forward to _____ (go) on vacation.

8. I hate _____ (eat) cold pasta.

Expressing future time

It is important to be aware that, strictly speaking, English does not have a future tense. Rather, the language has a number of verb forms that can be used to express future time, events, predictions, intentions, promises, and so on.

1. *Will* and *shall* (*shall* is British English) are commonly used as auxiliaries with verbs that express prediction or when we expect something to happen:

   On the first of next month, *I'll* be twenty-one.

   Will is also used in weather forecasts:

   It *will* be colder tomorrow. There will be rain in the Northwest.

2. *Be + going to* is used to talk about intentions or plans. Often the speaker has already made the decision about the future action:

   What *are you going* to do next weekend?

   I'm going to visit a friend in New Orleans.

3. *Be + going to* is used to predict a future event or condition on the basis of present evidence:

> *It's going* to rain. (Evident because at present the sky is full of dark clouds.)

4. The *simple present* is used to express future certainties:

> The plane *departs* at 8:30 a.m. tomorrow.

The simple present is also used in conditional sentences in the subordinate *if* clause (see page 88):

> *If* you boil water, it *turns* to steam.

5. The *present continuous* is used to express future arrangements that are not as fixed or as certain as with the simple present:

> *I'm seeing* her this evening.

> Next summer, *we're taking* a holiday in Hawaii.

6. *Is/are + infinitive verb* is a formal way of expressing a future arrangement:

> The President *is to visit* Argentina in the fall.

7. The *future continuous (will + be + verb + -ing)* is also used to express a future arrangement:

> At 8:00 p.m. tomorrow, *we'll be leaving* for Thailand.

8. Modal verbs can express a range of certain and uncertain futures:

> I *may/might go* there if I have time.

Remember, when teaching future time, it is best to select the meaning or purpose to be expressed and then match this to the verb form.

Task 16:
Understanding
future
expressions

A. The first part of this task is intended to increase awareness of the verb forms that are used in context and in realistic situations. Read the scenes in Chart 1 and decide on an appropriate verb form for each blank. Then complete Chart 2 with the verb form you have chosen. In the third column of Chart 2, describe the function (intention, suggestion, promise, etc.) and a reason for the form (present simple to express future certainty, etc.). The first few in Chart 2 have been done for you.

Chart 1

1. *January Saturday Morning* On Main Street, Jenny says to her friend Chloe: "Let's plan our vacation. _____ we get some brochures from the travel agent?"	2. *Saturday Evening* At Jenny's flat, Jenny says to Chloe while leafing through brochures: "I think _____ go to Bulgaria. Would you like to come with me?"	3. *Monday Morning* At her office, Jenny says to a colleague: "Chloe and I _____ visit Bulgaria in July."	4. *The Next Saturday* In the office of the travel agency, the travel agent says to Jenny & Chloe: "If you go to Bulgaria, you _____ need a visa. Your plane _____ take off at 8:00 a.m. and _____ arrive at noon."
5. *July* *Saturday Afternoon* Jenny and Chloe's list of things to do: Renew passports Get visas Pay for tickets Get traveler's checks Jenny says to Chloe: "We _____ need to do all these things really soon!"	6. *Monday Morning* At Jenny's office, Jenny says to a colleague: "We _____ leave on Friday. Look at these pictures of Sofia. I can't wait to go. It _____ be a really great trip!"	7. *Thursday Morning* On the phone, Jenny tells Chloe: "Just think, this time tomorrow we _____ (fly) over the Alps."	8. *One Week Later* In a nightclub in Sofia, Jenny says to her new friend: "I ____ not forget you and I ___ write often when I get back to my office."

Chart 2

Situation number	Form	Function
1.	Should	make a suggestion
2.	I'll	make a decision at the time of speaking
3.	are going to	
4a.		
4b.		
5.		
6a.		
6b.		
7.		
8a.		
8b.		

A. The following utterances use verb forms that native speakers would not choose. In each sentence, change the verb forms to more appropriate forms.
1. I feel awful. I think I'll faint.
2. I don't like the idea, but I'm giving him the keys if you insist.
3. She hasn't studied very much, but I expect she's passing the exam.
4. I listened to the weather forecast today. They say it's raining tomorrow.
5. I'm sorry but I won't come to class tomorrow.
6. 'Bye, I'm going to see you tomorrow.
7. I have an appointment at the dentist's. I'll go this afternoon.
8. My plane leaves San Francisco for Denver at 7:00 a.m., so at about 8:30 a.m., I'm going to fly over the Rockies.
9. I'm sorry I can't go to the movies because I'll have a party tonight.
10. Don't be late! The train is going to leave at 6:30 a.m.

Conditional sentences

Conditional sentences differ in terms of what is likely or unlikely and real or imaginary ("unreal"). They also differ in their reference to time (past, present, or future). Conditional sentences can be divided into four different types:
1. The *present conditional*
   If + simple present . . . simple present (main clause):
   If you *heat* metal, it *expands.*
2. The *future conditional* (also referred to as the *first conditional)*
   If + simple present . . . *will/won't* (main clause):
   If it *rains* tomorrow, we *won't* go to the beach.
3. The *would conditional* (also referred to as the *second conditional)*
   If + simple past . . . *would* (main clause):
   If you *worked* hard, *you'd* pass the exam.
4. The *would have conditional* (the "unreal or hypothetical conditional," also referred to as the *third conditional)*
   If + past perfect . . . *would have* + past participle (main clause):
   If you *had listened,* you *would have heard* the announcement.

Task 17:
Understanding
conditional
sentences

A. Read the following two sentences. How would you explain the differences between them to a student?
   1. If you come in July, you'll meet my sister.
   2. If you came in July, you'd meet my sister.

B. Which of the following sentences expresses greater expectation that the job is likely to be offered?
   1. Will you accept the job if they offer it to you?
   2. Would you accept the job if they offered it to you?

C. Which statement is hypothetical because it's too late to change what happened or didn't happen in the past?
   1. If you ask me, I'll try to help you.
   2. If you had asked me, I'd have tried to help you.

D. Write the letter of the clause in Column II that goes with the clause in Column I.

Column I	Column II
__ 1. I'll tell you the first letter of the word	a. I could have gotten the job.
__ 2. If you don't like this food	b. it wouldn't have been broken.
__ 3. Unless you pay the ransom	c. if you give up now.
__ 4. You'll regret it later	d. unless I was really desperate.
__ 5. If you asked your brother	e. they might be able to help you.
__ 6. If you went to the embassy	f. I'll make you an omelet.
__ 7. If you were offered frog's legs	g. you'll miss your plane.
__ 8. I wouldn't stay in a place like that	h. he'd probably lend you his car.
__ 9. If the manager hadn't seen me	i. you'll never see her alive again.
__ 10. If you hadn't been so impatient	j. I'm sure I would have gotten
__ 11. Unless you leave right now	away with it.
__ 12. If I had had the experience	k. would you eat them?
	l. if you want a clue.

E. Now read the previous sentences again. If the order of the clauses in each sentence is reversed, is the meaning changed or affected?

F. Put the twelve sentences into three groups according to the similarity of structure (write the sentence numbers below):

Group 1	Group 2	Group 3
(For example, future conditional sentences)		

G. Look at the twelve sentences again and decide which of the following functions fits each sentence. Write the sentence number next to its function.
   a. threatening or warning
   b. expressing regret
   c. giving advice
   d. blaming
   e. offering
   f. imagining

H. Read the following sentences. What functions do they express? Write the appropriate function below each sentence.

   1. If all goes well, we'll be back by this evening.

   _____

   2. Would you mind if I gave him your address?

   _____

   3. If you stopped interrupting me, I'd get this done.

   _____

4. If I'd worked harder, I'd have passed the exam.

    _____

5. I wish you wouldn't shout!

    _____

**Task 18:
Understanding
other
conditional
sentence patterns**

A. In addition to the four basic conditional sentence types, there are others. You'll find a few of the common variations in the following chart (in addition to the basic four). Fill in the numbered blank spaces following the example in the first row.

Example	Structure (If *clause and main clause*)	Function/Meaning
1. If you freeze water, it expands.	1. simple present/ simple present	1. statement of fact/ general truth
2. If you'll buy the food, I'll get the wine.	2. future/future	2.
3. If you are to succeed, you'll have to work harder.	3. *Be + will + have to*/ infinitive + main verb	3.
4. If I had invested in Microsoft, I'd be very rich by now.	4.	4. Possible results of hypothetical past action
5.	5. Simple imperative/ present	5. Giving instructions

B. In the sentences below, write the correct form of the verb in parentheses in the blank. *Note:* There may be more than one possible way. (This type of task is also suitable for high-intermediate to advanced students.)

1. If you _____ (finish) your work, give it to the student next to you.

91

2. If my wife _____ (call), tell her I'm on my way home.

3. He would be pleased if you _____ (invite) him.

4. If you _____ (peel) the potatoes, I _____ (slice) the carrots.

5. If your little boy _____ (do) as he was told, he wouldn't be in trouble.

6. If you _____ (fill in) your application form, leave it with the secretary.

7. If you mix orange juice and cranberry juice, it _____ (taste) delicious.

8. If our team _____ (win) yesterday, we would be in the World Cup semi-finals.

9. We _____ (be) very pleased if you _____ (come) to our party.

10. If you polish your car with this special car shampoo, it _____ (look) wonderful.

Review questions

1. What is the difference between *lexical* and *structure* words? Underline the lexical words in the following song lines:

   Oh, when the saints go marching in

   He's got the whole world in His hands

   I'm singing in the rain

   Which words or syllables in the lexical words are stressed? Mark each syllable with a small box.

2. Is a question always *functionally* a question? What communicative function is expressed by the statement, "Why don't you see a doctor?"

3. Write a sentence using each of the following verb tenses:

    simple present:

    _____

    present continuous:

    _____

    present perfect:

    _____

    present perfect continuous:

    _____

    simple past:

    _____

    past continuous:

    _____

    past perfect:

    _____

    past perfect continuous:

    _____

4. What is a *passive* sentence? Give an example.

5. What form of a verb is used after a preposition: the infinitive form or the verb + *ing* form? Give two examples.

6. Name several ways to express future time. Use examples.

7. What are the four main types of *conditional* sentences?

Further reading

Celce-Murcia, M. and Hilles, S. *Techniques and Resources in Teaching Grammar.* Oxford University Press, 1988.

Close, R. A. *A Teacher's Grammar.* Language Teaching Publications, 1992.

Eastwood, J. *Oxford Guide to English Grammar.* Oxford University Press, 1994.

Leech, G. *An A-Z of English Grammar and Usage.* Edward Arnold, 1989.

Lock, G. *Functional English Grammar.* Cambridge University Press, 1996.

Swan, M. *Practical English Usage.* Oxford University Press, 1995.

Ur, P. *Grammar Practice Activities.* Cambridge University Press, 1988.

Wajnryb, R. *Grammar Dictation.* Oxford University Press, 1990.

TEACHING PRONUNCIATION

Sounds

Vowel sounds and diphthongs

Helping learners with sounds

Common errors in producing sounds

Stress

Stress and polysyllabic words

Rhythm

Intonation

Catenation

Glossary of phonetic terms

Review questions

Further reading

TEACHING PRONUNCIATION

TEACHING PRONUNCIATION HELPS STUDENTS LEARN to pronounce the sounds of English and to understand native English speech. It is *not* realistic to expect students to learn perfect pronunciation or to be able to speak like native speakers. Rather, you should make two realistic goals for teaching pronunciation: to learn enough about the sounds of English to be able to present them clearly and to help students learn to understand most of what they hear *and* be understood when they speak.

How can you prepare for the task of teaching pronunciation? First familiarize yourself with the three main areas of pronunciation:

♦ **Sounds.** You should be aware of the *sounds* of vowels, diphthongs, and consonants, especially those that are different and a challenge for most English language learners.

♦ **Stress.** You should be aware of *stress* on syllables and on words in connected speech.

♦ **Rhythm and intonation.** You should be aware of *rhythm* and *intonation* patterns in a flow of speech.

Sounds
There are a great number of possible *sounds* in languages; each language uses a limited set (usually between 20 and 60) consisting of *vowels* (voiced continuing sounds like *ee* or *ah*) and *consonants* (sounds like *b, d, g,* and *k).*

The English *alphabet* (a set of symbols for writing the words of a language) is not a good guide to the sounds of English. This is because English has forty-four *distinctive sounds*, and the alphabet has only twenty-six letters. This discrepancy results in two kinds of problems:

1. A single letter can represent several different sounds. For example, the letter *e* sounds quite different in m*e*n and wom*e*n than in th*e* and r*e*n*e*w.

2. The letters do not show the differences between sounds represented by the same letters. For example, the sound of *th* in *this* and *these* is different than the sound of *th* in *thistle* or *thank.*

To handle these problems, a *phonetic alphabet* was created. This special alphabet, usually called the *IPA* (International Phonetics Alphabet), makes it possible to show clearly how native speakers of standard American English pronounce words. The IPA is available in good dictionaries and used worldwide by language teachers. Following is a version of the IPA that is easy to understand and use:

The Phonemic Chart
General American

iy	ɪ	ʌ	a	ɔ	ow
b<u>ea</u>t	b<u>i</u>t	b<u>u</u>d	b<u>o</u>b	b<u>ou</u>ght	b<u>oa</u>t
	ɛ	æ	ʊ	uw	ə
	b<u>e</u>t	b<u>a</u>t	b<u>oo</u>k	b<u>oo</u>t	<u>a</u>bout
ey	ay	aw	oy		
b<u>ay</u>	b<u>i</u>ke	c<u>ow</u>	b<u>oy</u>		
p	b	t	d	k	g
pen	Ben	tip	dip	cat	gun
l	r	m	n	ŋ	h
lip	red	me	neat	si<u>ng</u>	hat
f	v	θ	ð	s	z
fish	vest	<u>th</u>in	<u>the</u>	see	zoo
š	ž	č	ǰ	y	w
ship	leisure	chew	judge	yes	win

Note: This modified and condensed version of the IPA (with 39 sounds) is in accordance with generally accepted symbols used in American textbooks and guides to American pronunciation.

Learning the IPA is not as hard as it may seem. If you take a look at the *consonants*, you will see that there are many similarities between the IPA symbols and the regular English letters of the alphabet:

	IPA Symbols
the *b* sound as in the word *bob* is written	/b/
the *d* sound as in the word *dog* is written	/d/
the *f* sound as in the word *fit* is written	/f/
the *g* sound as in the word *got* is written	/g/
the *h* sound as in the word *hit* is written	/h/
the *k* sound as in the word *cat* is written	/k/
the *l* sound as in the word *lit* is written	/l/
the *m* sound as in the word *mom* is written	/m/
the *n* sound as in the word *none* is written	/n/
the *p* sound as in the word *pop* is written	/p/
the *r* sound as in the word *rock* is written	/r/
the *s* sound as in the word *sis* is written	/s/
the *t* sound as in the word *tip* is written	/t/
the *v* sound as in the word *vim* is written	/v/
the *w* sound as in the word *win* is written	/w/
the *y* sound as in the word *yes* is written	/y/
the *z* sound as in the word *zoo* is written	/z/

Note: In the IPA, the *y* sound is sometimes represented by /j/.

These seventeen symbols for sounds (out of the possible forty-four) are easy to recognize; therefore learning the IPA is much easier than you think. You will find that there are only a few new symbols you need to learn in order to teach pronunciation.

The IPA is worth learning and remembering. It is useful when studying English for several reasons:

♦ The IPA makes learners aware of the distinctive sounds in English. It helps them focus on sounds that do not exist in their native languages.

- Learners can *see* as well as *hear* that sounds are similar or different in English to those in their own language.
- A visual representation helps learners with errors. Learners cannot always hear their mistakes; the symbols help learners realize that remedial work is needed.
- The IPA helps learners use dictionaries more effectively. Students learn how to pronounce new words without the teacher's help if they know the IPA symbols in the dictionary.

For the teacher, the IPA is worth knowing and using because:

- The IPA is a more professional way to show students that you know something about practical phonemics.
- Knowing the IPA gives the learner more confidence in you as a teacher.
- The IPA helps with remedial work. You can reinforce the correct sound by pointing to the chart or writing the transcription on the board.
- Seeing is believing! It is easier to teach sounds when they are graphically represented.
- It's almost the only way to introduce students to certain features of connected speech (like intrusive sounds, omission, and elision).

Note: You'll get to know the chart as you use it and teach with it. Don't worry if at first you can't remember all the symbols. It is most important to learn the symbols for the sounds students have the most problems with.

Sounds naturally occur in words and in a flow of connected sounds. In these natural environments, individual sounds are modified or changed by other sounds. When you say a word like *butter* (or even a short word like *but),* it's not easy to separate the individual sounds out of the word. A sound can occur in three possible positions in a syllable or in a word: at the beginning (initial), in the middle (medial), and at the end (final). The sounds /p/ and /b/, for example, have different qualities at the beginning of a word than at the end. Say the words *pop* and *bob.* Now hold a tissue in front of your lips when you say the words. You will notice that the initial /p/ or /b/ is a bit different—the amount of air released with the initial /p/ is greater than with the final /p/.

Try to notice the difference in voicing with the /p/ and /b/ sounds, too. If you lightly place your fingertips on your voice box (at the front of your throat) and say *pa* and *ba*, you'll feel more vibration with the *ba* sound. But look at yourself in a mirror and whisper *pa* and *ba*, and you won't see any difference in the way your lips form the sounds.

The formation of sounds is called *articulation*. Where you form the sounds is known as the *point of articulation*. In technical terms, the /p/ and the /b/ are both called *stops* because the air that we breathe out (from our lungs through our mouths) is stopped by the closed lips and then pushed out suddenly. These sounds are also called *plosives* (in phonetics). You have, however, noticed a difference between the /b/ and the /p/ in the vibration of your voice box. The /b/ sound can be described as a *voiced plosive* and /p/ as an *unvoiced plosive*. Voiced plosives like /b/ and /d/ are accompanied by actual sound and vibrations of the voice box. Unvoiced plosives, on the other hand, have air expelled but no sound.

How do sounds change meanings? Take a simple word like *bin* (transcribed by the IPA as /bɪn/). It's closely related in sound to the word *pin* (in IPA: /pɪn/). In fact, this pair of words differs in only one sound. This characteristic is called a *minimal difference*. Because the only difference between word sounds like *pin* and *bin* is the /p/ and the /b/, *pin* and *bin* are called a *minimal pair*.

One of the main reasons for teaching pronunciation is to help learners to be understood. The native speaker will not understand a word spoken by a learner if it sounds like another word that has a different meaning (for example, what if the learner says "I gave him a *bat* on the head" instead of a *pat?*) Therefore, minimal pairs can be used to help students learn to produce the *minimal* differences and thus understand the *meaningful* differences between words.

The individual sound that makes a difference between two words is called a *phoneme*. In language teaching, we show that a word is written in its basic, distinctive sounds by using diagonal slashes. For example, /pɪn/ consists of three phonemes: /p/, /ɪ/, and /n/.

Task 1:
Practicing
phonemic
transcription

A. Match the *first* sound in these words with their phonemic transcription:

1.	Thomas	/ǰ/
2.	jump	/k/
3.	sugar	/n/
4.	those	/y/
5.	contract	/f/
6.	united	/ɪ/
7.	physique	/t/
8.	pneumonia	/š/
9.	enough	/θ/
10.	thank	/ð/

B. Match the last sound in these words with the phonemic transcription:

1.	cowboy	/ey/
2.	thumb	/oy/
3.	watched	/t/
4.	wealth	/z/
5.	bags	/θ/
6.	weigh	/m/

C. Match the following words with their phonemic transcriptions:

1.	puff	/pam/
2.	pole	/puwl/
3.	palm	/pʌf/
4.	put	/powl/
5.	pool	/pʊt/

Vowel sounds
and diphthongs

By using the IPA, you are able to show that American English has tese vowel sounds:

b<u>ea</u>t	b<u>i</u>t
b<u>u</u>d	b<u>o</u>b
b<u>ou</u>ght	b<u>e</u>t
b<u>a</u>t	b<u>oo</u>k
b<u>oo</u>t	ab<u>ou</u>t

In addition, the IPA has three combined vowels called *diphthongs* (sometimes called *glides* because the two vowels glide smoothly into one combined sound):

> h<u>ou</u>se /haws/
> v<u>oi</u>ce /voys/
> f<u>i</u>ve /fayv/

Task 2: Transcribing vowel sounds

Read the following list of minimal pairs. The words in this list show the ten different vowel sounds (the *vowel phonemes* of English). Using the IPA chart on page 98, write out the phonemic symbol for each vowel sound.

1. bad   /   /
2. bed   /   /
3. pit   /   /
4. pot   /   /
5. bud   /   /
6. bird   /   /
7. bard   /   /
8. board   /   /
9. pull   /   /
10. pool   /   /

Task 3: Transcribing diphthongs

A. Look at the five words listed below and note their vowel sounds. Write out their transcriptions using the IPA chart:

1. name   /   /
2. time   /   /
3. note   /   /
4. noise   /   /
5. now   /   /

Task 4: Working with vowel sounds and diphthongs

Match the seven phonemic symbols (vowels or diphthongs) with the seven color words in which these sounds occur:

1.	/ɛ/	green
2.	/uw/	blue
3.	/ay/	red
4.	/aw/	white
5.	/ey/	grey
6.	/iy/	gold
7.	/ow/	brown

Note: The short vowel sound called schwa is the most frequently used vowel in English. It is the vowel sound in *the* and *a* and the first sound in *about*. Its phonemic symbol is /ə/. It occurs in unstressed words and syllables, such as in prepositions like *to* or *of*. For example:

She went <u>to</u> school.   /tə/

She's the Queen <u>of</u> England.   /əv/

Task 5: Practicing pronunciation of vowel sounds

1. How is the *u* in *but* pronounced in the following? (The sentence should be read fairly quickly with normal stresses.)

   He's an intelligent student but not hard-working.

   Transcribe *but*:   /   /

2. How is the *a* in *at* pronounced in the following?

   They're at home this evening.

   Transcribe *at*:   /   /

3. How is the *o* in *from* pronounced in the following?

   She comes from Mexico.

   Transcribe *from*:   /   /

Task 6: Awareness of the sounds of the past tense -ed

There are three different sounds of the past tense -*ed*:

   /d/ in *played*

   /t/ in *asked*

   /ɪd/ in *ended*

A. For each of the following past forms, put an X in the column
    which indicates the appropriate pronunciation of -ed.

		/d/	/t/	/ɪd/
1.	asked			
2.	skated			
3.	watched			
4.	posted			
5.	laughed			
6.	refused			
7.	missed			
8.	stayed			
9.	bored			
10.	mended			

B. Using the chart above, try to think of the rules for the three
    different sounds of -ed. Note the sound of the consonant at the
    end of the verb before the past ending is added. Is it voiced or
    unvoiced? If the verb ends in a vowel or diphthong, what is the
    sound of -ed? Once you have thought about this, complete the
    rules below.

1. After a verb ending in *t* or *d*, the final -ed is pronounced /   /.

2. After a verb ending in a voiceless consonant other than *t* (/p/,
    /k/, /f/, /s/, /š/, /č/ or /θ/), the final -ed is pronounced /   /.

3. After a verb ending in a voiced consonant (/b/, /g/, /l/, /z/, /v/,
    /ǰ/, /ž/, /m/, /n/, or /ð/, /ŋ/) or vowel sounds, the final -ed is
    pronounced /   /.

**Helping learners
with sounds**

Remember, recognition first! Before asking learners to produce new
sounds in words that may be unfamiliar, give them *recognition* exercises.
The most simple of these exercises is to ask students, "Do these words
sound the same or different?" *(Note:* Make sure they understand the
meaning of the words they are going to hear and later see.)

Use minimal pairs for sounds that may cause problems for students whose native language does not have the same contrasts. For example, Spanish and Italian learners have a problem with the short vowel /ɪ/ and the long vowel /iy/. Therefore, they may *not* pronounce the words *eat* and *it* differently. The following is an example of an exercise with minimal pairs.

Using a tape recording or your own voice as the model, ask learners to make a check mark for same or an X for different.

	Same	Different
1. ship/sheep		
2. meet/meat		
3. chip/cheap		
4. seat/sit		
5. sea/see		

Note: With exercises like the one above, it's a good idea to go over the list of words with learners, listening and repeating the pairs of words in chorus and individually. Such exercises can be done with pictures to illustrate the differences in meaning (*ship* and *sheep, bin* and *bean*). A fun way for young learners is to ask them to clap when the two words have the same vowel sound or shake their heads when they are different.

Common errors in producing sounds

Awareness of the problems various language or ethnic groups have with producing sounds is helpful in identifying and anticipating the types of practice needed. The following tips should help you help learners with these errors.

Vowels/Diphthongs	Examples	Nationalities/Language Group
/ɪ/ sounds like /iy/	*ship* pronounced sheep	Greek, Italian, French, Spanish, Slavonic

What to do: Recognition practice to show that /ɪ/ is a much shorter sound than /iy/ and get learners to spread their lips and smile for the long vowel /iy/, as in "Say cheese" (for a photo)!

Vowels/Diphthongs	Examples	Nationalities/Language Group
/ɛ/ sounds like /æ/ /æ/ sounds like /ɛ/	*men* pronounced *man* *man* pronounced like *men*	Russian, Hebrew, German

What to do: Demonstrate that the mouth only opens a little for the sound /ɛ/, but for /æ/ the mouth opens more to allow the lower jaw and chin to drop right down.

Vowels/Diphthongs	Examples	Nationalities/Language Group
/æ/ sounds like /ʌ/	*hat* pronounced like *hut*	Italian, Spanish, Greek

What to do: Demonstrate that although for both sounds the mouth opens widely (with lips spreading), with /ʌ/ the lips are pulled back more to allow the sound to be formed further back towards the roof of the mouth.

Vowels/Diphthongs	Examples	Nationalities/Language Group
/ey/ pronounced /ɛ/	*sale* pronounced *sell*	Spanish, Greek

What to do: Get learners to recognize that /ey/ is a longer sound than /ɛ/ as it is a glide from /ɛ/ to /ɪ/, and is in fact two sounds. Ask learners to say /ɛ/ and then /ɪ/ as quickly as possible, which should produce the diphthong /ey/.

Vowels/Diphthongs	Examples	Nationalities/Language Group
/ow/ pronounced /ɔ/ or /a/	*coat* sounds like *caught* *old men* sounds like *all men*	Greek, Italian, Spanish, Turkish, Japanese, Portuguese

What to do: Similarly (as in /eɪ/) get students to say /ɔ/ and then quickly follow with /ʊ/ to merge into /ow/.

Vowels/Diphthongs	Examples	Nationalities/Language Group
/ʌ/ confused with /a/	*cut* sounds like *cot* *hut* sounds like *hot*	Greek, Italian, Slavonic

What to do: See the note above about /ow/. For /a/ the lips are slightly forward, the jaw is loosely dropped, and the sound is held longer than /ʌ/. Depending on the learners' cultural background, you can ask for the "ah" sound required by doctors, or other appropriate stimulus to produce /a/.

Vowels/Diphthongs	Examples	Nationalities/Language Group
/l/ sounds too close to /r/ /r/ confused with /l/	*light* sounds like *right* *Jerry* sounds like *jelly*	Chinese, Japanese

What to do: Demonstrate that both /l/ and /r/ are made by moving the tip of the tongue. The difference is that for /l/ the tongue touches the roof of the mouth so that air is expelled from the sides of the tongue, whereas for /r/ the air is funneled over and around the tongue to the front of the mouth. For the /l/ sound (a laterally spread tongue position), the lips are spread to the sides of the mouth and relaxed, but for /r/ the lips are tighter and pushed forward more. For some groups of learners, you could show the "kissing position" of the lips. Remember that in some cultures, like traditional Japanese, moving the lips like that is not polite.

Vowels/Diphthongs	Examples	Nationalities/Language Group
/b/ pronounced like /v/ /v/ sounds like /b/ in initial position	*civil* sounds like *sybil* in the middle of words *vest* sounds like *best*	Spanish, especially Latin American

What to do: Show learners how to produce /v/. The top teeth are gently pressed on the bottom lip. As /v/ is voiced, there should be vibrations in the Adam's apple and the bottom lip.

Vowels/Diphthongs	Examples	Nationalities/Language Group
/y/ confused with /ĵ/	*yellow* sounds like or pronounced *jello*	Spanish, Latin American

What to do: Concentrate on producing /y/ in words like *yes*, *yet*, and *yellow*. First practice the vowel /ɪ/ (tongue up high in the mouth near the ridge behind the teeth but not touching the roof of the mouth). Then move the tongue very quickly to make /ĵ/. Do recognition exercises to clarify different sounds of /ĵ/ and /y/ (for example, *jam* and *yam*, *joke* and *yolk*, *jeers* and *years*).

Vowels/Diphthongs	Examples	Nationalities/Language Group
/θ/pronounced /s/ /ð/ pronounced /z/	*mouth* sounds like *mouse* *thin* sounds like *sin* *breathe* sounds like *breeze* *withered* sounds like *wizard*	German, Russian, Slavonic, French

What to do: Get students to hiss like a snake for the /s/ sound. Next get them to move the tongue forward (not necessary to put it between the teeth) behind the top teeth. This should produce /θ/. For /ð/, get students to hum as in /m/. Then ask them to move the tongue forward and behind top teeth (as in /θ/) but with the voice to produce /ð/.

Vowels/Glides	Examples	Nationalities/Language Group
/s/ pronounced /z/ (especially before l, m, n) /z/ confused with /s/	*slick* sounds like *zlick* *eggs* sounds like *eks*	Italian, Arabic, Russian, Slavonic

What to do: Show that the unvoiced /s/ has no vibration in the voice box nor on the tongue, whereas for /z/ there is vibration. Practice with pairs like *bus/buzz, Sue/zoo,* and *sip/zip.*

Stress Where the emphasis is placed on words and syllables it is referred to as *stress*. Generally in a sentence, the lexical words carry most information and are stressed (see *Structural and lexical words,* Chapter 5, page 61). Word stress in sentences is important, but it is also important to realize that any word in English with two syllables or more has one syllable that has greater stress than the others. Look at the words that have more than one syllable in the telegram below:

> Chinese delegation arrives Kennedy Airport 9:00 a.m.
> Monday March 2

Native speakers will invariably stress the second syllable in *Chinese;* the third syllable in *delegation;* and the first syllable in *Kennedy, Airport, Monday,* and *second.*

Although English has various patterns of syllable stress, a large number of words (perhaps 80%) have the primary stress on the first syllable. It is important for the learner to realize this dominant pattern, though there are many common words with primary stress on the second syllable (such as verbs with a prefix: *remember, prepare,* and *consider*).

Task 7: Awareness of stress

A. For each of the following words, mark the primary stress by underlining the syllable with the stressed vowel. The first one is done for you.

1. inter<u>na</u>tional

2. revision

3. education

4. examination

5. constitution

6. revolution

7. computerization

All the above words end in *-ion (-tion* or *-sion)*. Can you see and hear the pattern? How would you describe it to learners? *Hint:* Try counting the primary stressed syllable from the end of the word, not from the beginning.

B. Each set below shows words derived from the same root. Mark the primary stress by underlining the syllable with the stressed vowel. Notice the shift in primary stress in the words.

1. democrat   democratic   democracy

2. photograph   photographic   photographer

3. educate   education   educational

4. telegram   telegraphic   telegraphy

5. intellect   intelligence   intellectual

C. Underline the syllable with the primary stress in the following words. Note the shift in meaning and/or grammatical change in each set. What is the pattern?

1. a digest   to digest

2. an accent   to accent

3. a contract   to contract

4. a permit   to permit

5. the produce   to produce

6. the desert   to desert

Note: The pronunciation of the unstressed vowel in verbs is often reduced to *schwa* /ə/ as in /kəntrækt/.

Task 8: Noticing stress: words in sentences

As an awareness exercise, read the following sentences aloud and notice the pattern and rhythm of the stressed and unstressed words.

> Are you <u>mad</u> at me?

> I didn't <u>see</u> you there.

> I didn't <u>ask</u> you to.

Think of more sentences with these stress patterns:

☐☐☐☐☐☐ or ☐☐☐☐☐☐   Write them below.

_____

_____

_____

Task 9: Practicing contrastive stress

Read the following dialogues aloud with a friend (native speaker) and then underline the word in B's reply that has extra stress.

1. A. You're from South Carolina, aren't you?

    B. No, I'm from North Carolina.

2. A. I bought you a grey tie.

    B. Well, I wanted a red one.

3. A. So, you've been living here for ten years.

    B. Well, no. I've been living here for two years.

Now make up your own examples using the sentences below. Underline the contrastive stress. The first one is done for you.

Is that 5132?	No, this is <u>4</u>132.
Is that 332?	No, this is _____.
Is she your cousin?	No, she's my _____.
Is he your husband?	No, he's my _____.
Are you the boss?	No, I'm the _____.

Stress and polysyllabic words

Polysyllabic words are words with three syllables or more. In polysyllabic words, beyond the *primary* stressed syllable there are unstressed syllables or a syllable that carries a *secondary* stress. In many dictionaries and books on pronunciation, the syllable with *primary* stress is marked with a short line before and above the syllable, whereas the syllable with *secondary* stress is marked before and below the syllable:

ˌinterˈnational, ˌpolyˈtechnic, ˌpolysylˈlabic, ˌrefeˈree, ˌsubjecˈtivity

One of the differences between British English and American English is that American English keeps the secondary accent on the *penultimate* (the one before the last) syllable in words like *temporary, secretary,* and *laboratory* with a full [e] vowel:

British English: ˈtemprɪ,   ˈsekrətrɪ

American English: ˈtempəˌrerɪ, ˈsekrəˌterɪ

For teaching and learning purposes, concentrate on *primary* stress and the contrast with unstressed syllables. The stress patterns in *polysyllabic* words in English are complex and should not be introduced to students at the beginning level. As a teacher, you will need to take time to become aware of the patterns.

Rhythm

English is a *stress-timed* language, meaning the beats on the primary stresses follow each other at roughly equal intervals. This timing, and the fact that spoken English shows strong contrasts between its stressed and unstressed syllables, gives English speech its characteristic *rhythms*.

There's a marked difference in rhythm when we compare sentences with many lexical words (usually stressed) to sentences comprising mainly structural words (usually unstressed). For example:

Bob's friend Jean has just bought two very good paintings.
(10 words, 9 stresses)
What would you have done if he had attacked you in the street?
(13 words, 4 stresses)

The shorter sentence takes more time to say than the longer one. In the longer sentence, the unstressed words are compressed between the steady stress beats and are spoken quickly. The shorter sentence is packed with stressed syllables that cannot be compressed.

In many traditional songs, verses, and nursery rhymes, you can hear the regular stress-timing even when the number of words or syllables differs from line to line. Read the following verses and note the number of stressed syllables in each line:

Verse 1
Ten green bottles
Hanging on the wall.
If one green bottle
Should accidentally fall
There'd be nine green bottles
Hanging on the wall.

Verse 2
Lavender blue, dilly dilly, lavender green
When I am king, dilly dilly, you'll be my queen.

In *syllable-timed* languages (French, Spanish, Japanese), roughly equal timing is given to each syllable. Try saying the following aloud with natural stress and rhythm:

I've got to go.
I've got to go now.
I've really got to go now.
I've really got to go right now.

The following phrases show a number of lexical words stressed in sequence. Ask learners to listen and then repeat the phrases in a steady rhythm. It's a good idea to beat the rhythm by clapping or tapping with a pen. Note that the rhythm of English tends to be eight beats long. Count out 1-2-3-<u>4</u>-5-6-7-<u>8</u>.

a truck, a heavy truck, a heavy truck with a load
a heavy truck with a load of wood
a heavy truck with a full load of wood

Soda,
Cherry soda,
a bottle of cherry soda
a can of cold cherry soda

Intonation   When we communicate orally, we don't just string phonemes together to make up words. We use *pitch*—high and low tones similar to the variations in music—to convey emotions and attitudes. *Intonation* encompasses the moments in which we change pitch. It enables us to express surprise, pleasure, disappointment, irony, excitement, and other feelings.

Intonation has two other main functions:

1. It shows grammatical contrasts, such as between questions and statements:

    Bob called. (falling tone/statement)

    Bob called? (rising tone/question)

2. It marks new information (the pitch falls onto the important word or sound):

    A. Let's go to the movies.

    B. I'm going to the movies tomorrow.

    A. She's from France.

    B. Oh, I live in Paris.

Task 10:
Understanding
rhythm and
intonation

A. How would you use intonation to sound friendly in the following one-word responses? Mark the intonation of each response (person B) with an arrow (rising or falling).

A: Hi Tom! How are you?

B: Fine.

A: Quite a while since I saw you.

B: Yes.

A: I've moved to Denmark.

B: Oh.

B. In the following dialogue, mark the intonation of person B (the person who hasn't heard the statement properly).

A: I met Joe Brown.

B: Who?

A: Joe Brown. He's leaving on Thursday.

B: When?

A: Thursday. He's going to Moscow.

B: Where?

C. With a friend, act out the three different dialogues indicated by the faces. Notice how the intonation changes in each dialogue.

The three stages of marriage

Stage One *The honeymoon*	Stage Two *After one year!*	Stage Three *After seven years!*
Wife: Darling? Husband: Mm? Wife: Coffee? Husband: Mm!	Wife: Dear? Husband: Mm? Wife: Coffee? Husband: Mm.	Wife: Bill? Husband: Mm? Wife: Coffee? Husband: Mm?

D. Read the following dialogues. Notice how the intonation changes.
The tip
A: Here's twenty dollars.
B: Thank you.
A: Here's three dollars.
B: Thank you.
A: Here's one dollar.
B: Thank you.

Catenation   In normal discourse, the native speaker naturally moves smoothly (it sounds quick to the non-native listener) from one stressed syllable to the next. In fluent speech, therefore, the pronunciation of the final sound of one word and the initial sound of the following word is changed or lost. This is known as *catenation* or *linking*. Following are specific examples of catenation with their technical names:

Technical Name	Description	Examples
Elision	Loss of a sound, often when some consonants are the same or similar	We've visited Guatemala. (Only one *v* is pronounced.) He'd decided to leave. (Only one *d* is pronounced.) I can't type. (Only one *t* is pronounced.)
Intrusion	An additional sound is inserted, often to link two vowel sounds	He's going to Italy. (/təwɪtəliy/)
Assimilation	Sounds are changed to make it easier and smoother to pronounce the next sound (or the previous sound)	Ten pennies (/tɛmpɛniyz/) Get out! (/gɛdawt/)

Task 11:
Understanding
catenation

Transcribe the underlined words in the following sentences (it helps to read them out loud).

1. So you <u>want to</u> go!

2. What <u>did you</u> do yesterday?

3. How <u>did you</u> get there?

4. Where <u>did they</u> go in Asia?

5. What <u>can't you</u> understand?

6. Why <u>did he</u> go?

Glossary of phonetic terms	Affricate:	Any stop or plosive where the release of air is performed so slowly that considerable friction occurs at about the same place where the stop is made (for example, /č/ or /ĵ/).
	Alveolar:	A place in the mouth (otherwise known as hard palate) where when the tip of the tongue touches, these sounds are produced: /t/, /d/, /s/, /z/, /n/, /l/.
	Articulation:	Description of how and where particular speech sounds are made. An active articulator is the part that moves; a passive articulator is the part that is touched or approached.
	Bilabial:	Description of sound produced when the lips are together. In a bilabial sound, the lower lip is an active articulator; the upper lip is a passive articulator. For example: /p/, /b/, /m/.
	Continuant/ semi-vowel:	A rapid vocalic glide on to a syllabic sound of steady duration. In English, semi-vowels like /y/ and /w/ glide from positions approximately /iy/ and /uw/. Semi-vowels are treated as consonants because their function is consonantal rather than vowel-like (marginal, not central in the syllable).
	Dental:	Description of the sound produced using the upper teeth. In a dental sound, the tip of the tongue (active articulator) is against the upper teeth. For example, /t/, /d/.
	Fricative:	Description of the sound produced when the two articulators (teeth and lips) close together, forming a restriction through which air can escape, making a hissing sound. For example. /f/, /v/, /θ/, /ð/.
	Glottal:	Description of the sound produced when only the vocal cords are being used. For example, /h/.

Labio-dental: Description of the sound produced when the lower lip is against the upper teeth. For example, /f/, /v/.

Lateral: Description of the sound produced when the soft palate is in a raised position (shutting off nasal resonator); the tip of the tongue is in contact with the upper teeth ridge, allowing air to escape on both sides of the tongue. The English lateral phoneme is /l/, which is alveolar.

Nasal: This sound is similar to a plosive except the closure is not released; air escapes through the nose. For example, /n/, /m/, /ŋ/.

Palatal: Description of the sound produced when the tongue is towards the front of the mouth and near the hard palate. For example, /y/, /s/, /z/.

Plosive: A complete closure of the articulators (such as lips) in which the articulators are suddenly released. (Also called *stop*.)

Velar: Description of the sound produced when the tongue moves back and up towards the velum (soft palate). For example, /k/, /g/, /h/.

Review questions

1. What are the three main areas of pronunciation?

2. In what ways is the written alphabet in English an imperfect guide to the sounds of the language? Give two or three examples.

3. What's the main difference in sound between a simple vowel and a diphthong?

4. Why should language teachers get to know the IPA? What are the most useful phonemic symbols to know?

5. Why use minimal pairs in teaching pronunciation?

6. Which words in a sentence usually carry greater stress than others?

7. How can a change of syllable stress change the meaning of a word?

8. What is intonation? Catenation?

Further reading   Baker, A. *Introducing English Pronunciation: A Teacher's Guide to 'Tree or Three' and 'Sheep or Ship.'* Cambridge University Press, 1982.

Celce-Murcia, M. *Teaching Pronunciation.* Cambridge University Press, 1996.

Cook, V. *Active Intonation.* Addison Wesley Longman, 1980.

Harmer, J. *Teaching English Pronunciation.* Addison Wesley Longman, 1987.

Laroy, C. *Pronunciation.* Oxford University Press, 1995.

TEACHING LISTENING

How to teach listening

Preparing a listening task

Types of listening tasks

- Predicting through vocabulary

- Student-generated questions

- Listening for specific information

- Putting events/items in the right order

- True/false statements

- Open-ended questions

- Multiple-choice questions

- Note-taking

Authentic readings

Review questions

Further reading

TEACHING LISTENING

LISTENING, WHICH MEANS PAYING ATTENTION TO and understanding what you hear, is an essential skill for communication. Teachers and students often underrate the importance of listening because the more obvious goal of a language course is to learn how to *speak* the language. However, you cannot converse with someone without understanding what you hear. Listening is in some ways more difficult than speaking. After all, you can control what you say; you cannot normally control what is said to you.

Successful listening depends on our ability to understand sounds in particular contexts and circumstances. The setting or social situation (the listening context) plays an important role in helping us to work out the meaning and interpret what we hear.

The listening context determines the listening strategy that one uses. The way we listen, therefore, varies according to our listening purpose. For example, we will probably listen more closely to a dramatic dialogue in a television show than to the commercial that follows; our purpose is to watch the show, not the commercials. As a teacher, you need to realize that students do not really listen unless they have a *purpose*—a reason to do so.

This chapter is intended to help you understand how to teach listening and how to carry out various listening activities.

How to teach listening

Following are tips and advice for helping you develop listening activities and tasks:

◆ **Help, don't test.** There is a difference between *helping* learners to develop listening skills and *testing* their listening ability (their ability to understand what they hear). The purposes of listening tasks should not be primarily to test the learners or to set traps for the learners to fall into. Learners need to reduce their fear of not being able to understand a listening task. To help learners feel more confident about the listening task on hand, keep in mind the following:

- introduce listening material with a simple global understanding question like, "Is the dialogue about a football game or a tennis match?" This is a simple and effective way to help reduce students' fear.

- assure students that they will hear the tape more than once. This tends to help them relax and listen openly with less stress.

- place learners in pairs or small groups. This enables them to share their individual difficulties in finding the answers.

- check and reconfirm students' answers and ideas. If tasks are unchecked and answers not confirmed as acceptable (or not), students feel insecure and wonder why they were asked to listen in the first place. Checking does not have to be done in the conventional teacher-directed mode. Answers could be handed out, or alternative answers could be given to different pairs who then re-divide and check each other's answers (such as an information-gap activity).

◆ **Be aware of different listening strategies.** It's worth reiterating that people use different strategies to deal with differences in content. We do not listen in the same way to airport announcements as we do to radio news. You must keep these differences in mind when choosing listening tasks for your students.

◆ **Select appropriate material.** There are many listening materials available for creating listening tasks. It's important to understand the difference between *authentic* listening materials and materials that are specially prepared for the language learner. The latter are easier to cope with; they are usually graded for particular levels and include both audiotapes and corresponding textbooks. Authentic materials are more challenging. They require special attention and the development of well-prepared tasks in order to be successful.

However, the aim of listening tasks should be to prepare students for interaction in the real world, not in the classroom. Students learn to communicate and participate in the real world by developing skills and strategies needed to cope with authentic listening materials. Hence, authentic language must be presented in the classroom, even though it may be more difficult to understand. The authentic text cannot be altered, but it can be shortened. In addition, the task can be made simple and within the students' competence. If the task is do-able, students are more likely to be successful, which in turn builds their confidence.

An example of a task using authentic material is to first show a short news broadcast from a TV program (this provides visual clues to the meaning). Then show the broadcast a second time without the visual background (such as a radio broadcast recorded on audiotape). Ask beginning and intermediate students to match the topics mentioned on the broadcast to items in a category list (politics, sports, crime, etc.) and to show global understanding of the different news subjects. Ask more advanced students to answer detailed questions on the content. Always make sure that the task is appropriate to the interests and levels of the students, whether you are using authentic texts or not.

◆ **Have a listening purpose.** Students need reasons for listening. It's not motivating to be confronted by a text without something specific to focus on. Listening to a foreign language is daunting enough; often learners try to understand every word, which usually means they don't achieve a global understanding. They don't realize what is unimportant and what is important. To avoid this, always give students specific reasons for listening and specific information to listen for. Anxiety is reduced when the students feel assured that they are not expected, nor do they need, to understand every word in the listening text.

Generally there are four purposes for listening:
1. listening for gist (or global understanding)
2. listening for specific information (for example, listening to an announcement at an airport)
3. listening to establish a context (Where is this happening? What's happening? Who is speaking to whom?)

4. listening to provide information for later discussion, role-play, or information exchange

Preparing a listening task

To prepare a listening task, answer the following questions:
- What is the purpose of the task?
- What listening skills will be practiced?
- Is the task suitable for the learners' level?
- What language do students need in order to do the task (key vocabulary)?
- How can I create interest in the listening text?

When creating listening tasks, it is important that *listening* skills are being practiced or tested, not other language skills or aspects like cultural knowledge. However, what students have learned from a listening task can form the basis for the practice of another skill, such as role-playing.

Remember that the main functions of a listening task should be to help learners gain confidence in their listening ability and to build strategies that help learners make sense of what they hear. The success of a listening task also depends on your attitude. Be positive towards the learners' attempts to carry out the task. Make sure your tasks are clear, focused, and not too difficult.

The following tasks are designed to help you when creating a listening skills lesson. They highlight two important points: *staging* the activities and clarifying the *purposes* of the stages.

Task 1: Staging a listening skills lesson

Think about the following ten stages and number them in an appropriate order for a listening lesson:

___ a. Play the tape for the first time.
___ b. Warm up (set the scene).
___ c. Play the tape for the second time.
___ d. Teach key vocabulary.
___ e. Pair up students and ask them to compare their answers.
___ f. Give follow-up activities (such as written work).
___ g. Have students report back to the whole class. Check and confirm their answers.
___ h. Monitor student activities.
___ i. Set questions/tasks for general or gist comprehension.
___ j. Set questions/tasks for detailed comprehension.

Task 2:
Understanding
the purposes of
the stages

Now read the following list of purposes and match them to the stages given above (except for *a*). Put the letter of the appropriate stage in the blank next to each purpose. *Note:* Some of the stages can be used more than once for a particular purpose.

___ 1. To give students a reason for listening.

___ 2. To use the information.

___ 3. To equip the students with essential vocabulary for managing the task successfully.

___ 4. To motivate students to listen and to create interest in the topic or theme of the tape.

___ 5. To make students feel secure and confident towards doing the task.

___ 6. To confirm students' answers as acceptable or not.

___ 7. To monitor students' progress. *(Note:* While students are actively engaged in pair work, the teacher should circulate around the classroom, checking the students' participation, facial expressions, and body language to get an idea of their individual abilities to cope with the task).

___ 8. To focus students on specific aspects of the listening text.

Types of listening
tasks

Read the following dialogue involving an English woman, Sue, talking about living and working in New York. This dialogue is used to show you a variety of tasks that students could do before, during, and after listening to it.

An Englishwoman in New York

Bill: Hi! My name's Bill. What's yours?

Sue: I'm Sue.

Bill: You sound British.

Sue: I am British. I'm from London.

Bill: Do you live in New York now?

Sue: Yes, I'm here for a year or two.

Bill: That's great! What do you think of New York?

Sue: New York's a wonderful city but it's difficult to get used to.

Bill: I bet it's quite different from London.

Sue: Yes, it is—but I like the difference. I came here to find an interesting job and a more exciting life—and I found all that and more!

Bill: We call it the "Big Apple."

Sue: Well, I've come to take a bite! However, New York is dirty and noisy. Though most New Yorkers are friendly, many are not polite. The cab drivers either don't talk or talk too much. But there's so much to do and to see ... theaters, movies, clubs open all night.

Bill: The city never sleeps! Do you know many people here?

Sue: I know the people from my office. We go out together in the evenings. We've been to several bars and restaurants, and they've introduced me to a lot of their friends.

Bill: Where do you work?

Sue: On Madison Avenue. A friend in London recommended me to an advertising agency and they gave me the chance to work for them. That was luck—it isn't easy to find a job here. I get more money than I used to earn in London, but renting an apartment is expensive.

Bill: Well, food is cheap and there are so many choices—food stands on every street corner and thousands of delis where you can buy enormous sandwiches. I feel like you can eat twenty-four hours a day!

Sue: I know, I'm gaining weight by the hour! You certainly can find anything you want here.

Bill: And a lot you don't want!

Sue:	*(laughing)* Now that's the truth! One of the best days I've had in New York was on a Sunday a few weeks ago. A girl I know at the agency invited me to a picnic in Central Park in Manhattan with two of her friends. I just moved from Brooklyn to an apartment near the park on East 77th Street, so it was easy to join them. Her friends brought bagels, smoked salmon, and wine from California. We had so much fun—it was my first picnic in the park. The day was beautiful—sunny and warm. Summers are a lot hotter here than in London.
Bill:	Yes, and the winters are probably much colder!
Sue:	I know—I've never seen so much snow. This winter it was freezing on the streets. Though the subway is crowded, I was thankful that I didn't have to stand in the snow and wait for a taxi!
Bill:	The subway is a quick and cheap way to get around—it's slow and difficult to drive many places. Do you always get to work on time when you take the subway?
Sue:	Well, I overslept one morning last week and I missed an appointment with an important client. My boss was furious. He called me a 'lazy Brit.' I got really angry—it was an unpleasant scene. Later he apologized and I finally confessed that it was my fault, not the subway's!
Bill:	So things are better now?
Sue:	Yes. I did extra work for him that evening and he seemed pleased.
Bill:	So it sounds like New York is treating you well.
Sue:	Oh, yes. I've been here for a year now, and a couple of weeks ago I had my first birthday in the States. My boyfriend took me to a musical at a theater on Broadway to celebrate. Afterwards we went to a beautiful Italian restaurant and then finished the evening at a jazz club in Greenwich Village. With so many things to do, New York has definitely been a wonderful experience for me!

Predicting through vocabulary

To motivate students to listen and to create interest in the topic or theme of the recorded text, give students a list of key vocabulary items and ask them to predict or guess what the dialogue is about. This task actually pre-teaches vocabulary used in the listening material while preparing learners for the semantic field.

Student-generated questions

In pairs, have students write questions they would like to ask Sue about her life and work in New York. Then have students listen to the recording and check how many of their questions she answers. This kind of mental preparation works well as a *first* listening task. Since students are responsible for generating questions (their task), they have increased personal investment in listening carefully.

Listening for specific information

Give students the following list. Students must listen to the dialogue and check off the items that are mentioned:

1.   The weather in New York   ❑
2.   What Sue does in the evening   ❑
3.   The apartment she lives in   ❑
4.   What she likes about her job   ❑
5.   The traffic in Manhattan   ❑
6.   A picnic in Central Park   ❑

Putting events/ items in the right order

Give students the following list of items or events mentioned on the tape. Ask them to read the list, listen to the dialogue, and number the events in the order that they hear them.

1.   _____ The day Sue missed a business appointment
2.   _____ A picnic she had in Central Park
3.   _____ Her first birthday in the USA
4.   _____ A disagreement she had with her boss

Note: Vary this type of task by using pictures or drawings. When the tape describes a narrative, for example, the pictorial story could be put in order. To make a pictorial story easier to manage, cut apart the pictures. This way they can be moved around individually rather than all being on the same sheet. Similarly, items like those on the above list could be written on separate slips of paper so that students can physically manipulate their order.

True/false statements

True/false statements are a relatively straightforward task format for teachers to produce. Ask students to listen and circle *True* or *False* after each statement:

1. Sue prefers living in New York to living in London. True or False
2. She finds New York people very polite and helpful. True or False
3. The cost of living is very high in New York. True or False
4. She never goes out in the evening. True or False

Note: Task formats like true/false statements work well because they require a maximum of listening and a minimum of writing.

Open-ended questions

Select details from the written text or tape. Form questions about the details, then tell students to use short answers such as "yes, she did" and "four weeks." Here are some sample questions from *An Englishwoman in New York:*

Did Sue like New York immediately?

Where did she live when she first arrived?

How long was it before she got her first job?

Multiple-choice questions

As multiple-choice questions restrict the options and therefore make the task of finding an answer easier, this task type is suitable for the beginning levels. You could use the same open-ended questions above to create the following:

1. Did Sue like New York immediately?
   a. Yes
   b. No
   c. She has mixed feelings.
   d. She doesn't say.
2. Where did she live when she first arrived?
   a. Manhattan
   b. Brooklyn
   c. Queens
   d. The Bronx

Note-taking

Focus students' listening by introducing several topics. Give the following directions (this type of task could also be given to the students in the form of a grid that they complete):

As you listen, take notes on what Sue says about the following topics:

the food
the weather
the people
transportation
entertainment

Note: The first four listening task types may be done before or while the students are listening to the dialogue for the first time. True/false statements and multiple-choice questions are more appropriate after students have had two or more chances to listen. Note-taking almost always requires several "listenings."

Authentic listening

Following is another example of a task that requires listening for specific information, but this one is more authentic. It's based on a situation in which students might find themselves. After listening twice to the recorded text, *At the Airport*, (or the teacher reading it aloud), students fill in the details on the grid and answer questions.

At the Airport
PAN.USA announces the departure of Flight 301 to Hong Kong. Boarding now at Gate 17.
This is the final call for Pacific Airways, Flight 702 to Manila. Boarding now at Gate 25.
Urgent call for passenger Jonathan Berg.
Would Mr. Jonathan Berg please go to the Information Desk.

Airline	Destination	Flight Number	Gate Number
PAN.USA			
Pacific Airways			

Who was the urgent call for?
What was the passenger asked to do?

Review questions

1. What are the main functions of a listening task?

2. Should you use authentic material for listening tasks? Why or why not?

3. What are the four general purposes for listening?

4. Name an activity that would be suitable for pre-listening. What activity would be suitable for students to do while listening? After listening?

5. Think of a post-listening activity that would lead to practice in another language skill.

Further reading

Mendelsohn, D. and Rubin, J. *A Guide for the Teaching of Second Language Listening.* Dominie Press, 1995.

Nunan, D. and Miller, L. *New Ways in Teaching Listening.* TESOL Publications, 1995.

Underwood, M. *Teaching Listening.* Addison Wesley Longman, 1989.

Ur, P. *Teaching Listening Comprehension.* Cambridge University Press, 1984.

White, G. *Listening.* Oxford University Press, 1998.

TEACHING SPEAKING

Eliciting

Making corrections when eliciting responses

Restricted oral practice

- Repetition

- Echo questions

- Questions and answers

- Simple substitution

- Combining sentences

- Chaining

Developing oral fluency

Types of fluency activities

- Warm-up activities and icebreakers

- Drama activities

- Games

- Role-play cards

- Information gap activities

Review questions

Further reading

TEACHING SPEAKING

FOR MOST STUDENTS, the main aim of learning English is to *speak* the language. After all, when we say, "I speak a language," we mean we know the language well enough to be able to communicate easily in speech and hold a conversation in the language. But the achievement of speaking skills depends largely on being able to listen and understand what is said to us. A learner will have difficulty speaking English if he or she doesn't receive the proper training and organized practice in both listening and speaking.

This chapter introduces speaking through three stages: eliciting, restricted oral practice, and developing oral fluency. The first stage is designed to help you develop the teaching skill of not talking too much while at the same time giving learners guided practice and stimulating them to speak. In this phase, you should aim to develop the students' confidence in responding to specific questions or prompts. This is the beginning of the development of *fluency;* it's not the time to concentrate on accuracy and highlight errors. In the second stage, you should focus on accuracy through restricted oral practice. This type of practice used to be called *drilling.* This stage is basically an enabling phase; controlled practice is essential in learning any skill. Think of it as practicing the scales when learning to play the piano. The third stage, developing oral fluency, is the most interesting for you and your students. In this stage, you should be able to introduce topics that are stimulating, controversial, and relevant to students' lives and aims.

Remember that a conversation lesson can't be done successfully without preparation and planning. You may cause embarrassment and frustration for yourself and your students if you expect them to speak on subjects or topics they cannot cope with. If you introduce speaking in stages and with planning and preparation, students will enjoy the speaking lesson—and so will you!

Eliciting   A teacher who can *elicit* or draw out appropriate verbal language from students rather than *tell* them what to say gets students more actively involved, increases their motivation, and enhances their learning satisfaction. When eliciting functional language, it's important that learners *sound right*. For example, when apologizing, students should sound as if they feel sorry and are not just using the words without meaning. In order to sound right, of course, students need to learn to use appropriate word stress and intonation. It's also useful to teach and elicit suitable responses:

"I'm really sorry."

"Oh, that's okay," or "Never mind," or "No problem."

It is also important that students are aware of *register* (whether the functional language is formal, neutral, or informal). Without this awareness, learners often sound too formal or too friendly. Eliciting can be done in the following ways:

- ◆ **Ask questions.** Use *wh-* questions (*what, who, where, why, when,* and *how*) rather than yes/no questions. "Where does he come from?" elicits information *and* checks understanding. "Is he from Zimbabwe?" only elicits "yes" or "no" answers.

- ◆ **Give instructions that require verbal interaction.** Examples are: "Describe what you can see in this picture," or "Tell the person next to you where you live."

- ◆ **Use real objects (realia).** For example, show students a credit card and a checkbook and ask, "What are these called? What's the difference between them?"

- ◆ **Use visual aids (drawings, flashcards, videos, etc.).** Video tapes can be used to elicit responses by "freeze-framing" a dialogue situation and asking the students, "What do you think the actor is saying at this moment?" (For more information on using visual aids, see Chapter 12, *Teaching with Visual Aids).*

- ◆ **Give definitions.** For example, to elicit the word *bachelor,* ask a question using the word's definition: "What do we call a man who has never married?"

- ◆ **Use synonyms and antonyms.** Ask questions using the synonyms or antonyms of a lexical item: "In the dialogue, which word is similar in meaning to *slim?* Which word is opposite in meaning to *dead?*"

◆ **Use gestures and mime.** Many verbs and adjectives (*sad, happy, angry*) can be easily elicited using gestures and facial expressions. It's also possible to elicit a short story or sequence of actions with appropriate but exaggerated actions. This simple drama technique is fun and enjoyable if you are comfortable with its use.

◆ **Use prompts, cues, and questions in social situations.** Establish a context that invites students to talk. For example, how would you respond to the following situations:

It's my 21st birthday today!

Look at my new watch. What do you think?

Alternatively, you can establish a context by describing a social situation:

You are passing a place that serves coffee, and one of your friends suggests stopping to have an espresso. What would you say?

You are in a hardware store and want to buy a hammer. What would you ask a sales clerk?

◆ **Fill gaps in tables, scales, or diagrams.** For example, put up a diagram representing a thermometer and indicating the position of *hot* and *cold*. Elicit other words that would fit between, above, or below the markers.

◆ **Review key vocabulary.** Make a list of words from previous lessons. You could write this list on the board or write the terms on cards and have each student take one. Remind the students of related words or structures and ask questions that will elicit use of the key vocabulary:

— Hot

— Cold

• to re-elicit sets of related words, such as the words for family relationships, supply one or two known words, like *mother* and *father*. Ask students to fill in the rest of the set.

• to re-elicit structure patterns or grammatical forms, use a simple substitution table with blanks that will remind the students of the order of words but will require them to supply the missing items (see the substitution tables on page 213).

- to re-elicit functional exponents, review how to say them in suitable situations. Prompt the situation by supplying cues similar to the ones presented in the original practice: "How does one refuse an invitation politely? What do you say?"

♦ **Use translation.** Translation should be used sparingly (see Chapter 1, page 8). Be aware that this method of eliciting can only work in monolingual classes (if, for example, you are teaching English in a Spanish-speaking country). You need to speak and understand the native language well enough to check the accuracy and appropriateness of the translation. Eliciting an equivalent word can be useful in checking that false cognates are not being assumed as correct and being used by students. For example, "What's the English word for *simpático?*"

When eliciting responses, remember that you can only elicit what students know and remember; you can't elicit what students don't know or can't remember. Make it clear who is to speak if you want individual students to contribute, and give feedback to confirm whether responses are okay or not. A response like "yes" or "thank you" is simple and effective. Once the correct form has been established, it's useful to elicit it one more time.

Task 1: Ways of eliciting

A. How would you elicit the following words?
   1. to jog
   2. to feed someone
   3. jealous
   4. a refund
   5. above and below
   6. bald
   7. a banana
   8. depressed
   9. a costume
   10. a lion

B. Think of simple ways to elicit examples of the following:
   Making an apology
   Warning someone of danger
   Congratulating someone

Making corrections when eliciting responses

When eliciting responses from learners, do not be too rigid or disapproving of how they answer. If the response isn't right but it's not totally unacceptable, then say "try again" or "yes, but... ." Don't just reject and discourage the students' attempts. Above all, avoid setting up a situation in which students are trying to guess "what the teacher is fishing for."

You should anticipate what learners are likely to say (or not be able to express) *before* the lesson. This aspect of planning is essential because your knowledge of pitfalls forms the lesson. Furthermore, thinking about what learners might say helps you clarify what is acceptable or unacceptable in your mind.

Study the following examples as ways to make corrections when eliciting responses from students:

A. Teacher: Imagine you are late for a class. What do you say to me or to another teacher?
    Students: Sorry, I'm late.
    Teacher: Okay, and what would you say if you were the teacher?
    Students: You're welcome.
    Teacher: That's not suitable. Try again.
    Students: Okay. Try to be early tomorrow.
    Teacher: Good. That's much better.

B. Teacher: I didn't work or study hard at school. Now I'm sorry I didn't. How can I say this in English?
    Students: I wish I had studied at school.
              If only I'd studied at school.

C. Teacher: My little sister is going to touch a hot coffee pot. What do I say to stop her?
    Students: Don't touch it! Look out!
    Teacher: Yes, don't touch it. 'Look out' is not right. Why? When would we say that?

Restricted oral practice

Learning a specific language structure requires intensive practice. It's better to think of this practice as *restricted oral practice* rather than drilling. Drills tend to become mechanical and meaningless. Eliciting responses in short periods (3-5 minutes) is one way to make certain that the language structure being practiced means something to the students. For example, if you want students to use an agreement response such as "So do I," then say, "I like swimming" to a student who likes that particular sport. Avoid making students say something that isn't true (don't say, "I smoke cigars" to someone who doesn't). This kind of intensive, restricted oral practice can be done for longer periods in the language lab, where students can work alone at their own pace on their individual problems (twenty minutes is usually the maximum for such practice).

When doing restricted oral practice, make use of eliciting techniques. You should also give the cue or the model sentence before you ask a particular student to respond. Don't point to one student and then give the cue or the prompt. By posing the situation first, you can get all the students to formulate the response mentally and not "switch off" because they're not going to be asked. Finally, don't think of oral practice or drilling as boring. It isn't boring for the students unless the practice goes on for too long and requires nothing much from them. Remember that being able to use a foreign language accurately can be very satisfying, and you can't do it without practice. Vary the exercises and use games which are excellent ways of drilling painlessly (see Chapter 13, *Teaching with Games)*.

Following are types of restricted oral practice.

Repetition   The most basic type of oral practice is simple repetition:

Teacher:	He lives in Vietnam.
Students:	He lives in Vietnam.

This kind of oral practice is useful to beginners and is not boring if it's done with attention to detail. It can be used to help learners improve their pronunciation as well as to correct common faults (like the tendency to omit the *s* in the third person verb form). Vary the repetition by using choral and individual practice (divide the class in half, groups, or pairs). Like the conductor of an orchestra, you need to be demanding and insist on the correctness of students' responses. This is the time for accurate speaking practice (but not too much at a time!).

| Echo questions | Make statements that have to be transformed into questions by a change in intonation. This practice is useful because learners may often hear statements that they don't understand. The *echo question* is a way of getting clarification and/or confirmation: |

Student A:	She went home two days ago.
Student B:	Two days ago?
Student A:	Yes, two days ago.

| Questions and answers | This type of practice can be used to follow up repetition practice: |

| Teacher: | Where does he live? |
| Students: | In Vietnam. |

| Simple substitution | Substitution practice requires more careful listening by the students. It can gradually be made more difficult: |

Teacher:	Do you have a car?
Students:	Do you have a car?
Teacher:	A computer.
Students:	Do you have a computer?
Teacher:	A video-recorder.
Students:	Do you have a video-recorder?

A more demanding type of substitution practice requires students to make their own response based on a pattern already taught. Keep in mind that the practice should be related to a certain situation or topic:

Teacher:	Your hair is getting very long.
Cue:	Cut.
Students:	Yes, I'm going to get it cut tomorrow.
Teacher:	Your pants are very dirty.
Cue:	Cleaned.
Students:	Yes, I'm going to get them cleaned tomorrow.

Substitution practice can also be carried out in four-line dialogues. First, establish a simple model in a situation. For example, you could talk about food and various ethnic varieties:

| Student A: | I really think <u>American</u> <u>food</u> is great! |
| Student B: | Really? I don't think so! |

Student A: What do you like?
Student B: I like <u>French</u> <u>food</u>.

Then continue the practice by substituting the underlined words with the following items:

Italian	coffee
Turkish	desserts
German	pancakes
Swiss	bread
Japanese	sushi

Combining sentences

This exercise is useful practice in using relative pronouns (*who, whose,* etc.) Note that the exercise can only be done successfully *after* the students have learned how to use relative pronouns in sentences.

Cue: An actor won an Oscar. He's Scottish.

Response: The actor who won the Oscar is Scottish.

Cue: An athlete won a million dollars. She's Australian.

Response: The athlete who won a million dollars is Australian.

Cue: He's a neighbor. His wife is a ballet dancer.

Response: He's the neighbor whose wife is a ballet dancer.

Cue: She's a student. Her father is the governor of Texas.

Response: She's the student whose father is the governor of Texas.

Combining sentences involves using language artificially, so it's important to make drills as meaningful as possible by using *context*, however brief, and by eliciting true statements of known facts:

Cue: Pete Sampras plays football.

Response: No, he doesn't. He plays tennis.

Cue: Americans play cricket.

Response: No, they don't. They play baseball.

Note: In combining sentences, exceptions and irregularities should

144

be avoided. These need to be presented and taught separately, otherwise learners might do something like the following (practicing *adverb to adjective + noun change):*

Cue:	She plays well.
Response:	She's a good player.
Cue:	He dances well.
Response:	He's a good dancer.
Cue:	She sings well.
Response:	She's a good singer.
Cue:	He cooks well.
Response:	*He's a good *cooker.*

*(A person who cooks is a *cook;* in British English, a *cooker* is a stove for cooking.)

Chaining   This technique can be used when a phrase or sentence causes difficulty because of its pronunciation or length. For example:

Model (conditional sentence):

If I'd known you were here, I wouldn't have gone away.

Teacher:	If I'd known
Students:	If I'd known
Teacher:	you were here
Students:	you were here
Teacher:	I wouldn't have gone away.
Students:	I wouldn't have gone away.
Teacher:	If I'd known you were here, I wouldn't have gone away.
Students:	If I'd known you were here, I wouldn't have gone away.

The above example is called *forward chaining.* The major drawback of forward chaining is that intonation naturally changes—the native speaker drops his or her voice at the end of each response, though this isn't the way the complete sentence should be said.

Chaining can be done backwards just as effectively, and with *backward build-up* there is less chance of distorting the intonation. It's advisable to divide the sentence into sense-groups and not odd words to make for easier pronunciation and to help the students' memory:

Model (conditional sentence):
If I'd known you were coming, I'd have baked a cake.

Teacher:	a cake
Students:	a cake
Teacher:	baked a cake
Students:	baked a cake
Teacher:	I'd have baked a cake
Students:	I'd have baked a cake
Teacher:	you were coming, I'd have baked a cake
Students:	you were coming, I'd have baked a cake
Teacher:	If I'd known you were coming, I'd have baked a cake.
Students:	If I'd known you were coming, I'd have baked a cake.

Another kind of chaining is more like a game, which adds a fun twist to it. The teacher chooses a sentence structure and then says to one student, "I'm a teacher but I'd rather be a model." The student then says to another student, "She's a teacher, but she'd rather be a model," and adds a statement like "I'm a student, but I'd rather be a singer." The second student has to remember and repeat the first and second statements and add his or her own statement following the same structure. This enjoyable way of practicing a particular structure gives students the freedom to make up their own variations.

Developing oral fluency

Your students want to speak English, but most know neither how to improve their spoken English nor what activities and practice really help them achieve their aims. Teachers, therefore, need to be clear about the goals and techniques that promote *fluency* in speaking practice and oral activities. First of all, decide whether the speaking activity promotes fluency or accuracy. You cannot expect to develop learners' fluency if you are monitoring things like accurate grammatical use, precise and appropriate vocabulary choices, or correct pronunciation. To encourage learners to communicate, you must adopt an attitude that encourages fluency development and saves accuracy for another lesson.

In some English language schools, you may be expected to only teach lessons in English conversation. The fact that English conversation classes are offered reflects the demand of students who have learned to read, write, and probably translate English at schools in their own country, but didn't get the opportunity to speak English effectively and confidently.

Conversation lessons can be disastrous unless they are adequately prepared. You cannot expect to walk into a classroom with 15 to 30 adult students and start a conversation! If you are not fully prepared and just announce a conversation topic, such as *Cars and Pollution,* you will probably produce silence. Most of the students won't know what to say. They won't know related idioms and vocabulary, and many might panic at the thought. Because neither you nor the students are prepared, you then take over the role of talking about the subject and the conversation lesson becomes a mini-lecture. In such a lesson, asking questions will most likely elicit short answers from a few confident students—the rest will remain silent.

To avoid such disastrous lessons, keep in mind the following when preparing free-speaking activities to develop fluency:

◆ **Choose high-interest topics.** Choosing topics of interest to the learners is a crucial first step in achieving successful, motivated participation in free-speaking activities.

◆ **Pre-teach.** Introduce and explain essential vocabulary items, structures, and functions.

◆ **Stimulate interest.** This can be done in one of the following ways:

- Use visuals (pictures, short videotape clips, cartoon drawings)
- Display newspaper headlines and ask students to write details to fit the headlines
- Personalize the topic, relating it to students' experiences and/or their background
- Establish an "anticipatory set" through a warm-up with questions and opinions

◆ **Set the scene for discussion.** Arrange students' chairs for face-to-face interaction.

◆ **Give students time to think and prepare.** Students need this time to decide what they want to express. If they are going to be part of a role-play or simulation, having them read and understand their part is essential for their success.

- ◆ **Make a participation plan.** This plan should ensure that all students in the class participate in the discussion.
- ◆ **Organize the time.** Make sure that one activity does not take up too much time (see Chapter 19, *Planning Lessons).*
- ◆ **Make a recording.** If possible, make a recording on audio-cassette or video of the discussion or speaking activities. A recording gives useful feedback for the correction of common errors (which could be done in a later lesson). Make the recording as unobtrusive as possible so that it doesn't inhibit the nervous or reserved students.

Types of fluency activities

Following are activity ideas for helping students develop oral fluency.

Warm-up activities and icebreakers

A good icebreaker which focuses on fluency-building is to start a new class by pairing up students and asking them to interview each other. Give them a limited time (say, five minutes). Afterwards, have each student introduce the person he or she interviewed to the rest of the class or to another pair. If the students are beginners and cannot ask suitable interview questions, demonstrate the activity by asking a few questions and eliciting answers from the whole class first. Write sample questions on the board so that students can refer to them while they are doing the interviews (for more warm-up activities, see *Warm-up games* in Chapter 13, page 226).

Drama activities

Drama activities, like role-play and simulation, are particularly popular with learners and are excellent ways of getting learners to speak in lively situations (see Chapter 14, *Teaching with Drama).*

Games

Games are a great way to get students speaking fluently because students get wrapped up in playing the game and don't worry so much about *how* to speak correctly. Rather, they concentrate on *what* they have to say (see *Speaking games* in Chapter 13, page 235).

Role-play cards

Many students find it easier to speak about specific situations or problems of interest than about large, general issues. Journalists "personalize" these large, general issues by focusing on the individual human interest angle. You should incorporate this form of personalizing into your free-speaking lessons as well. One excellent way to do this is to prepare role-play cards. Role-play cards should give a brief description of each role and the problem associated with that role. Following are examples of such cards:

You are the manager of a large restaurant. The rent has just been doubled and you need to 'down-size' the staff. How do you economize on staff? Who would you get rid of first?

You are a non-smoker, but you live at home with your parents and your brother or sister, who are all heavy smokers.
How would you ask them to cut down on smoking in the same room that you all use? How would you persuade them to stop smoking?

You may distribute these cards within pairs or groups of students. Assign the various roles to students; have them switch roles as time permits.

Information-gap activities

Communication takes place naturally when one person has information, ideas, or opinions that someone else doesn't have. Of course, the need to exchange information, ideas, or opinions has to exist or be created. In the classroom, information-gap activities are a successful way to motivate students to talk to one another and exchange what they know.

Although the teacher sets up most information-gap exercises, they can be created in other ways. Real personal information provided by the students (information about their lives, their jobs, and their knowledge of the world) works well, or one can set up problem-solving tasks such as simulations and role-plays (see above). Following are examples of information-gap activities that are suitable for developing oral fluency:

A. Plan a vacation

For this information-gap activity, use cards similar to the role-play cards outlined on page 149. Pair up students and assign "A" and "B" roles. Student B will need time to collect information about airfares and package holidays in Mexico, or you can provide a handout of essential information.

Student A

You want to arrange a vacation in Mexico. You have saved up $1,000, and you need a cheap way to travel and inexpensive accommodations. Go to a travel agent and ask for the information you need.

Student B

You are a travel agent. You specialize in arranging vacations in Mexico. You answer any questions or concerns that travelers to Mexico might have.

B. Find out information

In this activity, each student (in pairs) must find out the information needed to answer the questions on his or her worksheet. The student does this by asking his or her partner. Once the partners have finished the first set of questions, they ask questions to complete the missing information in their grid.

Student A: Information Sheet

1. Which ocean is bigger?
   The Indian   _____
   The Atlantic   82 million square miles
2. Which river is longer?
   The Mississippi   _____
   The Nile   6,437 kilometers

3. Which of these mountains is the highest? The lowest?

Popacatepetl	5,542 meters
Mount Kenya	5,201 meters
Mont Blanc	_____
Mount Kilimanjaro:	_____

4. Which planet is the biggest? The smallest? Number them from smallest to biggest (1 = mass of the Earth).

__ Venus	0.82
__ Saturn	____
__ Mars	0.11
__ Jupiter	____

Using the Grid

Which country is the largest in area? The smallest?

_____

Which country has the largest population? The smallest?

_____

Country	Area (sq./km.)	Population
Australia	7,686,848	
Brazil		133,882,000
Canada	9,976,139	
China		1,012,358,000
India	3,287,590	
Indonesia		147,000,000
Japan	372,312	
Russia	17,075,400	
USA		226,505,000

Now put the countries in order from smallest to biggest:

Area	1. _____	2. _____	3. _____
	4. _____	5. _____	6. _____
	7. _____	8. _____	9. _____
Population	1. _____	2. _____	3. _____
	4. _____	5. _____	6. _____
	7. _____	8. _____	9. _____

Student B: Information Worksheet
1. Which ocean is bigger?
The Indian	73 million square miles
The Atlantic	_____

2. Which river is longer?
The Mississippi	6,231 kilometers
The Nile	_____

3. Which of these mountains is the highest? The lowest?
Popacatepetl	_____
Mount Kenya	_____
Mont Blanc	4,810 meters
Mount Kilimanjaro	5,895 meters

4. Which planet is the biggest? The smallest? Number them from smallest to biggest (1 = mass of the Earth).
__ Venus	_____
__ Jupiter	317.89
__ Mars	_____
__ Saturn	95.15

Using the Grid
Which country is the largest in area? The smallest?

_____

Which country has the largest population? The smallest?

_____

Country	Area (sq./km.)	Population
Australia		14,615,000
Brazil	8,511,965	
Canada		24,620,000
China	9,596,961	
India		698,332,000
Indonesia	2,027,087	
Japan		120,055,000
Russia		147,501,000
USA	9,363,123	

Now put the countries in order from smallest to biggest:

Area 1. _____ 2. _____ 3. _____

4. _____ 5. _____ 6. _____

7. _____ 8. _____ 9. _____

Population 1. _____ 2. _____ 3. _____

4. _____ 5. _____ 6. _____

7. _____ 8. _____ 9. _____

C. Make an Appointment

This is a more advanced information-gap activity that combines the tasks of the previous ones.

Student A
You are a business person, and you want to make an appointment with your banker. Here is your diary for next week. Try to arrange a time to meet. Do not show your diary to your partner.

	Morning	Afternoon	Evening
Monday	Visit to Boston		Theater
Tuesday		Meeting with Union	
Wednesday	Board Meeting		Dinner with Chairman
Thursday	Finance Committee		
Friday	Visit to New York (gone until Tuesday)	New York	New York

Here are some questions and answers that you might use:

Are you free on/at/during _____ ?   Let's say 2:30 or 3:00 p.m.

What about/how about _____ ?   Sorry, I can't do 3:00 p.m.

Could you manage _____ ?   Shall we say 3:30 in the afternoon?

I look forward to seeing you on _____ .   It'll be a pleasure.

Sorry, I'm tied up then.   Can we fix a date and time?

Sorry, I've got something on _____ .   That'll be fine.

Student B:

You are a bank manager, and you want to make an appointment with your client. Here is your diary for next week. Try to arrange a time to meet. Do not show your diary to your partner.

	Morning	Afternoon	Evening
Monday		Visit to Newport	
Tuesday	Medical check-up		Rotary Club dinner
Wednesday	Directors' meeting	Report to Head Office	
Thursday			Fitness class
Friday	Interviews for new cashier (all day)	Interviews	Interviews

Here are some questions and answers that you might use:

Are you free on/at/during _____?	Let's say 2:30 or 3:00 p.m.
What about/how about _____?	Sorry, I can't do 3:00 p.m.
Could you manage _____?	Shall we say 3:30 in the afternoon?
I look forward to seeing you on _____.	It'll be a pleasure.
Sorry, I'm tied up then.	Can we fix a date and time?
Sorry, I've got something on _____.	That'll be fine.

D. Pronunciation: An Information-Gap Activity

Information-gap exercises can also be used effectively for pronunciation practice. Although textbook exercises on pronunciation are not usually designed with communication in mind, it should matter whether learners hear sounds correctly when they are spoken. When learners practice minimal pairs (such as *pin/bin* or *chip/cheap*) even in dialogues, students who read them aloud are usually aware what other students are going to say, which leads to "artificial hearing."

The following information gap activity requires students (in pairs) to use real or made-up names of streets and shops. Each student needs to pronounce the names correctly in order for their partner to understand the directions. Give the appropriate map to each student. (See maps next page.)

The dialogue between the students might be along these lines:

Student A: Could you tell me how to get to Jane's Jeans Shop?

Student B: Jean's Shop. Sure. You go down . . .

Student A: No, no. Jane's Shop. That's J-A-N-E.

Student B: Oh, Jane's. Yes. Go east down Chip Street to Chid Street and turn left. Walk up Chid Street until it turns into Chittis Street and make a left at Ship Street. Walk down Ship Street. Jane's Jeans Shop is near the corner of Ship and Sheet Street.

Student A: Which corner?

155

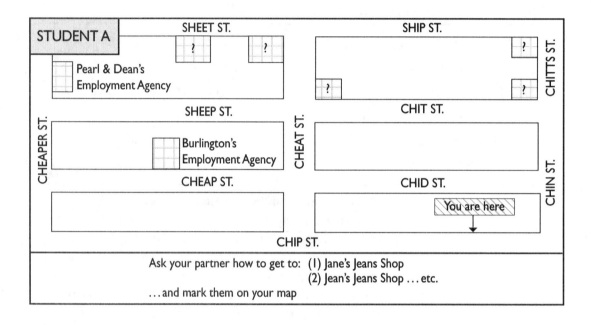

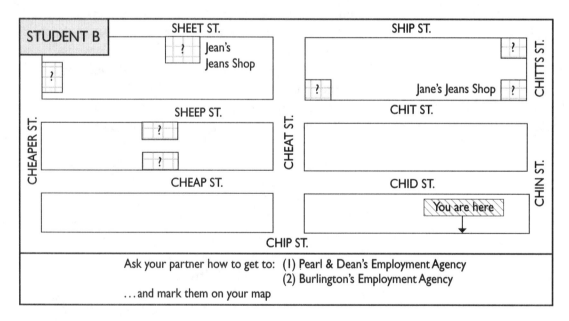

From *Modern English Teacher*, Volume 13, No. 2, Winter 1995-96.

This type of fluency activity has many advantages:

◆ It's enjoyable and life-like. Street names can be changed (made even more difficult and challenging!).

◆ It encourages students to echo questions and ask for clear pronunciation and spelling.

◆ It involves both partners in giving information, checking, and confirming.

◆ It's unpredictable and therefore interesting!

Acknowledgment for this idea goes to Robin Corcos, ELT Advisor, Jakarta.

Review questions

1. What are three ways of eliciting language? Why should you elicit language rather than tell students what to say?

2. What are the disadvantages of using drills?

3. What are *echo questions? Substitution practices? Chaining?* What stage of speaking can you use these types of exercises for?

4. What factors have high priority in preparing free-speaking activities? How can you stimulate interest in these activities?

5. Why are games useful in promoting fluency?

6. How can role-play cards be used to encourage students to speak?

7. What are information-gap activities? How can they be used to promote accurate pronunciation?

Further Reading

Bailey, K. and Savage, L. *New Ways in Teaching Speaking.* TESOL Publications, 1994.

Christison, M. and Bassano, S. *Look Who's Talking!* Alta Book Center Publishers, 1995.

Klippel, F. *Keep Talking: Communicative Fluency Activities for Language Teaching.* Cambridge University Press, 1984.

Martinez, R. *Conversation Lessons: The Natural Language of Conversation.* Language Teaching Publications, 1997.

Nolasco, R. and Arthur, L. *Conversation.* Oxford University Press, 1987.

Ur, P. *Discussions that Work.* Cambridge University Press, 1981.

Chapter 9

TEACHING READING

Reading strategies

Intensive reading

Follow-up activities

    - True/false statements

    - Yes/no questions

    - Either/or questions

    - Word search

    - Asking questions

    - Cloze activities

    - Guided writing

    - Finish the story

Extensive reading

Graded readers

Basic reading problems

Integrating reading and speaking

Integrating reading and writing

Review questions

Further reading

    - Published readers

    - Jigsaw reading activities

    - Cloze activities

TEACHING READING

WHY TEACH READING? Reading is an important means of communication. Readers and writers interact through the reading of a text. Reading also offers additional exposure to the language; an exposure that can often be stimulating, interesting, and up-to-date in terms of vocabulary (especially in newspapers, etc.). However, learning to read in another language can be a frustrating experience for the learner if the reading material is too difficult or unsuitable. Consider the following comments from native speakers of English who have experience with reading foreign languages.

- ◆ "I can read with difficulty in Spanish, but it's slow and boring. Unless I really have to read, I usually give up after a few minutes. I can't read without looking words up in a dictionary."

- ◆ "I only read German because I have to sometimes for my work. The kind of reading involves scientific and technical articles. It's hard work. I use a special dictionary."

- ◆ "I studied French at school and I can read a bit. I hardly ever do it because it's such hard work."

- ◆ "I do read books in Italian and Spanish. I've lived in Italy and in Mexico, and I like to keep up my knowledge of these languages. I usually read newspapers but sometimes I'll read a detective story."

Students learning English make similar comments. These comments present basic and important points for you to realize when integrating reading into your lessons:

- ◆ People read in their own language or in a foreign language for different reasons and for a variety of purposes.

- ◆ Reading a book for pleasure is an enjoyable experience if it's done at a reasonable speed, without having to look up too many words.

- ◆ Reading texts which are heavy in facts or processes (scientific and technical texts, for example) is a slow, tedious process often regarded as something learners *have* to do, not *want* to do. Special dictionaries are often required for such purposes.

◆ Motivation is easily destroyed if there's little satisfaction or pleasure in reading.

The wealth of reading materials seems to have no end; every day new publications come off the press. This leaves you with the overwhelming task of selecting reading materials and making them suitable for your class. The following sections are designed to help you with the challenge of selecting and using reading materials. This is outlined through strategies, two types of reading *(intensive* reading and *extensive* reading), techniques, and activities that will motivate the reader within all your students.

Reading strategies

There are three main strategies that skilled readers use:

◆ **Reading for detail.** Reading *all* of a particular text to find out specific information

◆ **Scanning.** Reading quickly in order to find a specific point or item (to successfully scan, the reader does not and should not read every word and line)

◆ **Skimming.** Reading quickly to get a general idea of what the text is about (once again, the reader does not and should not read every word and line)

These strategies depend on the purpose of reading and should be taught appropriately. Think of situations in which you have used each of the strategies above. Which strategy would you use to read a menu? To find a service using the Yellow Pages? How to read 100 pages of a textbook for a course, when you only have one hour before class starts?

Intensive reading

We read intensively when we are concerned about detail. The text may have particular interest for us because it contains needed information. We may need to know exactly what the writer means. This knowledge helps us answer questions like "Where is this taking place? Who committed the crime? Why?" We may need to know how characters in the text feel about certain actions or events. This knowledge helps us explore our own thoughts and feelings. When we read to gain this kind of detailed understanding, we are doing intensive reading. In language teaching, we often have other reasons for the intensive reading of texts:

◆ to examine the use of specific grammatical features, like verb tenses or forms (for example, reading a text designed to highlight uses of the past perfect)

◆ to infer meaning of new vocabulary and gain understanding of new words in context

◆ to learn about *discourse markers* (how phrases are used to introduce other phrases; discourse markers focus the reader's attention on what the writer considers important; examples include *such as, important to note, most of all, especially, a major . . .*)

Following is a step-by-step example of a reading lesson requiring *intensive* reading. The chosen text is on Sir Thomas More's *Utopia*, suitable for a high-beginning level (from *Junior Files 2* by Elite Olshtain, et al.).

A Great Dreamer

Optimism, originality, and wisdom make a person a dreamer. Dreamers can see changes they want to make in society. They are optimistic enough to believe that these changes are possible. They are original enough to have ideas about how they want to change the world.

Sir Thomas More was a dreamer. In 1516 he wrote a book about an **imaginary** island. He called the island *Utopia.* This word meant "a perfect, but unreal place." This was his dream:

In Utopia everybody will work six hours each day. Each person will do the work she/he knows best. Everything will belong to everybody. There won't be any poor people or any rich people. All people will be **equal.** There will be no **punishments.** Every family will have a house. Houses will be **divided** among the people every ten years. Every person will get a house that is just right for him or her. All the citizens will eat together in large **dining rooms.** Each person will be able to choose his or her own religion.

Nowadays, the word *utopia* is used to mean an **ideal** place, state, or political system.

◆ **Step One: Create interest.** Before you give learners the text, personalize the subject by relating it to their own experience or their plans. You might want to ask questions, or do an activity such as the following (for *A Great Dreamer*):

Do you agree with the following statements? Choose one statement and write two sentences explaining why you agree or disagree.

1. A dream can change the world.
2. Changes always make things worse.
3. In 2090 the world will be completely different.
4. "All is vanity, and there is nothing new under the sun." (King Solomon)
5. You can't stop the world from changing.

Another pre-reading activity is to get students to predict the content from the title. This works best when the title is fairly descriptive.

- ◆ **Step Two: Pre-teach key vocabulary.** Select words that are likely to be unknown and/or uses of words that may not be clear. In *A Great Dreamer,* these words are in bold. Pre-teach, explain, or elicit these words from students before asking them to read the text (for ideas on how to do this, see Chapter 4, *Teaching Vocabulary).* Generally, it's a good idea to keep the number of unknown words to a minimum; pre-teaching 7 to 10 words is usually good for reading preparation (remember the learners' comments—having to look up words decreases reading enjoyment). Keep in mind that the meaning of some words could be easily guessed from the context. Encourage guessing if the context helps to make the guess possible and accurate (see *Guessing,* Chapter 4, page 48).

- ◆ **Step Three: Give a reading task.** Give the students a few questions that you are going to use to check understanding after the reading. Standard questions that could be used for any text are:

  What is the text about?

  What is the writer's purpose?

  Did you find the text interesting?

  More detailed questions for *A Great Dreamer* might be:

  How does the writer define a dreamer?

What did Sir Thomas More believe?

How will people get houses in Utopia?

What does utopia mean today?

Allow students 2 to 3 minutes to silently read the passage. At this stage, ask students *not* to use dictionaries. If a student looks confused or gets stuck while reading, make a note of the word that is causing difficulty. If it's likely to be a problem for most of the class, explain it after the first reading.

Note: It's *not* usually a good idea to ask students to read the passage aloud. It tends to be boring and most students cannot read aloud in a lively way with good pronunciation—especially with correct stress and intonation. Though this practice checks pronunciation, it often reduces comprehension. Most students don't concentrate on *meaning* when they are reading aloud and don't enjoy it as much. Would you want someone to read your favorite magazine aloud to you? However, when there are problems with understanding, it may be helpful for the teacher to read parts of the passage aloud to the class.

◆ **Step Four: Give follow-up activities.** Follow-up activities for readings can involve everything from completing tables and questionaires to acting out roles and writing stories. Following are two activities to use for *A Great Dreamer.* More ideas are outlined in the next section.

A. In the list below, check the dreams that you think came true. Discuss your answers with a partner.

	Yes	*No*	*Part of it*
1. All people will be equal.			
2. There won't be any poor people in the world.			
3. Nobody is going to work more than six hours a day.			
4. People will do the work they know best.			
5. There won't be any punishments.			
6. Every person will be able to choose his or her own religion.			

B. Plan a "perfect life" for yourself. Decide if you need the following things in your life:

free time	equality	friends	a home	work
dreams	culture	power	a TV	imagination

Follow-up activities

Follow-up activities should focus on detailed understanding. You can do this through a concentration on vocabulary, structure, receptive reading skills and/or writing. Here are ideas for follow-up activities using a short simple text titled *A Date at Midnight*. These are intended to be "stepping stones" for you to build your own activities. Remember that part of the fun of reading is exploring the text through unique, interesting routes! (The following text is appropriate for beginning or low-intermediate classes):

A Date at Midnight

One night a young man couldn't sleep, so he got out of bed and cycled to his girlfriend's house. When he got there he called up to her window and asked her to let him in. She told him that her mother and father were not asleep, but the young man said he was sure that they were because all the lights were out. So the girl got up and opened the front door. Her father heard the noise and called out, "Who's there?"

True/false statements

True/false statements, as mentioned in Chapter 7, are a relatively straightforward task for teachers to develop. Ask students to read the passage again and circle *True* or *False* after each of the following statements:

The young man couldn't sleep.	True or False
He didn't go to his girlfriend's house.	True or False
The girl's father was not asleep.	True or False

Yes/no questions

Another easy-to-develop task is the use of yes/no questions (make sure that questions can be answered with a simple *yes* or *no*).

Did the girl open the door for her boyfriend?

Did she tell her boyfriend that her mother and father were asleep?

Either/or questions

More advanced than the yes/no question, either/or questions are also simple to develop:

> Did the young man walk to his girlfriend's house or ride his bicycle?
> Did the girl believe what her boyfriend told her or not?
> Were the girl's mother and father asleep or awake?

Word search

This type of task helps learners polish their skill of scanning a text. Find the word or phrase in the story that means the same as the following:

> was not able _____
>
> allow someone to enter _____
>
> was certain _____

Asking questions

A twist to the "answering questions" method, this task checks reading comprehension and the ability to ask questions. Here are some answers to questions about the story. Write the questions that would produce these answers:

> _____?
> He cycled to his girlfriend's house.
>
> _____?
> Her father and mother were not asleep.
>
> _____?
> The girl got up and opened the door.

Cloze activities

To create a cloze exercise, remove every 5th or 7th word from the text. The aim of this activity is to "cloze the gap" by filling the blanks with the missing words or phrases:

> One night a young _____ couldn't sleep, so he
>
> _____ out of bed and _____ to his girlfriend's
>
> house. _____ he got there, he _____ up to
>
> her window _____ asked her to let _____

in. She told him _____ mother and father

_____ not asleep, but the _____ man said

he was _____ that they were because _____

the lights were out _____ the girl got up _____

opened the door. Her _____ heard the noise and called

_____, "Who's there?"

You can also tailor the activity to learners' needs by removing key vocabulary, tenses, or structural items. For example, to use a cloze activity to test structure, ask students to put the verbs in parentheses into the right tense:

One night a young man _____ (can) not sleep, so

he _____ (get) out of bed and _____

(cycle) to his girlfriend's house . . .

For more examples and advice on cloze activities, see *Cloze procedures,* Chapter 17, page 290.

Guided writing

Make a list of key words and phrases, then ask students to write the story using the list for guidance (students cannot look at the story). This could also be a speaking activity; in pairs, have students retell the story using the key words and phrases.

one night	young man	cycled
girlfriend	called up	asked her
mother and father	not asleep	lights out
opened the door	father heard the noise	

Finish the story

To create this task, leave the ending off the selected text (mystery stories work especially well with this). Ask students what they think will happen next. Have them complete the story in their own words (writing or speaking about it).

Extensive reading

Reading fluently to get the gist or general understanding of a text is called *extensive* reading. Extensive reading is often done individually for the purpose of enjoyment, with little teacher involvement. This type of reading is important because it adds to and widens the learner's exposure to the language. Extensive reading aims at acquisition rather than conscious learning, at fluency rather than accuracy. In order for this kind of reading to help the development of fluency, the text must be within the learner's competence; it will not be an enjoyable or rewarding experience if the text is too difficult.

Advanced students should be encouraged to read magazines and authentic books extensively. Let advanced students choose what they want to read, but suggest that they start with short stories or novels written in accessible styles and vocabulary. For students at beginning and intermediate levels, it may not be appropriate to use authentic texts. For these learners, there is a wide range of *graded readers*, outlined in the next section.

Graded readers

Graded readers are texts that have been simplified for English language learners. They have been on the market for more than 40 years, so there's a wide range to choose from. A good library or resource center should give students access to graded readers. The readers are usually graded in the following ways:

- ◆ **Vocabulary.** Readers are graded by the frequency and range of meaning of their vocabulary. Priority is given to common words (such as nouns like *man, woman, car,* and *street* and prepositions like *to, from, in,* and *on).* Words with a wide range of meaning are used rather than words with a specific meaning. For example, the word *fruit* would be used instead of *blueberry; vegetable* instead of *broccoli;* and *book* instead of *tome.* For students of English for specific purposes, there are simplified readers on specific subjects like management, science, or technology. Such readers focus on the basic vocabulary of the subject. A reader on management, for example, would use the words *profit, production,* and *marketing.*
- ◆ **Grammatical structures.** The way the language is used in readers is carefully graded and usually follows the order of grammar introduced in most textbooks.
- ◆ **Idioms and phrasal verbs.** Use of these items is limited. Writers of graded readers usually avoid them at beginning and intermediate levels.

◆ **Controlled information.** The amount of information in each reader is carefully limited and the logical connection between items is made as clear as possible by means of transition words like *because, when,* and *however.*

There are two ways to use readers: by individual choice or as a group. For individual choice, ask each student to select his or her own reader and to read it at home. Set a time limit (for example, one week). Give students tasks to do while reading and after they finish. One task is to require a brief (60 to 100 words) review of the reader. For guidance, tell students that the review must mention the title, the author, the plot, the characters, and the setting. You might want students to then tell the rest of the class about their books. This oral activity produces helpful discussion that often leads students to recommend books for further reading or criticize books that are not worth reading or are too difficult.

For group reading, ask everyone in the class to read the same book. Set a number of pages per week for each student to read (you may want to go by chapters). Hold a group discussion at the end of each week to talk about the reading up to that point.

Whether you choose to do individual reading or group reading, keep in mind that the linguistic level of the text must match that of the students. By doing this, students are more motivated to read. Interest in the subject is essential. The learner who reads with interest tends to enjoy the process and acquire new language quicker than the learner who is bored or unmotivated by the text.

Following is an example and corresponding comprehension activities taken from the Heinemann Guided Reader, *Rebecca.* For more graded readings, refer to the titles listed in the *further reading section* at the end of this chapter.

Rebecca
by Daphne du Maurier
retold by Margaret Tarner
Introduction: The Dream of Manderley

Last night I dreamt I went to Manderley again. I stood in front of the iron gates at the beginning of the drive. When I had first seen those gates, they had been open wide to welcome me. Now, in my dream, they were closed. Behind them, the drive went on to Manderley.

In my dream, I was able to pass through the closed gates. I walked up the long winding drive. The trees and flowers grew near to the drive and grass almost covered it. As I came to the last bend of the drive, I felt the old excitement. I was near to Manderley again. At last, I could see Manderley. The old house was as beautiful as ever.

It was moonlight in my dream. The pale light shone on the windows and grey stone walls of the old house. And in my dream I saw the sea. It was silent and smooth as glass. For a moment, the house seemed full of light. I thought that we were living there, happy and secure.

The moonlight shone more clearly. Now I saw that Manderley was an empty shell. Only the grey stone walls remained standing. No one would ever live there again. We would never live there happily, Maxim and I. We would never live there free of Rebecca, free from thoughts of the past.

I woke up. Manderley was far away. Hard, bright sunlight shone into our bare hotel room. The long, empty day lay in front of us. Nothing much would happen. Nothing ever did. But we had a quiet peace, Maxim and I, that we had never known before. We did not talk about Manderley. I would never tell Maxim my dream. Manderley was no longer ours. It had been destroyed long ago by evil and hate.

We shall never go back to England. Even after nearly twenty years, the past is too near to us. We try to forget the fear and terror, but sometimes we remember.

We are often bored in this dull little hotel. But people who are bored are not afraid. We read the English newspapers, but we never meet English people, thank God.

This hot little Mediterranean island is our home now. We shall never again feel the softer warmth of the English sun. We shall never again stand in the Happy

Valley and smell the scent of its flowers. Here, the hard light of the sun shines on white walls. The trees are dusty. The sea is a clear blue.

We have lost a lot but I have at last grown up. I am very different from the shy, frightened girl who first went to Manderley. The fear and the terror made me a woman. A dull woman perhaps. But I am with my husband, and he is all I need.

Sometimes I see a strange, lost look in Maxim's eyes. I know that his thoughts are far away. Then he sits quiet and still in his chair. After a time, he begins to talk. We talk about anything in order to forget the past. We have both known fear. We have both known pain and loneliness. That is all over now. Manderley has been destroyed. But we are still alive and we are both free.

Note that the story of *Rebecca* is told by a woman whose name we never know. When the narrator marries Maxim de Winter, she becomes, of course, Mrs. de Winter. This name could cause some confusion as there are often references to the first Mrs. de Winter who was Rebecca. For this reason, the storyteller is referred to in the following questions as the narrator.

1. Which word in the first sentence tells us that the narrator has been to Manderley before?
2. At first in her dream, the narrator saw Manderley "as beautiful as ever." What did she see when the moon shone more clearly?
3. "We would never live there free from the thoughts of the past," said the narrator. What name was part of these thoughts of the past?
4. Where is the narrator living now? Who is she living with?
5. What has happened to Manderley?

Basic reading problems

A word of warning: bear in mind that the basic skill of reading is a serious problem with students who may not have a background of formal education and who may therefore not be fully literate in their own language. It will be difficult, if not impossible, to deal with an illiterate student in a class of fully literate students. In adult classes for immigrants in the USA, this situation may often occur. You should not attempt to teach reading in such mixed groups. The illiterate student needs special help and should be taught to read in private or special group lessons. You should also be aware that reading and writing are particularly difficult for students whose mother language is based on a different alphabet (such as the languages of Arabic, Farsi, and Hebrew) or has no alphabet (the Chinese, Japanese, and some other Asian languages have a large number of characters representing meaningful units). Fortunately for the Western individual teaching in Japan, most Japanese students have been well-schooled in the modern Roman alphabet and can read and write in it without difficulty by the end of their secondary school education (their problem, rather, tends to be listening and speaking). This knowledge of the Roman alphabet does not necessarily hold true in developing countries in other parts of Asia where literacy cannot be taken for granted. In these countries, students have no familiarity with the Roman alphabet.

Integrating reading and speaking

One of the most successful and adaptable ways to integrate reading with speaking is through *jigsaw reading*. This is a communicative activity that has much in common with information gap tasks (see *Information gap activities*, Chapter 8, page 149). To do a jigsaw reading, choose a text and photocopy it. Cut the paragraphs apart and mix them up. Give a paragraph to each student and ask them to read it. Then put the students into pairs or groups with those who have read different paragraphs. Ask students to share and discuss the content of one another's paragraphs until they have the gist of the story. Get students to move from one pair or group to another in order to piece together all the paragraphs.

There are many variations of the above activity. The essence of jigsaw exercises is to make students responsible for reading and understanding textual information. Jigsaw exercises also make students share their knowledge with others in order to solve a problem. This gives each student a chance to teach other students about something he or she knows and involves each student in speaking (especially since they have something needed by the other students!).

Integrating reading and writing

Cloze activities are a successful way to use reading texts to lead into writing tasks. The following activity is based on an advertisement that appeared in an English newspaper. First ask students to fill in each blank with a suitable word from the list at the end of the text.

Au Pairs in America

There are (1) _____ exciting benefits in store for those who (2) _____ *Au Pairs in America,* the world's leading *au pair* program. Here is an opportunity to (3) _____ a year in the United States, providing child care while learning (4) _____ American culture, (5) _____ new friends and studying part-time. In return for 45 hours of child care per week with one of our carefully (6) _____ American host families, you will be (7) _____ with a room of your (8) _____. You will (9) _____ be (10) _____ $150 (11) _____ week in pocket money. We (12) _____ sure that the families are (13) _____. Community counselors will keep in (14) _____ with you (15) _____ your stay. After you (16) _____ completed the 12-month program, you are (17) _____ to travel (18) _____ the USA for up to a month or, if you prefer, you can return home (19) _____. If you are interested, please write to the (20) _____ address:

> Au Pairs in America
> 37 Queen's Gate
> London
> SW7 5HR
> England

Word list:

spend	join	many	selected
given	suitable	are	making
provided	have	throughout	also
touch	in	free	directly
about	own	around	following

Once the above warm-up task is completed, give students the following scenario:

> You have decided to apply to the company, *Au Pairs in America*. Tell the company about yourself. What type of person are you? Why would you like to go to the USA? Write a paragraph (about 70 words) describing yourself and your reasons for wanting to be an au pair.

Review questions

1. What are the three main reading strategies? Describe their differences. When do we use these reading strategies?

2. What type of material is used for intensive reading? Extensive reading?

3. Name a task for each of the following stages of reading: pre-reading, during reading, and after reading.

4. Is reading aloud a good idea for learners? What are the disadvantages of asking students to take turns reading aloud?

5. What are graded readers? Are they suitable for students at all levels?

6. What should you be aware of with a learner who is at the basic literacy-level of reading?

7. Name several activities that integrate reading with speaking and/or writing.

Further reading

Feuerstein, T. and Schcolnik, M. *Enhancing Reading Comprehension*. Alta Book Center Publishers, 1995.

Grellet, F. *Developing Reading Skills*. Cambridge University Press, 1981.

Krashen, S. *The Power of Reading.* Libraries Unlimited, Inc., 1993.

Richards, J. *From Reader to Reading Teacher.* Cambridge University Press, 1997.

Silverstein, S. *Techniques and Resources in Teaching Reading.* Oxford University Press, 1994.

Published readers

Collins English Library (levels 1-6)
Heinemann Guided Readers (levels 1-4)
Longman Classics (stages 1-4)
Longman Fiction (intermediate to advanced)
Longman Originals (stages 1-4)
Oxford Bookworms (stages 1-6; the black series features classics like *Great Expectations* and *Jane Eyre*)
Oxford Progressive English Readers (intermediate to advanced)
Penguin Readers (true-beginning to advanced; very up-to-date selection with movie versions and cassettes; most popular with young students)

Jigsaw reading activities

Coelho, et al. *All Sides of the Issue: Activities for Cooperative Jigsaw Groups.* Alta Book Center Publishers, 1998.
Pollard, L. and Hess, N. *Zero Prep: Ready-to-Go Activities for the Language Classroom.* Alta Book Center Publishers, 1997.

Cloze activities

White, V. *Cloze the Gap: Exercises in Integrating and Developing Language Skills.* Alta Book Center Publishers, 1993.

TEACHING WRITING

Guided writing tasks
- Form sentences
- Substitution tables
- Model texts
- Short replies
- Questionnaires
- Scrambled sequences
- Narratives

Writing tasks by level
- Beginning and high-beginning level
- Intermediate level
- Advanced level

Fluency development and free writing
- Postcards
- Topic writing
- Detective and mystery stories
- Fables and folktales
- The personal, advice, and lonely hearts columns
- Writing games
- Diary writing

Correcting written work
Review questions
Further reading

TEACHING WRITING

WRITING, THE VISUAL REPRESENTATION of a language, is invaluable for helping students communicate and understand how the parts of language go together. Many students actually learn and remember more through the written word. This section takes a close look at writing skills and how to help students develop their ability to express themselves in writing. Keep in mind that writing almost always involves reading; the two skills, the receptive and the productive, are interdependent. Generally speaking, the student who reads with ease and reads widely finds writing easier than the student who doesn't read much and/or reads with difficulty. It doesn't necessarily follow that a good reader is good at writing, but most students find that, if they continue to practice reading, their writing improves.

Why can writing be difficult? Teachers who are quick learners of other languages should remind themselves that writing in a foreign language is a formidable task. Many native speakers find that expressing themselves in writing in their own language is more difficult than speaking. This could be for many reasons:

◆ To many people, writing seems artificial, whereas speaking seems natural.

◆ When writing, you are usually isolated from the feedback of another person (unlike when speaking and listening) and you can't use gesture, facial expression, or intonation to facilitate communication.

◆ A good writer must be sure of sentence construction, spelling, and punctuation, as well as style and appropriate register. Misusing vocabulary or grammar could easily obscure the meaning you are trying to express.

◆ Writing demands successful organization of ideas and information.

◆ A writer has to choose an appropriate style for the subject and the reader.

You need to remember these obstacles when preparing students for written work. If you've had experience learning a foreign language, did you find writing easy or difficult? How about when you were learning to write in school? Were you given interesting or boring exercises and tasks? Were these written tasks relevant to your needs?

Why teach writing? It is true that there are many other means of communicating with another person no matter how far away the other person may be. The telephone has made communication much quicker and easier than writing letters. Therefore, you need to think about *the need to write* and make writing tasks useful, realistic, and relevant to students' lives.

As a preliminary to teaching writing, ask yourself what you have actually written recently. Have you written letters, postcards, memos, messages, or filled out a job application? Now think about the following reasons for teaching writing and ask yourself the questions:

◆ Writing is necessary for some kinds of communication. What kinds?

◆ Writing helps in learning the language. How does it help?

◆ Writing helps the memory. What kind of writing helps students to remember vocabulary, grammar rules, or meanings?

◆ School exams are mainly written tests. How can you prepare students for these?

◆ Students need to take notes. When should notes be taken? For what purposes are notes useful?

When preparing a writing task, you not only need to focus on *why* you are teaching writing, but you need to focus on *what* students need to practice in order to improve their writing skills. Writing tasks should help students practice:

◆ **Transitions.** Writing helps students connect the language and make transitions between words. Students learn to write smoother sentences by combining sentences using words like *and, but, although, if, when, so,* and *therefore.*

◆ **Punctuation.** To write well, one must be able to use punctuation correctly. The basic rules of punctuation may or may not be the same in the students' native language and English.

◆ **Spelling.** Writing is one of the routes to improving spelling (as well as punctuation). *Dictation* is useful for drawing attention to English spelling and pronunciation. Use a variety of dictation techniques, and keep the passages short (see *Dictation*, Chapter 17, page 294).

◆ **Organization.** Organization is the key to developing a writing topic. The more powerful and creative the writer, the more advanced his or her organization skills generally are.

◆ **Form.** Through writing, students practice various forms and styles—from writing letters to stories. Students need to know these forms, especially business letters.

Guided writing tasks

Guided writing is writing done through the use of clues, information, or guidelines. At the beginning and intermediate levels, guided writing is a helpful way for students to build confidence in their writing ability. Following are several ways to do guided writing tasks (see also *Guided writing*, Chapter 9, page 168).

Form sentences

For this task, give items or clues to form sentences. For example, have students write complete sentences using the following sets of words:

1. He—America—American. He's from America. He's American.

2. They—Canada—Canadian. They're _____.

3. We—Mexico—Mexican. _____.

Substitution tables

Use a *substitution table*. This type of table contains items that can substitute each other in a sentence. First, draw the table on the board, then ask students to write at least ten correct sentences from the table:

	always		by car		quicker
she	usually	goes	by bicycle	as it is	cheaper
	often		on foot		not far
	never		by bus		too slow

Example sentence: She always goes by car as it is quicker.

For more information on substitution tables, see Chapter 12, *Teaching with Visual Aids*.

Model texts Give students a short text to read and to use as a model for connecting words in a similar way:

> New York is a very busy port. It's at the mouth of the Hudson River on the eastern coast. Although it isn't the capital of the USA, it is the second biggest city. The capital of the country is Washington, which is about 300 miles to the south of New York.

Using the model above, connect these sets of words into a paragraph:

> Rio di Janiero—Brazil—coast—capital—Brazilia—thousand miles
>
> Bristol—England—West Coast—capital—200 miles west of London

Short replies Give students a short letter to reply to (this also works with postcards, page 190):

The English Language School
201 Pine Street
San Francisco, California 94010
Phone: 415.692.9985 Fax: 415.692.3344

March 15, 2000

Dear Student:

Welcome to The English Language School! We are pleased that you have chosen our institute to study English. The staff and I look forward to meeting you and wish you a safe arrival in San Francisco. In the meantime, we would like to know some things about you. We would appreciate your taking the time to answer the following questions:

Why are you studying English?

Why have you decided to come to the USA?

What do you expect from our program?

For your convenience, I have enclosed a letter form for your reply. Please respond to the above questions in 100 words or less and return as soon as possible.

We look forward to meeting you!

Best wishes,

Franklin P. Ketch, Ph.D.
Director of Studies

_____, 2000

Franklin P. Ketch, Ph.D.
Director of Studies
The English Language School
201 Pine Street
San Francisco, California 94010

Dear Dr. Ketch:

Sincerely,

Questionnaires   A questionnaire is a useful and fun activity for both teachers and students. The student gets a chance to express his or her opinions, feelings, and ideas on selected topics, while the teacher learns more about what the student thinks and wants. Questionnaires can be developed from magazine quizzes, news events, and more. One of the most basic and helpful questionnaires is one that relates directly to the course:

> *Course Questionnaire*
> Use complete sentences to answer the following questions.
> 1. Why did you choose to take this course?
> 2. Why do you need to know English?
> 3. Are you getting what you want from the course? If not, what would you prefer to learn?
> 4. What is difficult for you in learning English?
> 5. What do you like doing in the lessons? What do you dislike?
> 6. What do you need more help with?
> 7. Why is writing useful or important to you?
> 8. Would you like to see other students' writing? Why?
> 9. Are the teacher's comments about your writing helpful? In what ways?
> 10. What kind of writing practice do you need?

Scrambled sequences

You can create scrambled sequences by simply photocopying a short text and cutting apart the sentences, or you can write your own. For example, the following sentences make up the opening of a story, but they are in the wrong order. Ask students (in pairs or in small groups) to put the sentences in order. To check the actual sequence of this story, see page 391.

> They were watching a man getting out of a black Mercedes.
> It was a bitterly cold day in Chicago.
> The two detectives looked at each other.
> Detectives Ryan and Schwarz were outside the Lake Motel.
> Was the murder weapon in the bag?
> The man was carrying an overnight bag that seemed unusually heavy.
> Schwarz said, "Could this be the guy we have been looking for?"

Narratives

Ask students to write a simple narrative based on a sequence of pictures or a cartoon strip. For example, look at the cartoon story below and write what is happening.

From *1000 Pictures for Teachers to Copy* by Andrew Wright.

Writing tasks by level

In addition to the general guided writing tasks above, there are various other tasks that work especially well for certain levels. These tasks are presented by level in this section.

Beginning and high-beginning level

◆ **Copying.** Using short texts already studied, ask students to copy a paragraph or more (or all of the text). This reinforces language learned orally, which is particularly necessary for students who are unsure of the Roman script.

◆ **Filling in Forms.** Ask students to complete forms or applications with correct details (names, addresses, telephone numbers, and other personal information).

◆ **Dictation.** This reinforces information learned from texts already read and understood (see *Dictation*, Chapter 17, page 294).

◆ **Short descriptions.** Ask students to write short descriptions of subjects they can easily relate to (for example, "describe yourself, your family, or your home in 50 words").

◆ **Writing messages.** This is the one task in which passing notes in class might be okay! Provide the beginning of a message and ask students to complete it. For example:

> I don't have my homework because . . .
> I can't meet you this evening because . . .

◆ **Combining sentences.** Combining sentences teaches students to use specific linking words, not just *and* or *but* (see *Combining sentences*, Chapter 8, page 144).

◆ **Substitution table.** This provides material for students to use in writing connected sentences (see *Substitution tables*, Chapter 12, page 213).

Intermediate level

◆ **Letter Writing.** A fun way to use letter writing is to give students an advertisement to answer. Examples can be taken from newspapers, just make sure they are short and understood. Apart from job advertisements, you can use or make up housing exchange announcements. For example:

> Couple with apartment in Miami wish to exchange with
> flat in Dublin. Please send details to:
> C. G. Keating; P.O. Box 23245; Miami, FL 85091.

◆ **Instructions.** Have students write instructions on how to use the domestic appliances in their homes (the clothes dryer, the dishwasher, the microwave, etc.). Give students a framework for guidance:

> First . . .
> Then . . .
> After that, don't forget to . . .

◆ **Writing a review.** Ask students to write reviews of movies, theater shows, or TV programs that they have recently seen. This is excellent for practicing the skill of summarizing.

◆ **Picture writing.** Ask students to compare two photographs, noting the differences and similarities.

Can you find **EIGHT** differences between these pictures?

From *Look Again Pictures* by Judy Winn-Bell Olsen.

This task is especially useful in consolidating vocabulary after preparation with key vocabulary.

◆ **Note-taking.** Ask students to listen carefully to an announcement and make notes of the most important facts. The announcement can be a tape recording of a weather forecast, a brief extract from the news (radio or TV), or an announcement at an airport (see Chapter 7, *Teaching Listening)*. This prepares students for university life and for business meetings.

◆ **Biography writing.** Give students some facts about a celebrity who died recently, then ask them to write a paragraph on the person. Questions about the celebrity will help students to remember the facts and put them in order: How old was she when she died? Where was she born? Why was she famous? This task keeps students in a personal mode without using their own personal information again.

Advanced level

Advanced students also need help, preparation, and stimulus when writing, although you should make it less obvious that you are guiding them. As a teacher, you need to provide context and be their resource person. Advise advanced students about preparing and organizing ideas for extended writing projects. Many advanced students need writing practice for exams or have to write letters that use English for specific purposes, such as a letter for medical school (such practice is usually given by teachers who have experience in the subject, although general English language teachers need not avoid such topics altogether).

◆ **Writing letters.** It's not difficult to prepare yourself and students to write letters. Most people at some time in their lives need to write a letter of complaint (about commercial service or about unsatisfactory goods), or write an editorial letter (when they feel strongly about a topic) to a newspaper, the mayor, or even the President. The preparation for writing such letters can involve discussion with other students or brainstorming for ideas. Integrating the skill of writing with reading and speaking is an excellent way for preparing to write a letter. Suggest that students look up the subject in the library or recommend relevant books, articles, or encyclopedias.

◆ **Biography writing.** As with the intermediate level, biography writing helps students write about personal aspects, but doesn't give advanced students facts about someone. Rather, give them questions and encourage them to find the facts. This assignment can also be done as an interview using questions like: What would you ask the celebrity? What might the celebrity's answers be?

◆ **Group writing projects.** These projects, such as publishing a class newsletter or magazine, involve many students in meaningful writing. Have each student in a group undertake a different topic or section of the newsletter (sports, daily life, international news, etc.). You could also have students work in pairs (remember to pair up weaker students with stronger ones).

◆ **Future job or profession.** This is an important topic that can serve as a springboard for composition. Ask students to write about what they are going to do after the course. Use questions like: *Why have you chosen that kind of work? What type of further study, preparation, or training will you need?*

◆ **Note-taking.** As mentioned previously, note-taking tasks prepare students for university life (note-taking at lectures) and for business meetings. For more advanced or realistic note-taking practice, ask students to listen carefully to mini-lectures or radio talks (make sure the topics are of interest) and take notes.

Fluency development and free writing

To help students get beyond the beginning stages and become fluent writers of English, they eventually need tasks that encourage creative or *free* writing. The language learner often has a mental block when asked to write freely, even when he or she has enough knowledge of the language to deal with the task. This is a similar block to the one that prevents students from speaking freely. These mental blocks often happen because students are afraid to make mistakes and expose their so-called weaknesses and failures. The person who doesn't speak, doesn't make mistakes and hence doesn't lose face publicly. Therefore, a student may only want to do guided writing, though that doesn't mean he or she writes badly. It just means they need practice writing freely, creatively, or naturally—and feeling good about doing it!

Fortunately, you can help students become fluent writers. Following are tips for helping most students with free or creative writing:

- Give students a choice of topics that relate to their knowledge and experience.
- Put students in groups to brainstorm a topic and develop it. *Note:* A further stage of preparation is necessary for students who don't get much out of brainstorming in groups. Have such students brainstorm in pairs instead of in groups, as they can more easily exchange ideas and explain what they want to say.
- Give students time to think and make notes.
- If students still have a mental block after the preparation time runs out, get them to talk to you or to one another about the topic for five minutes.
- If students are being asked to write extended pieces (compositions), make sure they prepare notes on the opening paragraph, the development paragraphs, and the conclusion. *Note:* Such composition writing should only be done at intermediate to advanced levels.
- Give examples of texts that deal with similar topics to the ones students have chosen to write about. This type of preparation is a good way to integrate reading and writing.

Following are a few tasks for encouraging free writing. They may not all work with students in all your classes, but keep trying (teachers must be creative, free thinkers too!).

Postcards

Postcards work well as a limited writing format that encourages students to write freely. Collect tourist postcards (used or new). Cut blank pieces of paper to postcard-size and stick them over the backs of the cards. You could also make postcards by gluing magazine pictures onto index cards, cardboard, or heavy construction paper.

Students may need some language preparation. Introduce vocabulary for describing places, including key adjectives (beautiful, boring, fascinating, pleasant, etc.). Review how to express approval or disapproval and structures like the present continuous, simple past, and present perfect. Discuss what kinds of things one would write to friends, relatives, or colleagues. Show examples.

Once students are prepared to write, give each of them a postcard and ask them to compose a short message (five or six sentences) in five minutes. Stop them after this time period, even if they haven't finished. Go around the class to see what each student has done, but don't attempt to correct mistakes. Remember that in a fluency exercise, speed matters more than accuracy.

Though pictorial postcards are a great stimulus in giving students something specific to describe and write about, you can also use postcards without pictures to help students gain confidence in writing short letters or messages to other students (simply use blank pieces of paper the same size as postcards). Keep in mind that it's not as daunting to write fifty words within a limited space as to write a composition of one or two pages.

Following are two other fun variations to using postcards:

Have students pretend that they are aliens from another planet. Ask them to write a postcard or a letter about the strange things they've seen on Earth. Tell them to describe ordinary people and their "extraordinary" behavior.

Have students write postcards or short letters on what life is like fifty, one hundred, or two hundred years from now. Help students by putting questions on the board:

Will there be any cars on the street?
Will we live in cities? Will there be any place to live in the country?
How long will people live (150 years)?
Who will work?
Will people live on other planets?

Topic writing   For topic writing, select a subject that most students can relate to and be interested in *(clothes, eating in restaurants, sports, etc.)*. Elicit words associated with the topic. Write them on the board and/or ask students to write them down. Then get students to write sentences using each of the words. When they have finished, allow five to ten minutes for them to make a story or a connected description using their sentences. If they have difficulty, write sentence openers or unfinished sentences on the board. These opening words need to relate to the topic. For example:

Clothes:
I always choose . . .
I never wear . . .
I prefer bright/dark . . .
I don't like expensive/cheap . . .

Sports:
My favorite game/team is . . .
The best player is . . .
I never watch . . .
The best match/game was . . .

After the students have written something, it's helpful if they work in pairs to try to correct each other's mistakes. You should monitor the correcting to ensure that it is helpful.

Detective and mystery stories

Almost always a favorite among students, detective and mystery stories are great motivators for writing. For a fun activity in writing short detective stories, use the game *Alibi* (described in Chapter 13, page 240). After the suspects are questioned, have each student write the story down, adding his or her own creative descriptions!

Fables and folktales

Well-known stories like *Cinderella, Sleeping Beauty, The Frog Prince,* and *Little Red Riding Hood* provide enjoyable writing material. Ask students to write an updated version of an original fable or folktale. A good (and funny) example of this is *The Little Girl and the Wolf* by James Thurber:

> One afternoon a big wolf waited in a dark forest for a little girl to come along carrying a basket of food to her grandmother. Finally, a little girl did come along and she was carrying a basket of food. "Are you carrying that basket to your grandmother?" asked the wolf.
>
> The little girl said yes, she was.
>
> So the wolf asked her where her grandmother lived, the little girl told him, and he disappeared into the woods.

When the little girl opened the door of her grandmother's house, she saw that there was somebody in bed with a nightcap and nightgown on. She had approached no nearer than twenty-five feet from the bed when she saw that it was not her grandmother but the wolf, for even in a nightcap a wolf does not look any more like your grandmother than the Metro-Goldwyn lion looks like Marilyn Monroe. So the little girl took a revolver out of her basket and shot the wolf dead.

Moral: It is not as easy to fool little girls nowadays as it used to be.

Ask students to discuss ways of modernizing *Cinderella* or one of the other classic tales. Make sure there is at least one student in each group who knows the story. You may need to suggest modern changes that would really change the ending of the old story. What would happen if the charming prince in *Cinderella* was really a princess in disguise? How would the story end? (The fairy godmother could be a feminist who inspired Cinderella to rebel!)

The personal, advice, and lonely hearts columns

There is plenty of material in the syndicated columns of newspapers to stimulate students to write letters. Ask students to find advertisements in the personal columns, or select one and distribute it to each student. Students then write ads based on the common needs expressed in the ads:

> Someone wants to meet a romantic, intelligent, warm-hearted non-smoker.
>
> Someone wants to meet a lively, young-at-heart companion.
>
> Someone wants to meet a sexy person with a sense of humor, professional job, and fast car.

The ads can be serious, realistic examples or slightly absurd and designed to cause a laugh (you'll find both kinds these days!). After students have written their ads, collect a number of photos of people from magazines (make sure the photos represent various types and ages of people—both men and women). Put students in pairs and give each pair a picture to discuss. Ask them to answer questions like: Who is this person? What's his or her job? How old is this person? What do you think the person's interests are? After the discussion, place the photos on the classroom walls or on a bulletin board. Ask students to walk around and try to match their ad with a picture. As a follow-up, get students to write letters to an advice columnist. Their problems can be personal or based on examples from the columns in newspapers or magazines. Encourage students to reply to the letters with suitable advice.

Writing games

Games add a fun dimension to writing. In Chapter 13, *Teaching with Games,* there are some ideas for using games to write. See especially the *Consequences* game (page 234). In this game, each student writes one sentence on a blank piece of paper and passes it on to the next student, hence "building" a story. As previously mentioned, it is important to give guidance in such tasks. The use of games for writing is most often to practice fluency. Students should be encouraged to write quickly and *not* be too concerned about being accurate.

Diary writing

Ask students to write down daily experiences in a notebook or keep a record of their language learning (new vocabulary, idioms, grammar points, etc.). With diary writing, do not expect too much; the important thing is to get students into the habit of writing something, no matter how brief, every day. Monitor the diaries once a week, but don't correct mistakes. Note errors for remedial practice in class.

Correcting written work

Before you correct students' written tasks, decide on a set of correction symbols (editing marks) and tell your students what the symbols mean. Encourage students to use the symbols to check their own work and correct their mistakes. As a rule when correcting written work, don't write out the correct form, just draw attention to the errors. This way, students must study their mistake and determine what is correct. Remember that correcting too many mistakes can discourage students. Use positive signs as well to show approval of good work. Following is a list of correction symbols that you might want to use (see Chapter 11, *Correcting Errors,* for a task using these symbols):

Sp	= Spelling mistake
T	= Tense error
G	= Grammatical error
WO	= Word order
WW	= Wrong word
P	= Punctuation
Cap	= Capital letter
!	= Read again and correct this one yourself (for obvious errors that the learner should know)
prep	= Wrong preposition
^	= Word omitted, insert a word
✓	= Good sentence, expressed well

Review questions

1. What things should you focus on when preparing a writing task?

2. What is guided writing? How can guided writing help beginning students? Give an example.

3. Think about the task of writing a letter. For each of the following levels, name an appropriate activity that will help students improve their letter-writing skills:

    Beginning: _____

    Intermediate: _____

    Advanced: _____

4. How is *free writing* different from *guided writing?* Give an example.

5. What strategy should you use in correcting written work?

Further reading

Reid, J. *Teaching ESL Writing.* Prentice Hall, 1993.

Raimes, A. *Techniques in Teaching Writing.* Oxford University Press, 1983.

Brookes, A. and Gundy, P. *Beginning to Write.* Cambridge University Press, 1999.

Frauman-Prickel, M. *Action English Pictures.* Alta Book Center Publishers, 1999. (picture sequences that could be used for narrative writing)

Taylor, E. *Using Folktales.* Cambridge University Press, 1999.

Tom, A. and McKay, H. *Writing Warm-ups.* Alta Book Center Publishers, 1999.

White, R. *New Ways in Teaching Writing.* TESOL Publications, 1995.

Winn-Bell Olsen, J. *Look Again Pictures.* Alta Book Center Publishers, 1998. (pictures that can be used for writing)

CORRECTING ERRORS

Sources of errors

How to make corrections

Correction effects on the learner

Review questions

Further reading

CORRECTING ERRORS

NOBODY'S PERFECT—we all make mistakes, even in using our native languages. As a language teacher, it is important for you to point out learners' errors carefully. You must keep in mind that correcting errors can interfere with the learner's development. Too much correction and too much negative feedback can be inappropriate and harmful; over-correction can discourage and even upset a student. Therefore it is necessary to have a strategy about correction that takes into account the learners' needs (whether or not correction is needed) and the effects of over-correcting. If the aim of an activity is to get students to verbally express their opinions on a topic, for example, then it is counter-productive to make corrections, especially if it means interrupting the students before they have finished talking. If, on the other hand, the aim of the lesson is remedial practice with a structure that the learners find difficult, then it is appropriate to emphasize accuracy and to use suitable correction techniques.

It is useful to make the distinction between an *error* and a *mistake.* If a learner has *not learned* a grammatical form or structure and consistently gets it wrong, the learner is making an *error.* For example, French students tend to say, "I have seen it yesterday," when they have not yet learned the uses of the simple past tense and the present perfect. In this example, the use of the wrong tense is an error. If, on the other hand, another student *has learned* when to say "I saw it yesterday" and when it is correct to say "I have seen it," yet sometimes uses the incorrect form, the deviation is called a *mistake* (given time, the learner can correct him or herself). A third term, a *lapse,* is used to refer to the wrong usage when it occurs because the student is tired, not concentrating, or suffering a momentary loss of memory. Of the three, errors are the most significant and require careful noting by the teacher. Remedial practice should be given at an appropriate time for the errors, especially those that are common to many students in a class. In this chapter, for simplicity reasons, the term *error* will be used (though it could be a mistake or a lapse).

The tasks in the first part of this chapter are designed to make you aware of some of the sources of errors, mainly native language interference. The second part of this chapter answers practical questions on how to correct and suggests techniques for making corrections in the classroom.

Sources of errors

Cognates are one common source of errors. A *cognate* is a word that is similar in form and meaning to a word in another language. For example, the word *telefon* in German is *telephone* in English. If the meaning and use of the two words is different in the two languages, they are called *false cognates.* For example, the word *sensible* in French looks like the English word *sensible* (meaning practical in outlook), but the French word means sensitive (easily hurt feelings). Another important source of errors is *over-generalization,* which results from the learner having learned a rule (such as plural nouns end in *-s*) but not having learned its restrictions (for example, some nouns, like *child* have a different plural form, *-ren).*

Task 1: False cognates

A. Choose one of the following lists of words in a language with which you are *not* familiar. Guess what you think would be the translation (an equivalent word or phrase in English) of each word.

> *French*
> passer un examen
> librairie
> furieux
> sensible
> histoire
> eventuellement
>
> *German*
> singen
> sympatisch
> aktuell
> menu
> werk
> bekommen

Italian
coincidenza
sensibile
controllare
straniero
assistare
di fronte a

Spanish
embarazada
profesor
constipado
contenta
padres
avisar

Now compare your guesses with others' guesses or look up the words in a bilingual dictionary (the correct translations are also given in the answer key). What do your translations tell you about cognates?

B. The following statements were all made by students learning English. Read each example, and then answer the comprehension questions.

1. I live in Sao Paolo which is a great city. (Brazilian)
   Does the speaker like Sao Paolo?

2. The old lady had a heart attack while she was crossing the road, so I stopped the circulation. (French)
   Did the speaker take any medical action? What did he or she do?

3. She didn't hear me at first so I cried. (French)
   Did the speaker get very upset?

4. I feel sorry for the people who live in the suburbs. (Spanish)
   Why does the speaker feel sorry for those people?

5. Can I borrow your toilet? (Japanese)
   Does the speaker want to remove the toilet for temporary use elsewhere?

6. I'm not sure if that's possible—I'll have to look at my agenda. (French)

   Is there a meeting going on?

Now compare your answers to the ones in the answer key, page 392. What does this exercise tell you about this kind of error? What is the common source of errors in these statements?

Task 2: Correcting various errors

What do you think the learner intended to say in the following examples?

1. She leaves Boston in a small apartment.
2. I have seen that film yesterday.
3. I will be a professor in school.
4. I have stopped to play football because of the damage to my leg.
5. I should like that you help me.
6. They are very exciting to see Switzerland.
7. Teacher: Where do you come from?
   Student: I am coming from Morocco.
8. He was a man who stole old ladies.
9. My mother is a good cooker.
10. She's beautiful, isn't it?

How to make corrections

Timing is first and foremost when making corrections. Choose the right time to correct—if accuracy is the aim of the activity, then make the student aware of the error soon after it occurred. But if fluency is the aim, don't stop the student in the middle of a sentence to correct him or her! For errors in fluency activities, make a note or record the errors and deal with them after the activity has finished.

There are three main types of correction:

- **Self-correction.** The student makes his or her own corrections.
- **Student to student correction.** Students correct one another.
- **Teacher to student correction.** The teacher corrects the students.

Following is an outline of the advantages and disadvantages of each type of correction:

Self-correction

Advantages

- If learners work out for themselves what is wrong and what is right, they help their memory and learning process.
- Self-correcting encourages independence and non-reliance on the teacher.
- Self-correcting increases motivation when students get it right, thus building self-confidence.
- Through self-correction, the teacher gets accurate, immediate feedback on students' abilities and knowledge.

Disadvantages

- Students who cannot recognize what the error is, or where it has occurred, cannot correct themselves.
- It's embarrassing or even humiliating for students who can't self-correct when their lack of ability is exposed to the whole class.
- The student may realize that there is an error but not know how to correct it; the correct model has not been learned.

Student to student correction

Advantages

- It may be easier to accept correction from another student than from the teacher—depending on how publicly it's done.
- The student who is able to correct another student gains confidence.
- The process encourages other students to listen carefully to one another, which keeps everyone involved.
- The process gives feedback to the teacher about other students who have learned the correct form or structure. Teachers find out if all members of the class need further teaching and learning of the item.

Disadvantages

- The student who 'corrects' may give an incorrect form.
- The student being corrected may not be able to understand or recognize the correction because of pronunciation difficulties of his or her peer.
- It may take too long to elicit the correct model from other students.
- The student who is corrected feels 'put down' by his or her peer who scores at his or her expense.

Teacher to student correction

Advantages
- The error is identified quickly and accurately; furthermore, students can participate in analysis of the error (why it's wrong).
- The correct model is given quickly and reliably.
- There can be a focus on errors common to many students in the group, thus avoiding concentration on individual errors.

Disadvantages
- The practice may lead to over-dependence on the teacher. Students will no longer need to try to work out the error themselves, nor will they know how to get it right without the teacher's help.
- Students may lose interest while other students are being corrected.
- All of the advantages of self-correction and student to student correction apply as reasons *against* teacher correction.

When making corrections, you need to make sure students *realize* that an error occurred and *understand* how to get it right. Following are several ways to make corrections. Read them and think about the questions.

- **Tell the students.** Simply say, "You made a mistake in that sentence" or "There was an error in that sentence." Which of the statements is personal? Impersonal? Which do you prefer? See *Correction effects on the learner,* page 206.
- **Signal.** Use your hands or a facial expression to indicate an error. For example, show surprise (raised eyebrows), a pained expression (plus say *ouch!*), or use both together (a gesture or facial expression with a verbal response). Think about the effect of using a 'stop signal' with your hands. In this way, you can capture attention and point out the error before students move on to the next sentence. Which of the examples would you prefer if you were the student who had made the error?
- **Use your fingers.** Fingers are useful correction tools! For example, in the sentence, "I must to do it," the third word should be omitted. Hold your third finger to indicate where in the five-word sentence the error has occurred.
- **Echo.** This is a risky technique and should *not* be used if the

teacher has developed the habit of repeating what students say, even when they have not made a mistake. If a student says, "I am coming from Croatia" in answer to the question, "Where do you come from?" it is not helpful to echo the error by saying, "You are *coming from* Croatia?" This indication of an error is unclear and could be misinterpreted by the students as approval of the statement. It is better to ask another student to use the correct form, and then give the first student a chance to correct his or her response. If this strategy doesn't work, provide a model such as: "I'm an American. Where do I come from? I come from America."

◆ **Use the board.** If an error is made in a sentence, write the sentence on the board but leave a space or a box where the error occurred. For example, if a student says, "Never I go there," write the sentence with an X where the word is placed in error and a checkmark where it should be: ___X___ I ___✓___ go there.

◆ **Draw arrows.** Arrows can be used to indicate which word is wrong. Draw an arrow pointing to the word that needs to be corrected, and ask students to make the correction. Resist always telling students what's wrong and correcting the error for them (this is a common, though not good, teaching habit). It's important to involve students in thinking about what's wrong and how to make it right.

◆ **Use video or audio recordings.** Recordings can be effective means of monitoring errors in speaking. The advantages of using recordings are:

1. Feedback and assessment of learners' performance involves the students.
2. The learners develop awareness of their strengths and weaknesses so that, without the teacher telling them, they can see/hear if they are making progress.
3. The feedback from recordings (if done in small groups or pairs) maximizes opportunities for student-to-student correction.
4. Recordings give good opportunities for the teacher to be

in an unobtrusive monitoring role.

5. Learners' needs are revealed continually and remedial tasks can be planned on the basis of this feedback.

Task 3: Making corrections in writing

Making corrections in writing is outlined in Chapter 10, *Teaching Writing*, page 195. Correct the following letter (written by a student). Use the correction symbols given on page 195.

Dear Alan,

Thank you for your invitation that I have received today. I enjoy myself and accept the invitation, but I'm afraid because I don't know very well the people who are invited to the party. I would like to know if I have the possibility of bringing a friend, he is very kindly, charming boy. I know him since ten years. My problem is that I don't know if I must put on a dress could you tell me? At what time the party starts? Please not too late because I must come on feet and the party is so far the house. I'm looking forward to see you Saturday night.

Bye Bye,

Mario

Correction effects on the learner

Corrections should be indicated and made in a supportive manner. Create an environment in which corrections are perceived as a necessary part of learning and developing. A well-known article, *You Can't Learn without Goofing*, by Dulay and Burt was very influential in the seventies and changed many teachers' attitudes about second language errors.

Although the study focused on children's second language acquisition, the title serves as a reminder to all teachers that "our job is to encourage the growth of the language (in the learner) by appreciating the learning steps" (Edge, 1989).

Teachers should especially avoid damaging the self-esteem of the learner. Don't pick on the person; instead, *highlight* the error. Make individual corrections on a one-to-one basis. If the individual error is a common one in the group, deal with it publicly without drawing attention to the person who "goofed." Most learners are sensitive to being corrected—some national groups more than others. Some students are fearful and inhibited because of the humiliation that results from making mistakes in public. Consequently, they would rather say nothing than risk making an error. This reticence presents a serious obstacle to learning, especially fluency development. For the teacher, learner fear of humiliation is a real challenge, as a teacher would prefer any output to no output.

Keep in mind that students who are continually making mistakes may have a *learning to learn* problem. In this case, you want to help the student improve as a learner. Teachers can certainly help by minimizing error correction and maximizing opportunities for practice. See the section, *What makes a good learner?*, Chapter 1, page 12 for more information.

Task 4: Making corrections

Correct the following sentences with a colleague or a native speaker. Ask your partner to say the sentence. Help him or her to correct the error. Use the techniques you learned in the *How to make corrections* section, page 202.

1. He likes tennis table.
2. I must to go to dentist.
3. She talk a lot.
4. He has the hair blond.
5. I see him yesterday.

Review questions

1. What are *false cognates?* Give an example in English of a word derived from another language and explain why it is often (or could be) misused.

2. When is the best time to correct students' errors?

3. What are the three types of correction? Give one advantage and disadvantage of each.

4. What are some good ways to indicate that errors have been made?

5. How can you avoid correction that causes negative effects on the learner?

Further reading

Bartram, M. and Walton, R. *Correction: A Positive Approach to Language Mistakes.* Language Teaching Publications, 1991.

Dulay and Burt. *"You Can't Learn without Goofing." Error Analysis.* Addison Wesley Longman, 1974.

Edge, J. *Mistakes and Correction.* Addison Wesley Longman, 1989.

TEACHING WITH VISUAL AIDS

Using the board

TEACHING WITH VISUAL AIDS

SEEING IS BELIEVING: a language learner depends on the eye for understanding context and the meaning of new words. Teaching new vocabulary and structures is much easier if you present the new items visually. Visual aids like real objects, pictures, and color photographs make a strong impact and capture the learner's attention. Teachers who rarely use visuals deprive their students of vivid and effective aids to learning and remembering.

This section presents a few of the most convenient and practical visual aids for classroom teaching, as well as advice and tips on how to use them. It also includes a special section on using the powerful medium of video in the language-learning classroom.

Using the board
The board (a chalkboard or white board) is still the most useful visual teaching aid in the classroom. To use the board well, you have to be organized and allow space for impromptu use (such as making a quick sketch to illustrate the meaning of a new word). Following are a few tips for making the board a successful visual aid:

- ◆ **Write as clearly as you can.** If your handwriting is difficult to read, practice on the board when you are not teaching.
- ◆ **Have students draw.** Some students may be able to draw better than you can. If a student really knows the item which needs to be drawn, let him or her draw it.
- ◆ **Use key words.** Write a few key words, a pattern, or a rule on the board after each activity. Don't put too much on the board at the beginning or end of the class; build up the notes at suitable points as you go through the lesson.
- ◆ **Don't overuse the board.** Some teachers think they are teaching because they are writing things up on the board. In fact, that may be some students' idea of what a good teacher does. Remember that oral/aural presentation is generally more

important in language teaching than writing/reading to convey meaning or for practice. Don't let your board work get in the way of giving sufficient speaking and listening practice.

◆ **Learn to draw stick figures.** Even if you're not an artist, you can draw! Often when students need a visual for understanding, it's better to draw badly than not at all. Stick figures can be quickly and easily drawn (and show a lot of character!):

From *Look Who's Talking!* by Mary Ann Christison and Sharron Bassano.

◆ **Involve the students.** In addition to having students draw, ask students to help you spell words that need to go up on the board. At the end of a lesson on a target structure, ask students to help you write up the pattern sentences in which the structure occurs.

The board is very suitable for substitution tables, drawing timelines, and practicing pronunciation. These three "board-friendly" visual activities are described individually in the next sections.

Substitution tables

Substitution tables contain items that can substitute each other in a pattern sentence. First draw the table on the board, then ask students to write correct sentences using items from each column. For example:

	glass		place?
	wine		building?
Is there any	wood	in this	room?
	metal		jug?
	liquid		

Example sentences:

> Is there any glass in this room?
>
> Is there any wine in this jug?

Substitution tables are a very effective way of showing students that there is a particular word order in certain sentence patterns. By using a substitution table, students can make a large number of correct sentences from one pattern.

Substitution tables can also be used to illustrate the use of *some* with countable nouns plus common adjectives:

	new	clothes		closet.
She has some	smart	shoes	in her	room.
	warm	gloves		drawer.
	white			suitcase.

Example sentences:

> She has some new clothes in her closet.
>
> She has some warm gloves in her suitcase.

213

A similar substitution table could be made using the word *any* (Does she have any . . .).

You could elicit other items to fit into the columns. This gets students contributing and participating in the construction of the table.

Make sure that your substitution table generates correct sentences only. It's easy with some patterns to generate wrong sentences, such as in the following table:

That's Those are	my	cup. T-shirt. keys. trousers.	Please give	it them	to me.

It has to be made clear to the students that if they start with *That's*, they must choose a singular or uncountable form and continue with *it*. *Those are* goes with plural forms and with *them*. This device can be useful in giving simple writing practice at beginning levels. It can also be used as a game: Who can write down the most correct sentences? For another example, see *Substitution tables*, Chapter 10, page 181.

Timelines   Drawing timelines on the board helps students understand the concept of the use of some tenses. Use appropriate sentences with your timelines. For example:

Present perfect continuous

I've been working in San Francisco for 5 years.

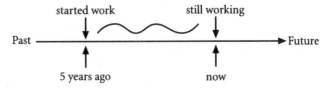

Used to

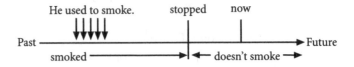

Pronunciation	Use the board to show phonological features: Syllable stress: comfort (<u>COM</u> fort) Consonant clusters: lu<u>x</u>ury /ks/ Weak vowels: was /wəz/

Task 1: Using the board

A. Draw a substitution table to give practice in making sentences with the simple past of *to be* with adverbials. For example:

You We	were	away	on the weekend

Complete the table with more choices in the first, third, and fourth columns.

B. Draw timelines to illustrate the difference between the following two sentences:
1. While I was having a bath, the phone rang.
2. While I was having a bath, my friend was watching TV.

Using other visuals

Besides the board, there are a great many other ways to use visuals. Following are a few suggestions and advice on using them:

◆ **Pictures and photos.** Magazines and newspapers have all kinds of pictures and photos that can be used in class. When choosing pictures, make sure they are big enough for everyone in the class to see. For pictures that are postcard-size and smaller, you should allow time to pass them around the class. Pictures also need to be clear and unambiguous (however, pictures that are ambiguous can sometimes produce discussion and generate various interpretations). Use simple, obvious pictures when defining vocabulary words (flashcards are common). If the meaning of a word isn't understood through the picture, do a quick sketch on the board or use an appropriate gesture or facial expression.

◆ **Realia.** Teachers of children are well aware that a box (or cupboard) with everyday, real objects and toys helps with active learning. Adults can also be helped by seeing and touching things. If you know about Cuisenaire Rods (colored pieces of wood of varying lengths used originally to teach mathematical concepts and languages—see *The Silent Way*, page 343), then by all means use them.

Collect aids like street or transportation maps, menus, and postcards.

◆ **Overhead projector.** Use an Overhead Projector (O.H.P.). This valuable teaching tool is easy to operate; it allows you to refer to the text or chart projected behind you while you remain facing the students. Overhead projectors work well for focusing the attention of the whole class on the teaching point. You can show the text line by line (use a piece of paper to cover up the rest) and get students to anticipate what comes next. You can also draw a picture in stages. Keep in mind that to use an overhead projector, you have to prepare the text on transparencies beforehand (most copy shops will make transparencies for you).

Task 2: Using visual aids

A. The objects listed below can be used to teach one or more of the language items *a-j* (structures, vocabulary, and functions). Match the objects with the language items by writing the appropriate letter or letters in the blanks.

1. A street map _____
2. A menu _____
3. A clock _____
4. A pair of gloves _____
5. A glass of juice or a bag of candy _____
6. Public transportation map or schedule _____

a. telling the time
b. offering
c. prices in restaurants
d. food and drink (vocabulary)
e. made in . . .
f. I've just . . .
g. How long does it take?
h. full/empty
i. next to/opposite/just past
j. giving directions

B. Decide what type of visuals would be useful in presenting and practicing the following:
    1. *Used to* (He used to—but doesn't now.)
    2. I prefer *X* to *Y*.
    3. Making complaints
    4. Giving advice on minor ailments
    5. *Some/any*

C. Using the verbs *watching*, *studying*, *sunbathing*, *talking*, and *exercising*, describe what the people are doing in the following drawings:

From *Action English Pictures* by Noriko Takahashi and Maxine Frauman-Prickel.

Using videos

Videos are a wonderful medium for presenting new material or for stimulating discussion in a vivid, dramatic form. However, as with all teaching aids, the value of videos depends on how you use them. Good video tapes have content that is lively, interesting, and entertaining and contain a clear language learning purpose. Television viewing habits have made many people passive in their attitude toward watching videos; language learners often approach video material with the expectation that they can relax and be fairly passive. Thus, when using videos, one of your first priorities should be to make the watching of videos an *active* learning process for students. This requires students to respond to the content of the video, either verbally or in writing. Prepare worksheets and oral questions for use before, during, and after the viewing. These tasks ensure that students get the maximum benefit from watching a video. Following are tips for using videos as visual aids in your lessons:

- **Prepare a viewing guide.** A viewing guide has the same function as a lesson plan, but it doesn't need to be very detailed. It should introduce the topic, keep to a few points (general details about the people, main events, story line, and language) and have questions about the content of the video. Distribute the viewing guide to students before watching the film.

- **Ask questions.** Get students to respond to both written and spoken questions.

- **Watch and listen for cues.** Tell students to watch and listen for specific items (for example, "What was the burglar carrying when he broke into the room?"). Listen for particular language items, such as vocabulary or structure ("Some newspaper headlines will be shown. Make a note of any passive forms").

- **Freeze frames for review.** The pause button on a VCR enables you to "freeze" or highlight the scene of your choice, making it easier for students to focus on a significant detail. Freeze-framing is best used during a second viewing of the video; it's usually better to run through the whole video or a naturally defined segment of it the first time. The second viewing gives students the opportunity to watch and listen for points they might have missed. If the video is long and demands a lot of concentration, divide it into segments, using natural breaks as stopping places. Encourage the students to make notes when the video stops, and ask them if they want a re-run of parts of the video.

◆ **Pronunciation and fluency practice.** The dialogue and the speech on videos can be used for pronunciation practice, especially intonation and stress on words or syllables. The dialogue is also useful for vocabulary learning and practice. New words or phrases are easier to understand in the context of a film. If students have trouble with a new word being used in the video, you can highlight it by stopping, reviewing, or freeze-framing the film.

◆ **Silent viewing.** This technique is used to encourage students to predict or speculate on what is being said by the characters in the film. For silent viewing, show the video the first time with the sound turned off and ask students to predict what is happening. The second time, show the video with the sound on and ask students to check whether their predictions were right or appropriate.

◆ **Note-taking.** Practice note-taking with videos. See Chapter 10, *Teaching Writing*. Taking notes is an important skill for university students and for commercial purposes (at business meetings). Students will need guidance and help with note-taking, so it's necessary to prepare them with questions on what to listen for. Highland Publishing has a video titled *The Real Thing* which presents real lectures for students to listen and practice their note-taking skills.

Types of videos

There is a bewildering variety of videotapes available. The most useful fall under the following categories:

◆ **Language-teaching videos.** These video materials are made by language teaching organizations especially for language learners. Examples include *On Track* and *Only in America* published by Oxford University Press and *True Voices* published by Addison Wesley Longman.

◆ **TV programs.** Recordings of soap operas, comedies, sitcoms, and news programs provide authentic language material.

◆ **Specialist films.** Some videos are made for specific purposes such as business English and English for tourism. For example, the *Focus On . . . Series: ABC News ESL Video Library,* published by Prentice Hall Regents, has videos that focus on specific areas like business, health, or the environment.

◆ **Teacher training tapes.** Some teacher-training programs and organizations have videos that demonstrate the teaching of particular basic techniques with classes of English language learners. Addison Wesley Longman publishes a video series called *Teacher Training through Video: ESL Techniques.*

Review questions

1. What are some ways to use the board? What should you *not* do when using the board?

2. What is the main use of drawing substitution tables on the board? What do you have to be careful of when constructing substitution tables?

3. How would you use time lines to show the difference between *I have been doing something* (present perfect continuous) and *I did something* (simple past)?

4. How can you use "freeze-framing" when showing a videotape to a group of students? How about silent viewing?

5. What criteria should you keep in mind when choosing pictures, photographs, or drawings to elicit comparative descriptions (such as "What's the difference between this picture and that one?").

Further reading

Frauman-Prickel, M. *Action English Pictures.* Alta Book Center Publishers, 1999.

Lonergan, J. *Video in Language Teaching.* Cambridge University Press, 1984.

Cooper, R. et al. *Video.* Oxford University Press, 1991.

Romo, R. and Brinson, B. *Easy Visuals for English Language Teachers.* National Textbook Company, 1993.

Shapiro, N. and Crenser, C. *Chalk Talks.* Command Performance Language Institute, 1994.

Wright, A. *1000 Pictures for Teachers to Copy.* Addison Wesley Longman, 1984.

Wright, A. *Pictures for Language Learning.* Cambridge University Press, 1989.

Wright, A. and Haleem, S. *Visuals for the Language Classroom.* Addison Wesley Longman, 1991.

Chapter 13

TEACHING WITH GAMES

Warm-up games
- Throw the ball!
- Get in order!
- Back-to-Back
- Find someone in the room who . . .
- Whose bag is it?

Action and mime games
- Simon says
- Charades
- Are you _____ing?
- Hotel problems
- Just done it!
- Picture description
- Blindman's buff
- Guess the adverb
- The robot
- Find your partner

Vocabulary Games
- Hangman!
- Spelling bee
- Crosswords

Writing Games
- Consequences
- Fictionary

Speaking Games
- Instructions
- Pyramid discussion
- The balloon debate
- Twenty questions
- What's my job?
- Coffee pot
- Bananas
- Big, bigger, biggest
- Alibi
- Just a minute!

Quizzes
Review questions
Further reading

TEACHING WITH GAMES

GAMES ARE AN ESSENTIAL INGREDIENT for varying the learning pace, relaxing, and motivating students. By using games, students can actively practice language and enjoy learning. Students feel less inhibited when they are participating in a game; most don't mind risking linguistic mistakes in a game context; rather, they focus on communicating to score points or win. This makes games an excellent route for building fluency.

Be aware that some learners, especially adults, have clear expectations about what should happen in a classroom and think games should *not* be a part of their learning. These learners often think of games as frivolous and a waste of time. They simply do not see the value of any activity called a game. In such situations, you need to prepare learners for games by explaining the purpose of games and convincing them that these activities have linguistic and communicative value.

Often for learners, the most difficult part of playing a game is understanding how to play it. When planning to introduce a new game, think carefully about how to do it. Demonstrate, rather than explain, whenever possible and always give clear instructions. You can plan for a game to be played at the beginning of a lesson (ice-breakers or warm-ups), during a lesson (to change the pace), or at the end of a lesson (as a closing or "wrap-up"). Games can focus students on the content of the lesson, act as revision, or simply serve as an activity that is an enjoyable way of practicing and using the object of the lesson.

As a teacher, you should gradually add to your "library" of games (include items that can be given as prizes—erasers, stickers, etc.). Examples of games have been used throughout this book (to show how to teach speaking, reading, etc.). Following are more game ideas, categorized in the following sections: warm-up games, action and mime games, vocabulary games, writing games, speaking games, and quizzes.

These games have been selected because of their popularity and the fact that they can be adapted to almost any level, age, and content. They also use little or no materials so that you can use them anywhere!

Warm-up games

Warm-up games or icebreakers are opening activities to "wake up" the class. They are often short, energizing, and designed to relax students and ease them into the lesson. Warm-up games also help students get to know one another, thus creating a supportive learning environment.

Throw the ball!

This is a great ice-breaker for finding out everyone's names on the first day of class. You'll need a ball or some type of object that can be safely thrown. Have students stand up and form a circle in the middle of the class. Demonstrate the activity by saying your name and then the name of the student to whom you throw the ball. The student who catches the ball repeats his or her own name and then the name of another student to whom he or she throws the ball. If a student doesn't know another student's name, he or she says "_____ (his or her name) to you." The "you" gives his or her name and throws the ball on until everyone knows everyone else's names. For example:

Teacher: Gilly to Masako! (Throws the ball.)
Masako: Masako to You! (Throws the ball to Kim.)
Kim: Kim to Luis! (Throws the ball to Luis.)

The ball continues to go around until the students learn each other's names. As a final check, ask the group to test themselves and see if they can remember all of the names. If not, they can simply say, "I'm sorry. I've forgotten your name."

Get in order!

This simple warm-up lets students get to know each other. Have students stand in a line (put themselves in order) according to age, height, order of birthdays, native country (alphabetical) etc. To find out this information, students have to mingle and ask questions such as "How tall are you?" and "When is your birthday?" In doing such an activity, students may incidentally use the language of comparatives: "Oh! So you're older than me. You stand next to Yoko."

Back-to-Back   Ask students to stand in the middle of the room and close their eyes. Then move each student so that he or she is standing back-to-back with a partner (remind them to keep their eyes closed!). When all students are back-to-back, ask them to open their eyes and guess their partner by asking yes/no questions. They cannot turn around and see their partner! You can also have students find out exactly what their partner is wearing by asking questions like: Are you wearing a pair of navy blue socks? Do you usually wear jeans? Is red your favorite color to wear?

Find someone in the room who . . .   For this activity, create a chart of descriptions or a set of questions using the phrase *Find someone in the room who . . .* . Give the information to each student and ask them to walk around the classroom (mingle) and find someone who fits the descriptions or can answer the questions. When the student finds someone, he or she writes that person's name next to the statement. This exercise has a dual function: it serves as an ice-breaking activity and can also be used for an informal tense revision or to practice question forming (the student has to make the statements into questions).

> Find someone in the room who ...
> has been to your country_____
> plays a musical instrument _____
> (See the next page for more examples.)

Whose bag is it?   This fun activity warms up students' imaginative thinking. Beforehand, you'll need to fill a bag with items such as a watch, a photograph, car keys, lipstick, a number of receipts, tickets, and the like. Put the bag in the middle of the classroom and pull out an item. Continue to slowly pull out items and ask students to create a picture of the character who owns the objects (they can write sentences about the person, draw the person, or talk about the person). This activity is often used to practice modals of deduction *(must, could)*, present and past tenses (for example, on seeing lipstick, students say "She *must/could* be a woman" or "She *must've/could've been* a woman").

... has a birthday in June.	... has three sisters.	... has never seen snow.	... likes kung-fu movies.	... likes jazz.
... believes people are smarter now than 1,000 years ago.	... likes tabouli.	... thinks it's all right for parents to hit their children.	... has at least one Madonna CD.	... has a driver's license.
... has never had a broken bone.	... knows what Hakeem Olajuwan does for a living.	... drinks a lot of diet Coke.®	... thinks it's okay for Americans to buy guns so easily.	... is an optimist.
... likes cats.	... is an atheist.	... has an American Express card.	... knows the value of pi (π) to six decimal places.	... believes other planets have intelligent life.
... believes people in America have too much freedom.	... knows how to sew.	... knows which country Mt. Kilimanjaro is in.	... would like to visit Mars.	... knows which century Mozart lived in.

From *Alarm Clocks! Weird and Wonderful Exercises for English Language Learners* by Douglas Milburn.

Action and mime games

A key to keeping students motivated is to keep their minds *and* bodies moving! Action and mime games work well to break the monotony of deskwork (we all get tired of sitting).

Simon says

This popular game (most often used for children) is a way of using Total Physical Response (see *Total Physical Response*, Chapter 21, page 344). It is useful for practicing the use of imperatives as well as vocabulary of body parts. It is most suitable for beginning and high-beginning levels. Start by asking one student to be Simon. Simon gives commands to the rest of the group, who must do exactly what he or she tells them every time that he or she says "Simon says … ." The trick here is that if the order *isn't* prefaced with "Simon says … ," the students do *not* do the action. The first student to make a mistake (do an action that Simon doesn't say) becomes Simon (or leaves the game) and the game continues. For example:

"Simon says put your left hand on your head."
(Students do so.)
"Touch your toes with your right hand."
(Students don't do this because Simon didn't say so; if a student does this, he or she becomes Simon.)

Charades

For this fun and often humorous game, write descriptions that need to be acted out onto slips of paper. Give each student a slip of paper. Each student then has to mime the actions on his or her slip of paper to the rest of the group and elicit the sentence from the group. Example sentence (advanced level):

You've lost your contact lens in a noisy crowded place, and you're looking for it.

Are you _____ing?

This version of *Charades* focuses on the present continuous form. Write sentences using the present continuous form (actions happening now). Once again, have students elicit their sentence from the class by miming. The other students have to guess the sentence by asking questions like

"Are you washing windows?" Continue the game until someone says the exact sentence. Example sentences:

You're washing an enormous elephant.

You're eating spaghetti with a knife.

You're watching a boring game of tennis.

Hotel problems

Another variation of *Charades,* this game requires the acting out of words, phrases, or parts of words to convey the meaning of a whole sentence. It works well to practice the present perfect and/or the language of urgent requests. On slips of paper, write sentences conveying urgent requests or messages. Ask one student to be the receptionist and another student to be a hotel guest. The guest has lost his or her voice and has to mime the urgent request or message on his or her slip of paper. Example sentences:

I've seen a cockroach in my room!

Call a plumber! The toilet has overflowed!

Call a doctor! My husband has had a heart attack.

Just done it!

As in *Hotel problems,* a student is given a slip of paper with a sentence on it. The sentence needs to be in the form *I've just ... !* The student has to elicit the exact sentence from his or her classmates by acting it out. The other students have to ask questions, using the form *Have you just ... ?* Example sentences:

I've just seen a ghost!

I've just won the lottery!

I've just spilled my drink!

Picture description

Picture description is an excellent game for practicing the understanding of instructions. Describe a simple picture to the class. The students have to draw it as well as they can. Once they have finished drawing, have them compare pictures. A picture description may be as follows: Teacher: In the middle of the paper is a hill. Above the hill is a big cloud. In the top left hand corner is the sun. There's a lake in front of the hill ... etc. (See the following drawing.)

This game can also be played in pairs, which increases each student's talking time.

Blindman's buff In this instruction game, students practice the language of direction in an amusing and meaningful way. Blindfold one student and tell him or her to find his or her way around a series of obstacles by following instructions given by the other students. The obstacles can be anything from desks and chairs to books and shoes.

Guess the adverb Adding fun to adverbs, this game is great for adverb practice and review. Send one student out of the classroom. Then ask the other students to think of an adverb, such as *slowly* or *carefully*. Decide on the adverb (it should be appropriate to the level of the class). Call the student back into the classroom. The student must guess the adverb (make sure the other students keep it a secret!) by asking the class to perform actions in the manner of the adverb. For example, the student might ask for the following actions:

Open the window.
Drive a car.
Peel a potato.

In turn, if the adverb were *slowly,* the class would mime all of the above actions in a *slow* manner. Continue until the student guesses the adverb.

The robot

Here's everyone's chance to have a robot—and practice imperatives! In this game, ask one student to be the robot. The rest of the class must give instructions that the "robot" has to obey by miming. Example instructions:

Take a shower.
Cook an egg.
Start a car.

Note: The instructions could also be more relevant to the classroom, such as "Sharpen your pencil" or "Erase the board."

Find your partner

Also called *Matching Pairs,* this game helps students to review and practice conditional sentences. Think of a number of sentences with two clauses (sentences which can be easily divided into two parts, such as conditional sentences, proverbs, etc.). Write each clause on a separate slip of paper. You can also write two halves of a response, such as a question and an answer. Give each student a slip of paper and ask them to memorize what's on it. Then ask students to walk around the room saying their part until they find their "other half." If their split sentences are part of a dialogue, ask students to continue the dialogue by writing a mini-situation or role-play (once they've found their other half). Example sentences:

I would've climbed Mt. Everest, but I was already suffering from frostbite.
(Dialogue)
Did you see the man in the supermarket?
No. What was he wearing?

Vocabulary games

Vocabulary games provide a fun alternative to the process of learning vocabulary (see Chapter 4, *Teaching Vocabulary*). Games especially help students to *remember* meanings, spellings, and the usage of words. For a game that gives students practice with using dictionaries, see *Fictionary*, page 235.

Hangman!

This classic children's game is a favorite for adults as well. Ask one student to think of a word and go to the board. He or she tells the rest of the group how many letters are in the word and writes the corresponding number of blanks on the board. Each student has to ask: "Is there a ___(letter of the alphabet) in the word?" If there is, the student at the board puts the letter in its correct blank or blanks, hence gradually filling in the letters of the unknown word. If the letter isn't in the word, the student draws the first part of a scaffold (the base). The point of the guessing is to get enough letters to know the word (fill-in the blanks) before the student completes the drawing of a scaffold (including the noose with a stick figure hanging from it). If someone thinks they know the word, they may guess it—but if they're wrong, the student at the board may add another part to the scaffold. This idea may sound gruesome, but it is good practice for using the alphabet and for spelling words.

Spelling bee   This traditional game is best played in teams. Prepare a list of words—preferably known items that have been taught or studied. Then divide the class into two teams (more if the class is large) and appoint a captain for each team. Choose a word from the list and ask the captain of one team to spell the word out loud. If the word is correctly spelled, the next word is given to the captain of the other team. Continue, giving every student a chance to spell a word. If a student misspells a word, he or she is eliminated from the game. The winning team is the one with the most surviving players.

Crosswords   Crossword puzzles are an entertaining way of reviewing language. You can write crosswords especially for your students as a motivating way to review vocabulary, or you can use computer programs designed to make up crossword puzzles.

Writing games   The use of games in writing is most often to practice fluency. Students should be encouraged to write creatively and not be too concerned about accuracy. See Chapter 10, *Teaching Writing*, for more guidance.

Consequences   This is a popular children's game that can be easily adapted for learning English. The object of the game is to get everyone involved in writing short stories. Each student starts with a blank sheet of paper. They write a sentence, fold the paper over, and then pass it on to the next student. Each student then writes a second sentence, folds it over, and passes it on. This "write, fold, and pass" process continues until the stories are complete. *(Note:* Pay attention to *how* the paper is folded. Students must only write on one side of the paper. Try it yourself first!) To ensure the stories have coherence, give students guidance in the form of half-finished sentences:

> Line 1: X met Y in a Z. (The students individually complete the sentence, for example Dracula met Boris in a swimming pool.)
> Line 2: S/he was wearing a _____ (pink tutu?), and s/he was wearing a _____ (gorilla costume?).
> Line 3: S/he said _____, and s/he replied
>
> _____.

Line 4: And the world said, "_____
_____."
Line 5: And the consequence was that
_____.

You can vary the framework to focus on a specific language structure. The final text is an amalgam of different ideas and is frequently bizarre and usually very funny.

Fictionary   This game, also known as *Call My Bluff,* is most suitable for high-intermediate and advanced students needing practice using dictionaries and writing (creatively!). Divide students into groups (teams) of three. Ask each group to find an unknown, difficult word in their dictionaries, or assign a difficult, unknown word to each group. Each group must write the dictionary definition of the word and make up two additional definitions (the object is to make all three definitions plausible). The group then writes the word on the board and reads out their definitions. The opposing teams have time to confer before submitting a group vote on which definition they think is correct. After the votes are collected, the leader of the group tells the other groups whether their definition is correct or incorrect. Each team that chooses the correct definition gets two points. If nobody gets the correct definition, the playing team gets one point. After several rounds, add up points and declare a winner.

Speaking games   Games are a great way to get students speaking fluently because students get wrapped up in playing the game and don't worry so much about *how* to speak correctly. Rather, they concentrate on *what* they have to say. For more ideas, see Chapter 8, *Teaching Speaking.*

Instructions   Ask students to think of a machine and then instruct others on how to use it. *(Note:* Make sure the students who are instructors understand the instructions first.) This exercise can be used for a lesson on driving a car or how to use the computers in the self-access center. In fact, some students may give better explanations on how to use computers than some teachers!

Pyramid discussion Pyramid discussions, though quite easy to organize, need to be based on problems that are simply stated and easy for students to relate to. Following is an example:

The Problem: You have survived a plane crash, and now you are left alone on a desert island (or in the middle of a desert, etc.). How do you survive until you are rescued? What are the five most essential things to have with you? You have a parachute and some other useful things that can be taken from the wrecked plane.

First Stage: Ask each student to think about the problem before discussing it with others.

Second Stage: Ask students to discuss the survival plan or the things they need with another student.

Third Stage: When the pairs have agreed on some items and a plan for survival, ask them to join another pair to make a group of four. In this group, they should compare their ideas and have further discussion.

Fourth Stage: Each group of four should present their ideas to the class. You should chair the discussion to help keep the focus on the best ideas or common agreement.

Pyramid discussions bring out a great variety of ideas and opinions by actively involving every individual in the class. They give students who are not good at expressing themselves a number of opportunities to repeat their ideas, arguments, or opinions in small groups and in larger groups. No single confident student is allowed to dominate, and the less confident students get chances to build their confidence.

The balloon debate

Another game that uses a dramatic problem is *The Balloon Debate.* Tell students the following scenario:

> You are all in a balloon which is quickly losing height over a shark-infested sea because there is too much weight inside of the balloon. Two or three students will have to jump in order to save the greater number. How do you decide who will go?

Ask each student to pick a job (doctor, taxi driver, journalist, etc.). Make sure no two students have the same job. Each student must then tell the class why he or she mustn't be thrown overboard because of the importance of his or her job. After each student has spoken, have the class discuss the relative merits of each profession. At the end, ask students to vote on which students must jump.

Twenty questions

Also known as *Animal, Vegetable, Mineral,* this game gives students practice in forming yes/no questions.

Ask students to think of something (a noun) that can be classified broadly as an animal (including human beings), a vegetable (any plant or vegetable product, such as wood), or mineral (including metals and chemicals; one example is a diamond). Select one student whose word the rest of the class must guess. The students can only ask questions that can be answered with a *yes* or a *no*. *Wh-* questions are not allowed. Give students a limit of 20 questions. If they have not guessed the student's word after 20 questions, then the student is considered the winner. A guess, of course, counts as a question. *(Note:* You may want to give students the following hint: The first question should be, "Is it an animal?" If the answer's *no*, then the next question should be "Is it a vegetable?" A *no* answer identifies the noun as a mineral.)

What's my job?
A variation of the *Twenty questions* game, this game requires each student to think of a job or a profession. Select one student whose job/ profession the rest of the class must guess. Allow the class 20 questions to guess. Remember that the questions can only have *yes* or *no* answers. Examples:

> Do you have to work outside?
> Do you need special qualifications for this job?
> Do you have to work with your hands?

As illustrated, various themes can be "plugged" into this game format. Try sports, countries, or famous people.

Coffee pot
Another guessing game, *Coffee pot,* requires each student to think of a verb (for example, *to sunbathe).* Select one student whose verb the rest of the class must guess by asking questions. The funny part is that students must substitute the words *to coffee-pot* for the missing verb. This game is especially useful for reviewing question forms and tenses. For example:

> Do you *coffee-pot* at night?
> No.
> Do you *coffee-pot* alone?
> I can.
> Have you ever *coffee-potted?*
> Yes, many times.
> Is *coffee-potting* some kind of sport?
> No.

Bananas

In this game, bananas aren't just a popular fruit—they're a popular response! This is an especially humorous way to practice *wh*-questions. To begin, choose one student to be the first subject. Ask the rest of the class to address personal questions to the student. The questions must be in the *wh*- form. The student has to answer every question with the word *bananas*. The object is to make the student laugh or smile. If he or she does, then someone else becomes the subject (or victim!). The questions should be designed to elicit ridiculous or embarrassing answers. For example:

> What do you wash your face with?
> Bananas.
> What do you wear under your shirt?
> Bananas.

Note: You may also substitute words such as *spaghetti*, *garlic*, or *onions* for *bananas*.

Big, bigger, biggest

This is the *best* game for practicing comparative and superlative forms! It works especially well with young students; when using with adults, make sure they don't feel uncomfortable with the physical comparisons.

Divide the class into two teams. Keep track of the score by writing points down on the board. Start by asking one member of a team to stand up and say, "I am the tallest in the class." If one of the opposing teams disagrees, someone on that team must stand up and say, "I am taller than you!" As the teacher, you then measure them and decide who is taller. Award a point to the team that has the tallest student. Before the game begins, suggest things that can be compared and review some of the adjectives or words that will be needed. Examples:

height: tall, taller, tallest
age: old, older, oldest/young, younger, youngest
shoe size: big, bigger, biggest

Alibi   This popular speaking game, also known as *Murder!*, gives students a chance for role-play in dramatic situations. The aim is to provide practice in asking yes/no and *wh-* questions and in using simple past and past continuous verb forms.

Tell students that someone was murdered on a particular day in a certain spot (pick a place familiar to the students) and the police are going to question two suspects on their whereabouts between certain times (for example, Friday from 7:30 p.m. until 2:00 the following morning). Ask two students to be the suspects. The suspects must leave the room and carefully prepare their alibi (what they were doing during the time the murder was committed). Meanwhile, the rest of the class acts as the police and prepares questions to ask the suspects. Example questions:

Where did you meet?
What did you do after the restaurant?
What was the movie?
What was Clara wearing?

Once both groups are thoroughly prepared, bring in the first suspect and have the rest of the class question him or her and take notes. Then bring the second witness in for questioning. If the two stories of the suspects correlate, the suspects are innocent. If the stories are different, the police (the class) have to decide whether they have enough information to hold the suspects.

Just a minute!　Talk, talk, talk is the object of this fluency game, most appropriate for advanced levels.

Students have to talk about a given topic for 60 seconds without pausing. Examples of particularly productive topics are the movies, eating in restaurants, traveling, and shopping. Students may need a minute to prepare their ideas and vocabulary. Be prepared to give help before the game starts, such as leading a brainstorming session and listing useful words on the board. Select a student to start and ask the rest of the class to listen to him or her closely. There are three things that the student cannot do:

1. Hesitate
2. Deviate from the topic
3. Repeat him or herself

If the student does any of the above, other students may stop him or her. If the student talks for a minute without any of the previous "stops," he or she gets a point. The student who stops the talking student for breaking one of the rules can continue where the other student left off and also receive a point if he or she can successfully complete the 60 seconds.

Quizzes　Quizzes are usually popular when done in a game-like manner. To do a general quiz, decide what language structure to focus on (for example, students could write *wh-* questions with the past tense of *to be* or other verbs). Divide students into teams and give each team time to write a number of general knowledge questions using the target language structure. You may want to write some examples on the board.

Examples using the past tense:

Who was the first president of the United States?

Where was Princess Diana killed?

Who were the first men on the moon?

Examples using superlatives or comparatives:

What is the highest mountain in the world?

Which is the largest country in the world?

Which is longer, the Nile or the Amazon?

Each team then "quizzes" the other teams. The team that guesses the right answer gets a point. Continue until all the teams' questions have been asked. The team with the most points wins.

Review questions

1. Why might some students object to playing games in the classroom? How should you deal with this resistance?

2. How can games be used to practice the use of verb tenses? Other grammar points? Give two examples.

3. What sort of game is more suitable for advanced learners?

Further reading

Bassano, S. and Christison, M. *Drawing Out: Creative, Personalized, Whole Language Activities.* Alta Book Center Publishers, 1995.

Christison, M. and Bassano, S. *Purple Cows and Potato Chips: Multi-sensory Language Acquisition Activities.* Alta Book Center Publishers, 1995.

Hatfield, J. *Elementary Communication Games.* Addison Wesley Longman, 1984.

_____. *Intermediate Communication Games.* Addison Wesley Longman, 1990.

_____. *Advanced Communication Games.* Addison Wesley Longman, 1987.

McCallum, G. *101 Word Games.* Oxford University Press, 1980.

Milburn, D. *Alarm Clocks! Weird and Wonderful Exercises for the English Language Learner.* Alta Book Center Publishers, 1998.

Pollard, L. and Hess, N. *Zero Prep: Ready-to-Go Activities for the Language Classroom.* Alta Book Center Publishers, 1997.

Rinvolucri, M. *Grammar Games.* Cambridge University Press, 1984.

Ur, P. *Five-Minute Activities.* Cambridge University Press, 1992.

Wright, A. et al. *Games for Language Learning.* Cambridge University Press, 1983.

TEACHING WITH DRAMA

Drama techniques

- Mime

- Improvisation

- Role-play

- Simulation

How to teach with drama

Student attitudes towards drama

Drama activities

- TV and radio programs

- Buy me a house

- Hotel reception

- Getting a job

Review questions

Further reading

TEACHING WITH DRAMA

DRAMA ACTIVITIES PROVIDE valuable opportunities for students to use their imaginations, their personalities, their voices, and their bodies in creating situations to practice the language they've learned. Drama encourages students to use or interpret mime and gesture, to mimic and imitate, and to express feelings. It also gives students a *mask* (an identity other than their own personalities) to hide behind; timid students often shake off their inhibitions and take risks.

Drama in English language teaching usually does not mean play reading or play production. For many students, such ambitious drama projects are often inappropriate for the basic needs of a language course. If, however, students have enjoyed creating amusing sketches or role-play interviews, putting on a performance for other classes at the end of the course can be fun and rewarding.

Drama transforms classrooms into real world settings and brings the language to life. Students can read a dialogue that is supposed to take place in a shop, a bank, a cafe, or an airport, but unless they act as if they are in such places, the words of the dialogue are lifeless and meaningless. Drama helps students to use their imaginations and bring the outside world into the classroom. By imagining and *acting* the roles rather than simply saying them, students come closer to understanding what needs to be said and *how* to say it.

Drama also increases fluency development. Drama activities are an excellent way of getting students to use the language freely. There is no need to devote a whole lesson to drama; it fits very well into the free-speaking or production phase of learning. Let's say you have taught some specific grammatical, lexical, functional, or phonological points, and you now want to give practice and application in these target structures. Instead of using the tightly controlled practice in which you elicit the responses required, set up dramatic situations which necessitate the use of these forms. For example, ask one student to play the detective and another student to take the role of a suspect (see the game *Alibi* in Chapter 13, page 240):

Detective:	Where were you at 9:00 p.m. on Saturday evening?
Suspect:	I was at the movies.
Detective:	What did you see?

It makes it easier if you prepare questions on role cards and a few suggested notes (not complete sentences) for the actors.

Though most teachers agree that drama offers many positive aspects to the language lesson, only a minority of experienced teachers actually uses drama and regularly explores the benefits that it offers language learners. The purpose of this chapter is to show that drama techniques are easy to use and to show that one doesn't have to be a drama specialist to use these rewarding ways of teaching.

Drama techniques

There are four main drama techniques: mime, improvisation, role-play, and simulation. These techniques are outlined in this section.

Mime

Although mime is a silent activity, it encourages a lot of student talking time and very little or no teacher talking time. A suggestion for miming that involves the whole class is an activity called *Auditions*. Describe the following situation to the students: they are casting directors for a film or play. Their job is to select actors. One student at a time auditions for one of the parts in the production. For example, the directors need an old and grumpy man or woman for a certain part. One of the students then has to audition for the role, acting "old and grumpy" (remember, this is mime, so they cannot talk—only show). The rest of the group, the casting directors, discusses each performance and decides which actor is the most convincing. For examples of other activities which use mime, see the section *Action and mime games*, Chapter 13, page 229.

Improvisation

Perhaps the most useful drama activities are those that involve the students in improvising. *Improvisation,* the act of speaking or doing something without prior preparation, is the very essence of communication in everyday situations (we do not *prepare* everything we say when talking to friends and family). In simple improvisation, students do not take on a role but rather they play themselves. Drama activities which involve improvising give teachers the most realistic and meaningful means of helping students to express themselves without a script, hence opening the doors to real communication.

For intermediate to advanced levels, provided that the students understand the situations and can cope with the required language, you can try amusing or "embarrassing" role-plays to be improvised. For example:

> *Talk Your Way Out of This Situation!*
>
> You have eaten a large meal in a restaurant. When you go to pay, you find you've left your wallet (or your purse) at home and you have no money. What would you say to the cashier or to the manager?

Ask students to find a partner. One student takes the role of customer and the other plays the role of either a waiter/waitress or a manager. Students should practice the improvisations before doing them in front of the class (other examples of improvisation are given in the following section on role-play).

Role-play   Role-play is probably the most popular use of drama, both with teachers and students. The most common type of role-play involves the teacher in simply preparing role-play cards. To prepare such cards, first decide on the characters, the setting, and a conflict. Here is an example:

> You are a customer in a big store. Just as you are leaving with your purchases in a bag, a salesclerk stops you and accuses you of shoplifting.

Note: This kind of role-play can also be done as an improvisation.

A successful use of role-play is a development of *Counseling Language Learning.* This activity is a way of giving students free practice in using certain kinds of functional language. To begin, ask some students to be counselors and some to seek advice. Those seeking advice need to think of a real or imaginary problem to discuss with a counselor. Often the problem is an accommodation one with their host family (they don't like the food, the bathroom, and/or the attitude of their host). Some students may choose a problem with smoking, drugs, or drinking. Teach the students how to express advice and warnings. Pair the students seeking advice with the student counselors and leave them to express their worries and receive advice. Encourage the pairs to use a tape recorder when they feel ready to record their dialogues—this recording isn't compulsory, but most pairs do in fact record their conversations. The recording (suggested by one of the phases of a CL procedure) proves very useful in a number of ways: it removes the role-playing from reality and gives the actors more freedom; it helps many of the students to act the part (knowing that the teacher and other students might hear what they have said); and it helps with follow-up remedial work on errors. You'll find *Counseling Language Learning* to be surprisingly successful with students who do not like expressing their real opinions or personal feelings to the whole class. Make sure and have a follow-up session in which the students exchange roles (and become counselors or the counseled).

Simulation

Simulation, the act of reproducing a real situation, is a complex form of role-play that is very suitable for students of Business English (intermediate levels and higher). The aim of simulation is to create a situation that could arise in the real world. It requires more information and preparation than the usual role-play activity. For example, you may want students to set up a simulated business meeting in a large company. Allocate roles to students for the management team and staff members who represent all the employees (union representatives, shop supervisors). Create a purpose for the meeting: perhaps the company needs to resolve a dispute between management and employees on pay and conditions of work. The students will need background information on the demands for better pay and working conditions. The two teams will have to prepare their tactics and what they intend to ask for. Although such simulations are quite demanding and need careful preparation, students find them stimulating and worthwhile.

How to teach with drama

If you want to use drama, you have to show enthusiasm and be prepared to overcome some initial resistance from the students. Enthusiasm and belief in what you are doing, whatever aspect of the language you are teaching, is infectious and makes students feel secure and prepared to go along with the activity.

One of the reasons for teachers' resistance to using drama may be that it seems risky. Teachers naturally prefer controlled activities that can be planned step-by-step and therefore be almost risk-free. This reluctance to risk may be understandable during a teacher education program, but teachers who cannot or will not take risks are not only restricting themselves and their students, but they are also in danger of becoming very predictable and dull. If you want your lessons to be less teacher-centered and your students to be more creative and active, you have to take risks. You can, however, reduce the dangers inherent in drama by *careful planning* and by building an atmosphere of *trust*. Trust, a basic necessity in a good relationship with your students, is essential with drama activities.

It's also necessary to make sure students build trust among each other. You can't launch into drama until the students feel comfortable with you and with one another. It's a good idea, particularly with a new class, to do extra warm-up activities if you intend to use drama. Introductions are very important: it's not enough for the teacher to know the names of the students and how to pronounce them satisfactorily. Students should get to know each other's names and feel a sense of community within the group. See *Warm-up games*, Chapter 13, page 226, for ideas to help students get to know each other. Many of the warm-up games are, in themselves, a way of using drama and of preparing for more risky and creative activities.

To be clear about the role of the teacher in using drama, remember that you don't have to act, nor do you need theatrical training. Your role in this kind of drama has much in common with a director or stage manager. You don't want to be in the center of the stage—that's where the students need to be.

You should create the space, set the scene and the situations, and provide the props.

Having space is a great help with any drama activity. It's difficult to do anything that requires movement if the furniture leaves no room for the students to move about freely. Even if the drama activity only involves two students talking to each other, their chairs should be facing and not side by side. As the teacher, you also need to be able to move easily around the room to monitor and encourage the students.

Simple props are very effective in lending a touch of realism to a role; furthermore, they often promote humor and enjoyment in the activity. A large box of unusual clothes, especially hats, cups and plates (for a restaurant scene), and large squares of colored cloth can serve as dozens of props for role-plays.

Above all, successful drama activities depend on planning and preparation. As with all good lesson plans, the teacher should decide beforehand how much time is to be spent on the various stages of the lesson. For a drama lesson, it's wise to consider whether the normal lesson period is long enough (in many countries, a lesson lasts less than an hour). You may need an hour and a half to allow adequate time for all the elements. An outline for a drama lesson should include the following steps:

- ◆ **Step One: Warm-up.** Use warm-up activities and games to relax the students. (5 to 10 minutes)
- ◆ **Step Two: Pre-teach key information.** Describe the situations and give background information. Elicit appropriate vocabulary and expressions especially for jobs or professions in the situations. *Note:* This is not the appropriate time to teach a lot of new vocabulary. You want students to use or to activate what has already been taught. (10 to 15 minutes)
- ◆ **Step Three: Discuss and choose roles.** Discuss the roles of the people in the dialogues or sketches. What are their attitudes and feelings? Choose and allocate roles. (5 to 10 minutes)
- ◆ **Step Four: Do the activity.** Remember that the activity could be a mime, improvisation, role-play, or simulation. Let groups who are not used to the activity think of the first run-through as a trial run. It is not a *rehearsal* (that makes it sound as if they have to be perfect when they do it the second time). *Note:* In everything students say and do when using drama activities, avoid the idea that there is only one proper way to act out the roles. Always encourage different interpretations. (15 to 20 minutes)
- ◆ **Step Five: Give feedback.** As the teacher, observe and note the pronunciation, grammar, vocabulary, and communicative functions during the fourth step. After the activity, correct errors or preferably elicit self-correction from the students. Although most adult students like to get this sort of feedback, it's important to keep negative points to a minimum. Praise the students for what they did manage to express. Point out their fluency achievements, thus de-emphasizing the lack of accuracy. This feedback stage is greatly facilitated by the use of a tape-recorder or, even better, by a video camcorder. Although the machines are a great help when they are available, you are still needed to aid each student's perception of his or her mistakes and, even more important, in the remedial work that is required.

Student attitudes towards drama

As with games, resistance to drama techniques often comes from students who don't expect to play an active role in the learning process. The shy and reserved student may not be the one who objects to drama; it's often those who are not willing to adapt to new styles of teaching and learning. They may come from a society or culture in which learning is normally passive in the classroom (there's a lot of homework assignments). These students expect teachers to teach in the traditional style, and they are unwilling or hostile to methods like drama that require active participation. Such students will express their resistance perhaps in terms of "we're not here to play games" or "this is a waste of time."

Fortunately, the student who won't try drama is in the minority, but almost all students are only willing to try new techniques if they can see that the techniques work in terms of language learning. A teacher who introduces a new activity must show that it's useful as well as fun to do. You shouldn't use drama if you have difficulty showing that it has a language learning objective or that it fits in with the goals of the students and the course.

On their side, the students should be expected to be active and not think that the teacher will do all the work. Encourage students to learn from other students and to interact with them. Show that drama activities can give them such interactive opportunities. Remember, one of the good things about using drama is the shift from teacher-led, teacher-centered classrooms to those where students take more initiative and more responsibility for their learning.

Drama activities

There is considerable overlap between using language games and drama. The importance of warm-up activities in preparing for drama has already been pointed out. Other activities are outlined in the *Action and mime games* section, Chapter 13, page 229. In addition, the following are more ideas for using drama in your classroom.

TV and radio programs

Prepare and produce a TV or radio program. Divide students into groups (if the class is big enough) and have them discuss the components of a TV or radio program and decide on a name for their program (example programs are *Today, The Good Morning Show,* or

Saturday Night Live). Ask each group to choose someone to be the anchor person or host of the show. Suggest items to feature on their programs (news, weather reports, sports, interviews, comedy clips, etc.). Let each group decide what they want in their program and who is to play the roles. Here is a possible outline:

> *The Latest and Greatest Show*
> Student A (the host) introduces the highlights of the program.
> Student B (the news reporter) reads the news headlines.
> Student C (the weather person) gives the weather forecast for the region for the next 24 hours.
> Student A then says "Who's in town today?" and introduces Student D, who plays the part of a famous pop singer, film star, or sports champion.
> Student E interviews Student D (the celebrity).
> Student F (the sports reporter) gives a wrap-up on all the sporting events that happened today.
> Student G (a health professional) shares his or her expertise on diet and healthy eating and gives advice on losing weight.

The program should not last more than 30 minutes, but it's important to include as many students as possible in the roles. The most confident students should be allowed to take the leading roles in the first program. The shy students should not be forced to take roles but could be asked to help with the video or tape recording, perhaps to insert some music between items, or to help with preparing the news or weather reports. As the teacher, you must interfere as little as possible and mainly be available as a resource for vocabulary. After the activity (and the recording) is completed, use the students' contributions as feedback material for remedial work.

Buy me a house In this fun activity, students role-play buying or leasing a house or an apartment. The roles include real-estate agents and prospective home buyers (preferably couples; put students in pairs). The students acting the part of real-estate agents will need to interview the buyers in the real-estate office first to find out what they are looking for. They should ask questions like:

> What kind of home are you looking for? A house or an apartment?
> How many bedrooms?
> What location do you prefer?
> Do you want to rent or buy?

The realtors should prepare descriptive material with photos or drawings of houses or apartments to show the prospective buyers.

Note: The time for this kind of simulation most likely requires a part of two lessons on different days. The second lesson can include the acting out of a visit to two or three different types of homes (if the classroom is large enough to allow for movement). If possible, the students should use other areas in the school. For example, the cafeteria or snack bar becomes the dining room or kitchen, the students' lounge or common room becomes the living room, and the school restrooms become the bathrooms!

Hotel reception

This is yet another opportunity for improvisation. For this activity, use a table as a hotel reception desk and assign several students to be receptionists. The rest of the students act the parts of hotel guests arriving at the hotel. Some of the guests are easy-going and friendly; some are difficult and demanding. The aim is to let the participants say whatever they think is appropriate. However, before attempting the improvised dialogues, lead a preparatory discussion to determine whether the students have enough key language to handle the situations they are going to create.

A variation of this drama could be based on complaints: a hotel manager has to deal with a number of guests who are not satisfied with the services or the rooms in the hotel. To prepare, ask students to suggest things the guests could complain about. These could be listed on the board (such listing helps with the language structures and vocabulary). Some of the complaints could be mimed; the other students then have to guess what the complaint is about.

Getting a job Using job advertisements, applications, and interviews can be a valuable drama activity that integrates reading, writing, and speaking. First get advertisements for jobs. The advertisements can be real (from newspapers, the internet, etc.), or you can make up your own. It is sometimes more fun to invent unreal jobs to amuse the students and encourage them to use their imaginations. An interesting variation is for the teacher to advertise for assistants. In a language school, there are ordinary maintenance tasks: a gardener waters the plants, an electrician turns off the lights and disconnects other electrical equipment, and a librarian takes care of extra reading materials. Students can then interview for real positions. Put the ads up in the classroom (on the bulletin board, a help wanted board, or the walls) before students arrive.

For the next step, ask students to choose an advertisement and tell other students why they want the job. This can be done in pairs or in small groups. Students should report back to you when they have chosen their jobs and given their reasons for the choices.

Finally, have each student write a brief résumé for his or her chosen job, based on the following outline (you should write this on the board):

> Name
> Address
> Phone number
> Objective
> Education
> Work experience
> Special interests

Review questions

1. Do you have to be an actor to use drama successfully in the classroom? What does *drama* mean in this chapter?

2. What are three benefits in using drama in the language-learning classroom?

3. What problems might you encounter when using drama activities? How can you avoid these problems?

4. What are the four main drama techniques? Give an example of how you could use each one.

5. What is the teacher's role in drama activities?

Further reading

Curran, C. *Counseling Learning.* Apple River Press, 1972.

Maley, A. and Duff, A. *Drama Techniques in Language Learning.* Cambridge University Press, 1982.

Watcyn-Jones, P. *Act English.* Penguin, 1978. (excellent for role-play)

Wessels, C. *Drama.* Oxford University Press, 1987.

TEACHING WITH SONGS

Choosing a song

How to use songs in the classroom

- Fill-in the blank

- Re-order key words

- Correct the lyrics

- Dictation

- Sing along

- Discussion

- Role-play

- Writing

Teaching with songs

Review questions

Further reading

TEACHING WITH SONGS

IT'S NATURAL TO LISTEN TO SONGS. Most people's leisure time and everyday life includes listening to music. Many students, before they even study English, are fans of singers and groups who sing in the language. They are often familiar with songs in English that they've heard on the radio, in movies and musical shows, or on recordings. Music and songs increase students' learning *enjoyment* and *participation*. Using songs in the language-learning classroom gives students opportunities to express their personal likes and dislikes. This especially helps them to gain and show understanding of certain language items and structures.

Songs are an excellent source of *authentic* English. The lyrics contrast vividly with the controlled language of textbooks and specially prepared tapes. Songs often use up-to-date idioms and phrases, although you have to be careful if they use regional accents or dialects.

Most songs are also deeply felt and passionate. This strong emotional content is more memorable than the input of texts and taped dialogues. The *rhythms* of songs also have a powerful effect on one's memory, therefore helping students remember difficult vocabulary and structures.

Choosing a song

It can be overwhelming to decide which songs to choose for your classroom. Following are tips to help you select appropriate songs for your students:

♦ **Be careful of unclear pronunciation.** It has already been mentioned that care should be taken about choosing songs and singers with regional, non-standard accents or dialects. The singer may be very difficult to understand, even for native speakers, and almost impossible for the learner who is used to hearing standard American English. There are plenty of suitable songs whose singers don't use extreme variations and distortions in their pronunciation.

♦ **Be familiar with non-standard forms.** Many songs use idiomatic expressions and slang. When choosing a song, make sure you can explain and pre-teach these items. Note that some items may be useful as passive knowledge and worth explaining, while others can be ignored if they are not necessary to understand the general gist of the song. Students have enough to do in trying to understand the key words and structures; they don't need to be overwhelmed by all the non-standard uses of language structures.

♦ **Choose a song that students will enjoy.** Most of us have distinctive tastes when it comes to listening to music. Make sure that your musical selections are ones that your students will enjoy listening to as well; however, don't be upset if your students don't like the song you've chosen. It can be very difficult to please everyone in a group, especially when students have diverse language and cultural backgrounds or are of different ages. Make sure to select a song that will not offend students or insult their culture. It's a good idea to involve students in choosing a song; your lesson becomes more learner-centered and students are more willing to learn the meaning of the words and the message. When students are choosing songs, give them guidance about new words, expressions, and structures. Point out that the song should be relevant to their learning objectives and level of language.

How to use songs in the classroom

As mentioned in the introduction, using songs helps students focus on the meaning of words and/or the use of structures. Many songs have choruses that repeat a certain pattern over and over, hence helping students remember it. Popular examples are *Singing in the Rain, When I'm Sixty-four,* and *Have I Told You Lately?* Songs also work well for integrated skills practice. They can be used to introduce topics such as types of work or political themes and then be used for vocabulary input, discussion, role-play, or intensive reading.

Before listening to a song, students need warm-up activities. These activities should prepare students to listen and they should include pre-teaching and checking of vocabulary. The activity could be a discussion on the theme or topic of the song, a reading of some of the lyrics (probably not all), or a mime showing the feelings expressed. You could also give a listening exercise to elicit the gist of the song. Ask general questions like "Does the singer sound happy or sad?" This exercise gives students a chance to become familiar with general features of the song (style, mood, and rhythm) before they've studied the words.

After warm-up activities, you need to decide what tasks students should do before, while, and after listening. Following are some ideas.

Fill-in-the-blank

Choose a song that has especially clear lyrics. Write down the lyrics and delete key words (leave blanks where the words should go). Words that rhyme with previous words are good items to choose. Give each student the lyrics and ask them to fill in the missing words while they listen to the song. You could also provide alternative answers for the fill-in-the-blank exercise (for each blank, give two choices from which students select the correct word). This variation works well as a predictive exercise.

Re-order key words

Once again, write down the lyrics. Then scramble the order of words and/or phrases. Allow plenty of time for students to read and re-order the items (you may ask students to do this activity in groups). There are many variations:

- Give groups of words (8 to 10 items) from various parts of the song to students on cards or write them on the board. Ask the class to predict what kind of song it is or what it's about from the groups of words. Then have them listen to the song and put the words in the right order (as they occur in the song).
- Cut apart the lines of the lyrics (one per slip of paper) and ask students to re-arrange them.
- Give each student one word and ask them to mime it individually or with a partner. The rest of the class must try to guess the word.

Correct the lyrics	Prepare a worksheet that gives the complete lyrics, but make mistakes in some of the words and phrases. Students must correct the mistakes before and while listening. Apart from the opportunities to be funny and to put in absurd items, this is a good way to check understanding.
Dictation	For songs that are sung slowly and have repeated lines, give students the task of writing down the lyrics. Then divide them into pairs or groups and ask them to check what they have written. For beginning levels, give the first word or phrase of each line and stop the song at appropriate intervals to give students time to write.
Sing along	Done with actions or gestures, singing along is very popular with young students, though you'll find adults enjoy it as well. As a follow-up exercise, adapt the idea of karaoke to get students to sing the words (either one confident student or the whole group). To do karaoke, you need to find a version of the song without the words. Show the words to the class by using an overhead projector (this also enables you to show one line of the song at a time).
Discussion	If a song has an interesting theme and has really involved the students, you would be missing an opportunity if you didn't try to get more out of it than just listening. After the song, discuss its meaning. What is it expressing? How is it significant to your life?
Role-play	If the song is appropriate, students could do a role-play. For example, in a love song, one student could act the part of the rejected lover and another student could act as a counselor, listening and giving advice.
Writing	As a follow-up activity, ask students to write an additional verse for the song or an alternative version. Get them to sing it!

Note: It's a good idea to share any songs (plus worksheets) you produce with other teachers. This way, you create a resource for all classes to use. Your tapes and worksheets could also be included in the school or program's resource library.

**Task 1:
Choosing and
using songs**

Following is a list of ten songs and the singers who made them famous. These songs have been used successfully with English language classes throughout the world. Read the list with a friend (preferably an experienced teacher). Discuss the songs you know, decide which level they would be suitable for, and think of language points and activities you could use with them. Then, using the codes for levels, write the level and write the letters of the language points or activities that fit each song in the blanks next to the songs. (*Note:* If you don't know any of these songs, match up the language points and activities to songs you're familiar with!)

The Levels:
   Elementary (E)
   Intermediate (I)
   High-intermediate (HI)

The Songs

   _____   1.   *Every Breath You Take* (Sting)
   _____   2.   *Should I Stay or Should I Go?* (The Clash)
   _____   3.   *Tom's Diner* (Suzanne Vega)
   _____   4.   *All My Loving* (The Beatles)
   _____   5.   *The Sweetest Feeling* (Jackie Wilson)
   _____   6.   *Under the Bridge* (The Red Hot Chili Peppers)
   _____   7.   *The Logical Song* (Supertramp)
   _____   8.   *You've Got a Friend* (James Taylor/Carole King)
   _____   9.   *Candle in the Wind* or *Good-bye England's Rose*
                     (Elton John)
   _____ 10.   *I Just Called to Say I Love You* (Stevie Wonder)

Language Points/Activities
   a.   vocabulary of character
   b.   future tense *(will)*
   c.   pronunciation (sound and spelling)
   d.   national customs (annual festivals)
   e.   giving advice
   f.   present simple with adverbs of frequency
   g.   comparatives and superlatives
   h.   present continuous
   i.   discussion on fame (vocabulary)
   j.   discussion on personal relationships (vocabulary)

Teaching with songs

Following are three songs and corresponding activities. You may use these songs in your classroom, or use them as guidelines when preparing your own song-related tasks.

Song 1: *I Know an Old Lady . . .* by Rose Bonne and Allan Mills
This is a traditional song which has been sung and recorded by many artists (I recommend the version recorded by Burl Ives). First read through the lyrics:

I know an old lady who swallowed a fly
I don't know why she swallowed a fly
Perhaps she'll die

I know an old lady who swallowed a spider
That wriggled and jiggled and tickled inside her
She swallowed the spider to catch the fly
I don't know why she swallowed a fly
Perhaps she'll die.

I know an old lady who swallowed a bird
How absurd! To swallow a bird!
She swallowed the bird to eat the spider
That wriggled and jiggled and tickled inside her
She swallowed the spider to catch the fly
I don't know why she swallowed a fly
Perhaps she'll die.

I know an old lady who swallowed a cat
Fancy that! To swallow a cat!
She swallowed the cat to catch the bird
She swallowed the bird to eat the spider
That wriggled and jiggled and tickled inside her
She swallowed the spider to catch the fly
I don't know why she swallowed a fly
Perhaps she'll die.

I know an old lady who swallowed a dog
What a hog! To swallow a dog!
She swallowed the dog to chase the cat
She swallowed the cat to catch the bird
She swallowed the bird to eat the spider
That wriggled and jiggled and tickled inside her
She swallowed the spider to catch the fly
I don't know why she swallowed a fly
Perhaps she'll die.

I know an old lady who swallowed a cow
I don't know how she swallowed a cow
She swallowed the cow to worry the dog
She swallowed the dog to chase the cat
She swallowed the cat to catch the bird
She swallowed the bird to eat the spider
That wriggled and jiggled and tickled inside her
She swallowed the spider to catch the fly
I don't know why she swallowed the fly
Perhaps she'll die.

I knew an old lady who swallowed a horse
She died, of course.

I Know an Old Lady . . . is an excellent song for adapting to all levels and ages of language learners. Finding songs like this makes it easier for you to prepare (for example, you won't need to write up the lyrics of three different songs if you have three classes of different levels). The tasks for this song have been categorized by level:

Elementary to low-intermediate

A prediction activity is a simple and fun way to introduce the song to beginners. Give students a list of the animals in the song and ask them to guess the order of the animals using comparatives/superlatives:

A spider is smaller than a bird.
A dog is bigger than a cat.
A horse is the biggest animal.

Intermediate

Practice infinitive of purpose. Have students ask and answer questions about the animals:

Why did the old lady eat the spider?
To catch the fly.

High-intermediate

Practice indirect questions. Have students ask and answer indirect questions:

Do you know why she ate the dog?
No, why did she eat the dog?

Students could also practice *wh-* questions by asking and answering information about the animals:

What did the spider catch?
The fly.
What ate the spider?
The bird.

Advanced

This song is a lively means for advanced students to explore commonly associated vocabulary items with similar sounds:

wriggle/jiggle
moan/groan
stagger/swagger
mumble/grumble
screech/scream

Ask students to think of more "similar sounding" pairs. Have them write additional verses using the new word pairs. They could sing their new verses, mumbling the word *mumble,* etc.

Song 2: *My Way* by Paula Anka, Jacques Revaux, and Claude Francois
A classic version of this song is the one sung by Frank Sinatra. Play the beginning of the song, and ask students if they recognize it. Do they think it's an old or a new song? How do they think the singer feels? You can use questions like these as a warm-up activity to raise interest in the song.

For a task to do while listening, try an activity which involves correcting the lyrics. Before listening to the song, give each student a worksheet with the incorrect lyrics. Explain that there are ten mistakes. Play the whole song and then give the students (in pairs) ten minutes to find the mistakes. After this, listen to the song again and have students check (and correct) their worksheets. Following is an example of a way you could change the lyrics. The mistakes are in bold (for the actual words, see the answer key).

And now, the end is **here,** and so I face the **fine old** curtain.
My friend, I'll say it clear, I'll state my case, of which I'm certain.
I've lived a life, **you fool,** I've traveled each **uneven highway**
And more, much more than this, I did it my way.

Whiskies, I've had a few, but then again, too few to **get drunk.**
I did what I had to do, and **so, threw up** without exemption.
I planned each chartered course, each **carefree** step along the byway,
And more, much more than this, I did it my way.

Yes, there were **mealtimes,** I'm sure you knew,
When I bit off more than I could chew;
But **I chewed** it all when there was doubt,
I ate it up and spit it out
I **faked** it all and I stood tall and did it *My Way.*

In addition to the above activity, ask students (in groups) to devise a version of the lyrics with their own mistakes (the mistakes need to make sense, as in the example). Ask each group to sing their new version to the class. Is it an improvement?

Song 3: *You are Not Alone* by R. Kelly

A popular version of this song is the one sung by Michael Jackson. Prepare a worksheet with the lyrics. Wherever there is a key word, insert another plausible word. The task is for students to choose which word is suitable from each pair. First, pre-teach any difficult or unknown words (such as *burdens),* then give students the worksheet and ask them to read the lyrics before doing the task. Once they've read through the lyrics, they can listen to the song and choose the most suitable words (underline or circle the correct word). Following is an example of a way you could change the lyrics. The word pairs are in bold (see the answer key for the correct choices).

Another day has **gone/come.**
I am still all **alone/asleep.**
How could this be?
You're not **near/here** with me?

You never said **hello/good-bye.**
Someone tell me **why/who.**
Did you have to **know/go?**
And leave my world so **cold/hot?**

Chorus
Everyday I sit and **ask/tell** myself
How did it slip away?
Something whispers in my **phone/ear** and says . . .

You are not alone.
I am **there/here** with you.
Though you're **far/not** away.
I am here to **say/stay.**
You are not alone.
I am **not/here** with you.
Though we're **now/far** apart.
You're always in my **heart/mind.**
You are not alone.

Just the other **night/day.**
I thought I heard you **say/cry.**
Asking me to go.
And hold you in my **arms/hands.**
I can **hear/say** your prayers.
Your burdens I will bear.
But first I **need/hold** your hand.
Then forever can begin.

Repeat chorus
Whisper **three/two** words.
Then I'll come **walking/running.**
And girl you **know/think** that I'll be there.

You may want to play the song again and encourage students to sing along with their corrected lyrics. Follow up with general questions like:

Do you like this song?
What feelings does it express?
What do you think the three words are that the singer wants to hear whispered?

For discussion, ask students to talk about loneliness. Do they miss anyone? Do they love the person they miss? Make sure the students aren't uncomfortable with this discussion. Try to keep it general (not too personal).

Review questions

1. Why use songs in teaching English? Give at least three reasons.

2. What factors should you keep in mind when choosing songs for use in a multilingual class?

3. Name three ways you could use songs in the classroom.

4. What are three songs that aren't mentioned in this chapter that you think would be appropriate for teaching English? What language points and activities could you use them for?

Further reading

Cranmer, D. and Laroy, C. *Musical Openings.* Addison Wesley Longman, 1992.

Murphey, T. *Music and Song.* Oxford University Press, 1992.

LEARNING WITH SELF-ACCESS

Setting up a self-access center

The challenges of self-access centers

Types of self-access equipment

- CALL (Computer Assisted Language Learning)

- Video

- Language laboratories

- Reference sections

Review questions

Further reading

LEARNING WITH SELF-ACCESS

SELF-ACCESS CENTERS PROVIDE MATERIAL for students to learn independently of the classroom. Such centers encourage students to take responsibility for their own learning and become better learners. This does not mean, however, that students don't need teachers; self-access material is most effective when used as supplementary learning to the classroom.

Setting up a self-access center

A well-equipped language school or program usually provides facilities for self-access learning in a library or special learning center. These facilities include:

- ◆ **Computers** (the use of computers for language learning is most commonly referred to as Computer Assisted Language Learning or CALL)
- ◆ **Cassette recorders** (for individual listening)
- ◆ **Language laboratory** (also referred to as an Audio Active Comparative Lab or AAC; enables students to record and listen to their own voices)
- ◆ **Video players** (VCRs and monitors with headphones)
- ◆ **Reference section** (this section should have several types of reading materials)

On the following page is a layout of a self-access center. If your program doesn't already have such a center, you should consider the possibility of introducing one. Are there any rooms not being used? Is there a library that the center could be a part of? A self-access center is only useful if it is efficiently maintained and run within an organized framework; above all, it must be accessible.

Setting up a self-access center can be a lot of hard work; however, once a center is established, you'll find that it provides practical solutions to many language teaching and learning problems. First and foremost, students are individuals who differ in their learning styles,

SELF-ACCESS STUDY CENTER
Layout based on 4 connected areas or separate rooms

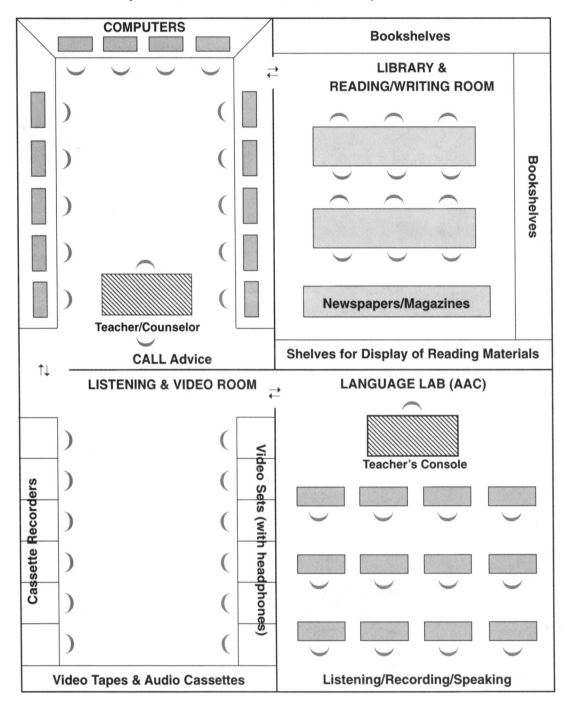

aptitude, and needs; they need different kinds of help in learning a language. A self-access center gives students this help; it allows them to concentrate on specific skills and areas they need to improve. The learner can go at his or her own pace and often get immediate feedback (most computer programs do this). Students also have different *purposes* in learning English. It's difficult to reconcile these different purposes when teaching a group of students in a class together; hence the value of a self-access center. What would you do if you had a class in which some students only wanted coaching for the TOEFL exam; others wanted English mainly for business; others wanted to know English for technical purposes; and a few only wanted to improve their ability to take dictation? By having facilities like computers and audio machines, you could make this situation less of a challenge; simply give individual advice to each learner on the kinds of practice material he or she should use in the self-access center.

The challenges of self-access centers

Some teachers are not comfortable with using facilities such as computers and language laboratories. The basic problem for such teachers may not be with the electronic equipment but with the need to *adopt* a different attitude to teaching. A teacher who has been trained to fulfill the traditional role of explainer (a father or mother figure) finds it hard to change to being a counselor/facilitator—to be on an equal level with the students (see *What Makes a Good Teacher?*, Chapter 1, page 10).

Students are not always eager to use a self-access center. Not every student wants to become independent and thus responsible for his or her learning. Many are inclined to leave the responsibility on the teacher. They want to be *taught;* they don't want to see that they need to work and contribute to the process of learning. This reluctance is not magically solved by having a self-access center; however, if you are involved with the self-access center and can advise and help students to learn how to use the facilities, you will greatly help students "warm-up" to the concept of learning on their own.

Types of self-access equipment

The general types of self-access equipment have been listed in the introduction to this chapter. This section takes an individual look at each type of equipment. It is intended to familiarize you with the ways in which students can learn through self-access.

CALL (Computer Assisted Language Learning)

Most students are familiar with computers, and in any case, quick to learn how to operate them. Once learned, computers provide an endless source of exercises and practice activities. Many language-learning programs also come with authoring kits, which allow you to design additional exercises for students. One excellent way to find language exercises to do on the computer is to search the internet. Websites like www.eslcafe.com are abundant with ideas and links to language exercises. Also take time to browse through software and CD-ROM programs (many software companies are now producing demos for this purpose) and decide which ones are suitable for your students. Following are general types of programs to consider:

- **Vocabulary-based programs.** These focus on individual lexical items often presented in games. An example is the CD-ROM series *English Vocabulary* published by CPI. There are also vocabulary sections included in a number of programs, such as Quartext (1985) and Wida (MS DOS Acorn BBC).
- **Text-based programs.** These present the learner with a text that they must re-build or restore. There are a number of reading skills programs for students preparing for university courses. For example, Clarity Software publishes a program called *Read It!*, and Wida Software offers two programs: *Storyboard* and *Storyboard Plus*.
- **Grammar-based programs.** These teach and test the learner on grammar points and uses at specified levels. One popular program is *Tense Buster*, published by Clarity English Software.
- **Test-based programs.** These focus on exam preparation and include practice tests for the TOEFL. Since the TOEFL is now computer-based, these programs are especially valuable preparation. They include *TOEFL Mentor*, *TOEFL Mastery*, and *Longman Preparation Course for the TOEFL CBT.*
- **Adventure programs.** Originally developed for entertainment on the home personal computer, these programs have become

an attractive format for language learning. Typically, they put the user into an imaginary world full of characters and settings like monsters, castles, and aliens. The imaginary world has quests and dilemmas that the learner must solve. Sometimes this process means surviving certain perils or finding one's way out of a maze. For the language learner, finding a way out or discovering a treasure by asking questions and giving the right instructions is a very rewarding, fun route to learning English. Examples include *Where on Earth is Carmen Sandiego?* by Broderbund Software and *The Hitchhiker's Guide to the Galaxy* by Infocom Apple II.

Video Videos (most often movies and shows), present an interesting range of materials for students. Teachers who monitor the use of videos should aim to make the watching of them an *active* process for the learner. For guidance on using videos, see the *Using videos* section in Chapter 12, page 218. When placing video equipment in a self-access center, make sure to include headphones so video-watching does not disturb other students. It is also important to use a VCR that has a playback function (so students can review certain sections). Video equipment in a self-access center may include camcorders, which enable students to film themselves in short dialogues and role-plays.

Language laboratories A fully equipped language laboratory is often called an Audio-Active-Comparative Lab (AAC) or a *listen-respond-compare lab*. These labs have student booths and a teacher's console, which is connected to each student booth or position. Each tape-recorder in the booths enables a student to listen to a master tape, to record his or her utterance, and then to compare it with the model response on the master tape. The control panel (the teacher's console) gives immediate feedback to each student through earphones. This kind of lab is used by individual learners as a type of library where they do additional listening and speaking practice in their free time. The learners can easily get immediate feedback (correct responses) and the chance to correct themselves. A teacher on duty at the console can also monitor the learner and thus offer help with remedial exercises.

The so-called *listening laboratory* is cheaper to install and yet a very useful self-access learning facility. It is often simply an area with several cassette recorders (fitted with earphones) in booths or desk areas. This basic laboratory serves as a quiet study space where students can get listening practice through a wide range of cassettes. Recordings with comprehension tasks are best in this type of laboratory; they ensure active participation from the learner (the learner must listen purposefully and attentively in order to complete the tasks). Dictation tapes are also useful and convenient for self-access listening, plus there are a variety of other activities such as matching pictures to descriptions on tape.

Reference sections

Books and reading materials are still the most flexible and convenient means for learners to develop their reading and writing skills. Students are attracted to computers and often prefer to do a reading exercise simply because it's on a visual display unit (VDU), but the range of software texts is usually much narrower and often less interesting than the range of readings in *books*.

If you are involved in setting up a reference section or library of a new self-access center or wish to help improve an existing one, the reading resources should include the following:

- **Reference books.** Dictionaries, encyclopedias, maps, atlases, grammar reference books, and travel guides (especially guides to the local region) are just a few types of reference books that can prove helpful to language learners.
- **Simplified or graded readers.** These texts, especially made for English language learners, provide material with graded vocabulary and grammar levels. See *Graded readers,* Chapter 9, page 169.
- **Literature/popular novels.** It's always fun to have a few literature classics available for more advanced learners. These could include light novels, thrillers, and crime and detective stories.
- **Non-fiction.** Select a few books of special interest to students learning English; often books on life and institutions in English-speaking countries are appropriate.

◆ **EFL/ESL section.** This section should feature English language textbooks and workbooks for self-study, including ESP materials and English for Academic Purposes.

◆ **Newspapers and magazines.** English language newspapers are not always easy to obtain overseas, though the school can order them. Many countries now have an "English language weekly" or daily papers in English. English language magazines are available worldwide.

◆ **Reading laboratories.** Published reading lab materials have been around for many years and are still a very useful and flexible aid to reading comprehension. Originally published by S.R.A. (Scientific Research Association), each *reading lab* consists of a set of boxes with graded texts, short enough to be printed on one side of an 8 x 10 inch card. Each box color-codes the texts by levels and provides detailed instructions, tasks, and a booklet of answers. The labs also have short tests that enable most students to find the right colored texts for their level. Students find it satisfying to progress from one level to the next. Reading labs like the SRA boxes can be put together by teachers, though the work involves collecting a considerable number of short, interesting texts from a variety of sources. If you have the time to create your own reading lab, include texts of special interest for ESP and EAP students. In addition to reading labs, there is a wealth of reading books written especially for English language learners. Some examples of these are *Reading Choices* by David Jolly; *In Context* by Zukowski/ Faust, *Reader's Choice* by E. Margaret Baudoin et al., and *True Stories in the News* by Sandra Heyer. Finally, if you are teaching abroad, don't expect a private establishment to provide a learning center on the scale of a university campus or a city library. Rather, programs should aim to provide select materials likely to be of interest and useful to students. If you have any say in providing or adding to the reading resources, decide on a limited number of useful categories (as indicated above) and help to improve the *quality* not the quantity of books in the self-access center.

Review questions

1. What are some of the benefits of having a self-access center?

2. What should be in a self-access center? List facilities and materials that you would like in such a center.

3. What is CALL? What are the advantages of using computers with adventure-like programs?

4. What are three kinds of reading you would recommend students to use in the school library? Why?

5. How can you develop the learning skills of your students? Is it relevant to draw students' attention to your teaching strategies?

Further reading

Gardner, D. and Miller, L. *Establishing Self-Access: From Theory to Practice.* Cambridge University Press, 1999.

Hardisty, D. and Windeatt, S. *CALL.* Oxford University Press, 1989.

Sheerin, S. *Self-Access.* Oxford University Press, 1989.

Sperling, D. *The Internet Guide for English Language Teachers.* Prentice Hall, 1997.

TESTING

Purposes and types of tests

Effects of testing

What makes a good test?

Ways to test

Examinations in English as a second or foreign language

A review of key testing terms

Review questions

Further reading

TESTING

TESTS AND EXAMINATIONS AROUSE FEAR AND ANXIETY in most learners. At best, these assessment tools seem like necessary evils; many teachers empathize with their students and share their dislike of tests. However, tests can be designed to be more enjoyable; some of the most popular game and quiz shows on TV are tests of general knowledge—and prove to be a lot of fun!

Including tests and testing in a language teaching program is an integral part of teaching. Tests are a means of checking the results of your teaching and whether the students are learning. By testing, you can find out what your students know and what they need to improve. In turn, tests and test results provide you with insights and answers to two valuable questions:

Has your teaching been effective?

Was the test well-designed for its purpose?

Without regular testing, it is hard to know if your teaching is helping learners. Testing, however, should never become an obstacle or a substitute for teaching.

The word *test* covers a wide variety of assessments and ways of evaluating the knowledge, skills, and achievements of the learner. Some tests, usually called examinations, are set by external bodies and are therefore not under the control of the teacher. The main purpose of this chapter is to present tests and forms of testing that can be devised, set, or chosen by the classroom teacher.

Purposes and types of tests

The three different purposes of testing are to determine appropriate placement, diagnose problems, and check on achievement and progress. Following are the types of tests that are most commonly used to address these purposes. For other test types, see *A review of key testing terms*, page 297.

Placement tests   *Placement tests* are used to place students in appropriate levels or classes. Although teachers are not usually responsible for the placing of students in an appropriate class or stage of learning, it is important that they be aware of the placement test used in their program. Placement tests that are devised by your program should be better than those that are provided by external educational organizations. After all, the faculty and administration of your program ought to know its teaching situation and its grading system better than any outside body.

Placement tests should assess the four basic language skills in an integrated way. For example, listening and speaking could be linked in an interview with an experienced teacher and reading a letter could involve the student in writing an appropriate reply.

Keep in mind that in most English language schools in English-speaking countries, oral skills development is the main aim of the learners. The placement test, therefore, must give due weight to assessing listening and speaking. Pre-course tests and placement-on-arrival tests are easier to administer if they largely consist of, for example, short multiple-choice questions (see the sample test on page 361 for 30 question examples) which can be quickly and easily marked. However, simply administering a placement test rather than interviewing the students could lead to distorted, unreliable results. In fact, if the new student is treated impersonally, the student is much more likely to be placed in the wrong class! For example, because of the emphases in the Japanese school curriculum, Japanese students usually perform well on reading tests or grammar-based tests, but they score lower on listening and speaking tests. Hence, if the placement test mainly measures their reading, writing, and grammar abilities, Japanese students will be placed at levels too advanced for their total language ability. Placement tests should, therefore, be designed so that they indicate students' strengths and weaknesses. In other words, they should have similar aims to *diagnostic* tests.

Diagnostic tests   *Diagnostic tests* are a sort of linguistic health check which enable teachers to find out learners' strengths and weaknesses in the macro-skills of reading, writing, listening, and speaking. The purpose of a diagnostic test is not to give marks or grades but to get feedback on students' knowledge or performance. Diagnostic tests are intended to discover what students need in terms of remedial teaching or what gaps need to be filled in redesigning the teaching or learning program. These tests often reveal that students in intermediate or advanced classes make elementary errors.

Unfortunately for new teachers, there are not many examples of diagnostic tests in published form. Experienced teachers usually design their own to meet the needs of the students in their teaching situation. What students have been taught in previous courses is not always a clear indication of what they know, thus teachers make up short tests to find out *what* their students know. Inexperienced teachers could use the school's placement tests as a model for such tests. The kind of guidance that a diagnostic test gives may also just as easily be obtained by giving students a standard achievement or proficiency test.

Achievement tests

Achievement tests are a way of assessing what students have achieved so far in the course. There are two kinds of achievement tests: *progress* achievement tests and *final* achievement tests.

◆ **Progress tests.** Progress tests should be constructed with twin objectives: to measure or assess the extent that short-term course objectives have been achieved by students and to measure how much progress is being made towards the final goals of the course. It is easier to assess progress if the test is based on well-defined short-term objectives, like the ability to write a connected narrative based on a series of pictures or (for the more advanced student) the ability to write a report based on the interpretation of information in graphs. Progress tests do not have to be formal or too serious, and scoring does not have to be strict or rigorous. For example, games and quizzes are enjoyable ways of testing how well students are using basic structures (see *Quizzes*, Chapter 13, page 241). Games which involve asking questions reveal to the teacher whether students are able to use question forms fluently and accurately (see *Twenty questions*, Chapter 13, page 237).

◆ **Final achievement tests.** A final achievement test should test whether students have achieved the course objectives or not. It has been generally accepted that the "content of a final achievement test should be based directly on a detailed course syllabus or on the books and other materials used" (Hughes 1989). A poorly designed syllabus or unsuitable course text materials may lead to results that do not indicate that the students have successfully achieved the course objectives. This is because tests constructed from poor objectives are more likely to reflect failure than success. This failure is hardly the responsibility of the teacher. Those who design courses need to be explicit about objectives and make them achievable and realistic; in turn, test writers need to create achievement tests that are based on the objectives and content of particular courses. If these objectives are not adhered to, you may find that final achievement tests are not significantly different from *proficiency tests.*

Proficiency tests

Proficiency tests are usually designed and controlled by external bodies. For example, the Test of English as a Foreign Language (TOEFL) is administered by the Educational Testing Service of Princeton University with the general objective of measuring the candidates' language ability without regard to the teaching or the course they have been following. The TOEFL is used to determine whether a student's English is good enough to cope with academic work at an American university; it is a proficiency test with a particular purpose. There are a number of proficiency tests related to other purposes, such as a test designed to find out whether the student could function efficiently as a technical translator or as an interpreter at international conferences.

Typically, the proficiency test is not related to any course of study nor to any particular occupation; it does not prepare the student, or relate to, any particular future course of study. Well-known British examples are the Cambridge First Certificate, Advanced Certificate, and Proficiency exams and the Oxford EFL exams. These proficiency tests are weighted towards the academic skills of reading comprehension, vocabulary use, and writing skills. The Cambridge exams include an oral and a listening comprehension test, though these sections play a smaller part than the written sections in the overall score of the exams.

From a teaching point of view, you must be aware of the effects and influence that these exams have on the content of the courses and on teaching methods. This effect, often referred to as *backwash*, is discussed in the following section.

Effects of testing

The direct or indirect effect of tests on teaching and learning is called *backwash*. These effects can be positive or negative. Negative effects are often due to differences between the teaching and testing objectives. For example, if the teaching objectives are to improve the communicative skills of the learners but the examination at the end of the course necessitates preparing the learners for academic exercises, the exam will divert attention from the need to develop communicative teaching aims. Exams traditionally have concentrated on reading and writing skills and grammatical knowledge; the backwash effect of traditional exams on language teaching has therefore been the neglect of the listening and speaking skills.

Backwash can, however, be remarkably positive. Some years ago a new kind of oral/aural examination, devised by ARELS (The Association of Recognized Language Schools), was introduced to adult students at private language schools worldwide. For the first time candidates were tested by means of recorded tapes on their ability to respond appropriately to a wide variety of everyday utterances in social situations. The ARELS ORAL exam tested six kinds of listening and speaking in realistic contexts. The backwash effect of the exam was extremely beneficial. Certainly in many schools, teachers and students alike were awakened to and also welcomed the opportunities it gave to practice listening and speaking. This new awareness helped adult students develop their communicative skills. The only disadvantage of this exam was the fact that it had to be taken in language laboratories so that a large number of candidates in many exam centers could take the same tests at the same time. (*Note:* The ARELS tests are now part of the Oxford range of EFL exams).

What makes a good test?

Tests need to be well devised, with clear instructions and questions that can be understood and answered. They need to give students a feel of whether they are making progress. Students should feel that they are in a class that has direction, *not* that they are just following a string of lessons without a plan and objectives. Tests emphasize this direction to students. The following are points you should consider when using or designing tests:

- **Tests should be fair.** To be fair to learners, tests must only cover material that is appropriate to the learners.
- **Tests should be valid.** As much as possible, a test should be *valid*. This means that the content of the test should be based on what has been taught and it should measure what it is supposed to measure. Evidently, a listening test should require the students to listen to a spoken test that can easily be heard. They should not be reading the text at the same time!
- **Tests should be clear.** As mentioned above, tests need to have clear instructions and questions.
- **Tests should be easy to mark.** The marking of a test should be *objective,* or at least, not depend too much on the individual judgment of the marker or scorer. In order for tests to have reliable results, you need to reduce the element of subjective testing. However, complete objectivity is only achieved when no judgment is required by the scorer, and this tends to produce too many tests based on techniques like multiple-choice questions. Therefore some element of subjective marking is unavoidable and necessary, especially when testing letter-writing or composition skills.
- **Tests should be reliable.** A test that measures consistently can be said to be *reliable.* If the results are *not* consistent when a test is administered again, the test probably lacks reliability. Of the many features in tests that might make them unreliable, here are a few: instructions are unclear; items encourage guessing; questions are ambiguous; questions have too many options (which may confuse the student and the tester).

Ways to test   There are many ways to create exercises and questions for tests. Following are a few popular and common ways, including examples.

Fill-in-the-blank   A common means of testing is to require the student to fill-in blanks, usually with a single word. If more than one word is allowed, other answers are possible and marking becomes more difficult. The instructions must be clear: if a phrase is a possible answer for the blank, then the instructions should state "Choose the word *or phrase* that best completes the sentence." An example of a fill-in-the-blank question is:

> They said it would be a good idea, _____?
> a. isn't it?   b. didn't they?
> c. no?   d. didn't it?

Multiple-choice   As in fill-in-the-blank exercises, the student is presented with a sentence with a blank to be filled, usually with one word or a short phrase. Multiple-choice exercises test learners' ability to recognize and select the correct or acceptable item in a context. The options (usually four or five) include the correct, or most appropriate word or phrase and other incorrect or inappropriate words (called *distracters*). One of the greatest advantages of multiple-choice is in the marking and scoring; this kind of test is reliable and can be done quickly and economically. No special knowledge is required for the marker or scorer. Furthermore, as the candidate only has to underline or mark a number or letter, many items can be included and tested in a relatively short period, which tends to result in increased test reliability.

Multiple-choice testing has been so popular with professional testers that for some time its limitations were disregarded. It's worthwhile noting the following drawbacks to multiple-choice tests:

- ◆ **Only recognition knowledge is tested.** If a student is required to identify the correct grammatical item and he or she gets it right, it doesn't necessarily show that the student can *use* the grammatical item without help. The ability to produce the correct form in speaking or writing requires a higher level of familiarity than simply being able to *recognize* forms.
- ◆ **It's possible to *guess* the right answer.** Because a guess has a one in four (or one in five, etc.) chance of being right, this

possibility introduces an unknowable factor and effect on multiple-choice test scores.

- ◆ **Backwash may be harmful.** Preparing and using too many multiple-choice tests is an inefficient and boring way of teaching and learning. Students may improve their guessing skills, but will not be developing their knowledge and command of grammar or vocabulary.

For examples of multiple-choice exercises, see *Multiple-choice questions,* Chapter 7, page 131.

Cloze procedures

In its classic form, the cloze test deletes a number of words from a text, leaving blanks to be filled by the person taking the test. The following passage is an example. In the first two sentences, the missing words are given in brackets. The other answers are given in the answer key at the end of the book.

Inventor of the Future

If one person can be said (1) _(to)_ have led the world into the (2) _(age)_ of technology it was Thomas Edison. (3) _(Not)_ only did he invent and perfect (4) _(many)_ of the technologies vital to the (5) _(modern)_ world, he also set the standard (6) _(for)_ how research and development is done (7) _(today)_.

Edison was guided by his belief (8) _____ genius is one percent inspiration and (9) _____ perspiration. Consequently, he worked day and night (10) _____ much of his life. By the (11) _____ he died in 1931, he (12) _____ patented over 1,100 inventions. Some were his (13) _____ but many were improvements he had (14) _____ to the inventions of others. One (15) _____ the telephone. Alexander Graham Bell invented (16) _____, but it was Edison who improved (17) _____ range and clarity of the instrument (18) _____ it could be put to practical (19) _____ by ordinary people.

Some of the (20) _____ attributed to Edison had already (21) _____ invented. One example is the light bulb:

this (22) _____ first demonstrated in London in 1878 (23) _____ its English inventor, Joseph Swan. However, (24) _____ Edison demonstrated his light bulb in (25) _____ U.S.A. the following year, it was he (26) _____ was credited for giving the world (27) _____ light.

From BBC English, July 1997.

The cloze procedure has been widely adopted as a test of reading comprehension. At first, for some enthusiasts, it seemed to be a valid test of the underlying language abilities of the student. Support for this claim came from a relatively high correlation between scores on cloze passages and total scores on much longer, more complex tests such as the UCLA English as a Second Language Placement Test as well as with the individual components of such tests (reading and listening). (Quoted in Hughes 1989, page 65.) Certainly, in order to fill in the missing words, one has to be aware of a number of linguistic features: syntactic structures (item 8), grammatical form (item 12), appropriate lexical words (item 2), and collocation and idiom (item 19). In other words, underlying language ability *is* being tested.

Cloze tests are relatively easy to construct and to administer. Marking and scoring, however, are often problematical. If you try out a cloze test with other teachers or any educated native speaker, you may find considerable variation in their ability to fill in the missing words. This variation raises questions about the reliability of the cloze test and whether it is a valid assessment of overall language ability. Nevertheless, cloze procedures are useful if you select the texts carefully and do some pre-testing. Many teachers and some exams (such as the Cambridge Proficiency Examination) have used passages with particular items deleted (such as prepositions) to test the candidates' knowledge and use of certain structural items. Although this procedure seems only to test grammatical ability, getting the correct answer almost always requires an understanding of other features in the text.

To create a cloze text, keep in mind the following:

◆ **Choose appropriate passages.** The reading level of the selected passage should match the level of the students who are going to take the test. If there is any doubt about the level, do some pre-testing.

◆ **Do not delete words in the first few sentences.** Give students a chance to be introduced to the topic before testing them. Deletions should be made at about every 7th to 10th word. Avoid deleting difficult lexical items or words and phrases that would be hard to guess.

◆ **Give clear instructions.** Be explicit about choosing the *best* word or the *most suitable.* Avoid giving the impression that there is only one possible correct item.

◆ **Advise students to read the whole passage before filling in the gaps.** It is important that students get the gist of the text before starting the task of filling in the blanks.

Statement and response

As with all exercises, the instructions for statement and response tasks must be clear. To use a statement and response way of testing, instruct students to fill-in blank spaces in dialogues (use only *one* word in each space). For example:

1. A.   Where _____ you going?
    B.   I'm going home.
    (Answer: are)

2. A.   _____ are you from?
    B.   From Japan. I'm Japanese.
    (Answer: Where)

3. A.   ____ do you come to school?
    B.   By bus.
    (Answer: How)

Using given words

After having taught some words from a particular text, you should check that learners know how to place them appropriately in a passage, as in the following fill-in-the-blank test:

Put one word from the list below in each blank:

learning
developing
unarmed

Karate is a science of _____ self-defense and counter-attack.

In many U.S. cities thousands of young people are _____

their minds as well as their bodies by _____ karate.

True/false or correct/ incorrect

These exercises are often used on tests to check students' understanding after they have listened to or read a passage. They can test students' awareness of correct or incorrect English. The instructions should clearly indicate that students need to circle (or underline) *true* or *false*, *correct* or *incorrect*. *(Note:* Make sure that students do not become confused between incorrect *grammar* and incorrect *information*. To avoid this confusion, do not put incorrect information in your grammar test items.) The following is an example of this way of testing:

> Put a check (✔) in the blank if the following sentence uses correct English. If it is not correct, put an X.
> They like very much games. _____ *(Answer: X)*
> Peter doesn't ever eat carrots. _____ *(Answer: ✔)*

For more examples, see *True/false statements*, Chapter 7, page 131 and Chapter 9, page 166.

Matching pictures with words and phrases

A good way to test vocabulary comprehension is to ask students to match certain words or phrases with their pictures. For example, show students pictures of vehicles and ask them to write down the appropriate word for each picture:

truck	motorbike	camper	bus
limousine	car	jeep	

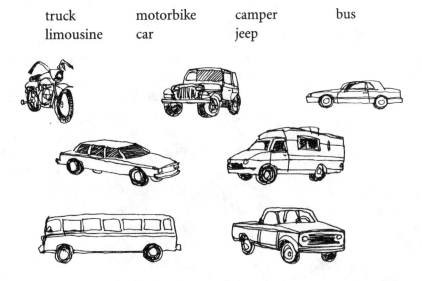

For more ideas on using visuals for testing purposes, see Chapter 12, *Teaching with Visual Aids*.

Scrambled
sentences

By scrambling (rearranging) lexical and structural items in a sentence, this simple exercise can test a student's comprehension of sentence order and grammar use. For example, instruct students to put the following items in order to make a sentence:

> brother intelligent more much her than she's
> (Answer: She's much more intelligent than her brother.)

Dictation

Dictation is a form of exercise in which students write something that is said by you, another student, or someone on a recording. A good way to do a dictation for testing purposes is to select (or rewrite to specifications) a passage of five to ten sentences. Each sentence should be about five to twelve words long and utterable in one breath. Before starting to dictate, read the whole passage through to the class at normal speed. Make sure that the students just listen (they should not start writing). Then tell the students that you are going to read each sentence three times and only three times. The first time you read the sentence, the students are to listen with their pens on their desks. The second time you read the sentence, the students should be writing it down. The third time you read it, all the students should have stopped writing and be able to use the third reading for checking their transcription. Do not read parts of sentences or re-read the sentences in parts. Read only whole sentences, with the same intonation each time (this dictation activity is most suitable for elementary to intermediate students).

Although dictation as a valid form of testing went out of fashion for a time, it has been widely recognized again as a helpful technique with many uses. Since its re-introduction, teachers are more aware that dictation has disadvantages if used too often or without careful thought about what is being tested by it. Dictation is a "global" test in that it tests a number of language features together, such as spelling, punctuation, meaning, recognition of sound segments and their relation to spelling, memory span, and lexical forms. Provided that teachers recognize that they are testing "globally," there are many good reasons for using dictation.

By using dictation, you are building language memory (this is why you should use relatively short sentences). After you have mastered the basic dictation procedure outlined previously, consider and try other ways of using dictation, especially for advanced level students. A useful book with practical suggestions is *Dictation: New Method, New Possibilities* by Paul Davis and Mario Rinvolucri, Cambridge University Press. Following are further tips to keep in mind when using dictation:

◆ **Use dictation to make students *active*.** Dictation is a way to get all students engaged in an activity.

◆ **Use dictation for student correction.** With the written text available, students are usually capable of correcting their own work or the work of other students (*Note:* Often, students are more capable of noting errors in the work of other students than in their own).

◆ **Use dictation for mixed-ability groups.** More advanced students can try dictation with little or no help; less advanced students can be given a handout of the text with some words omitted. The less advanced students then have to listen carefully to the whole passage and concentrate on filling in the missing words, while the advanced students write down the entire passage.

◆ **Use dictation with large classes.** In many language schools, teachers have to cope with groups of 20 to 40 (or even more) students. Dictation is one of the few techniques that works well with small *or* large groups.

◆ **Use dictation for young students.** Dictation helps with classes of young students who need settling down or who are undisciplined. It concentrates their attention and brings order and calm into the classroom.

◆ **Use dictation to relate sounds and writing.** The techniques of dictation are particularly useful with a language like English where the relationship between sounds and writing is difficult for most non-native speakers. Dictation draws attention to both the regularities and the irregularities of sounds and spellings in English.

Examinations in English as a second or foreign language

After you've had some experience in teaching, you may be expected to teach classes that prepare students for an exam. Keep in mind that many adult students are very eager to pass exams and put a lot of pressure on the teacher to do *only* exam practice work throughout the course. Clearly, an exam preparation course should include practice that is relevant to the knowledge and skills needed in the exam; however, it is important to maintain a balance so that all the language skills are practiced. Realize that students are not always the best judges of what they need and how to prepare for an exam. Doing exam question papers or mock tests all through a course will lead to boredom or fatigue.

Moreover, you need to constantly be aware of the distinction between teaching and testing: one cannot have output without input. Students who only want grammar and vocabulary because that's what is mainly tested in the exam still need practice in language use, including listening and speaking. Over a 12-week exam preparatory course, students should start with a lot of general English language practice, advice, and help with study skills. Towards the end of the course, students can be given more exam practice and techniques for successfully dealing with the areas of language on the exam.

You should be aware of the most common and/or popular exams in teaching English as a foreign or as a second language. The chart that follows gives brief details of exams set by US-based or British-based examining boards. These tests are known throughout the world.

TOEFL	The Test of English as a Foreign Language	Used as a criterion for admission to U.S. universities. Tests listening, reading, and grammar. No test of extended writing skills.
IELTS (British Council and Australian Universities)	International English Language Testing Scheme	Test for non-native speakers who wish to study at a British or Australian university.

Cambridge University Exams Syndicate	Preliminary English Test (P.E.T.) First Certificate in English (F.C.E.) Cambridge Advanced Exam (C.A.E.) Cambridge Proficiency Exam (C.P.E.)	Emphasis on communicative skills. Tests all four skills as well as vocabulary and grammar. Emphasis on authentic use of language. More emphasis on formal English.
Oxford University EFL Exams { ARELS Oral Exams {	Preliminary Higher Preliminary Higher Diploma	The Oxford exams focus on reading and writing skills, whereas the ARELS exams test listening and speaking.

A review of key testing terms

Cloze test:
Originally used for reading comprehension; this test requires that students first read a passage and then get a copy of the text from which every fifth, seventh, or -*nth* word is deleted. The student must insert the deleted word or a suitable word in each of the blanks. Cloze tests today are widely used to assess student knowledge of syntax, idiom, vocabulary, and the like.

Objective test:
Any test which can be marked mechanically or in which no linguistic judgment is required by the marker or scorer. Multiple-choice questions are a common form of objective tests.

Subjective test:
Any test that requires individual judgments by the marker or tester. Typical examples are composition, writing letters and summaries, and fill-in-the-blank exercises that are open-ended.

Reliability:
If the test measures consistently, it can be described as reliable. If the results vary considerably when the test is administered again, it probably lacks reliability.

Validity: A test has apparent (or "face") validity if it seems designed to measure what it is supposed to measure. For example, a listening test should test listening, not reading or writing skills, if it claims to be a valid test.

Review questions

1. What are the three purposes of testing? Give examples.

2. What is *backwash?* What do traditional exams tend to neglect?

3. What makes a good test? Name at least three things.

4. Pretend that you must create your own test. Do the following:

   - Design three fill-in-the-blank questions (one should use multiple choice).
   - Make up two true/false questions based on a short text of about 4 to 5 lines.
   - Make up two correct/incorrect questions based on a four-line dialogue.

5. Create a cloze test. Ask yourself these questions: Should cloze tests always be based on passages where every 5th, 7th, or *-nth* word has been deleted? Why and when should I use selective deletion in cloze tests?

6. Find a text that would be appropriate to use in class for a dictation. What is necessary to adapt it for dictation? Consider your feelings about dictation: is dictation an old-fashioned, bad form of testing? Are there good ways to use dictation? How else can you build language memory?

Further reading

Alderson, J. *Language Test Construction and Evaluation.* Cambridge University Press, 1995.

Hughes, A. *Testing for Language Teachers.* Cambridge University Press, 1989.

Law, B. and Eckes, M. *Assessment and ESL: A Handbook for K-12 Teachers.* Peguis Publishers, 1995.

Madsen, H. *Techniques in Testing.* Oxford University Press, 1983.

Underhill, N. *Testing Spoken Language: A Handbook of Oral Testing Techniques.* Cambridge University Press, 1987.

USING TEXTBOOKS

Advantages of using textbooks

Disadvantages of using textbooks

Choosing a textbook

Using a textbook

Review questions

Further reading

USING TEXTBOOKS

F OR LANGUAGE TEACHERS, TEXTBOOKS PROVIDE a *core* of language elements around which to build a course. For new teachers, a textbook is essential as a guide and can provide a well thought-out syllabus. Often, language programs think it is sufficient to prescribe certain core textbooks to meet the general needs of different levels and give performance objectives (see Appendix 2), but they do not provide a detailed syllabus. The core textbook can be a great help for creating a syllabus; it provides material to plan a *series* of lessons, rather than single lessons. In fact, a good textbook gives a plan for the entire course and helps with the achievement of long-term objectives.

Textbooks have advantages and disadvantages, however, which should be kept in mind when using them. Some teachers have positive attitudes towards textbooks, whereas others feel textbooks are inappropriate for their classes.

Advantages of using textbooks

- ◆ **Useful collection of material.** Textbooks provide useful, consistent, and exploitable material. For many teachers, they help lighten the need to collect material.
- ◆ **Sequence of activities.** Textbooks give a *sequence* of activities related to a particular theme or topic. These activities enable you to include skills development, communicative functions, relevant structures, and appropriate vocabulary into each lesson.
- ◆ **Context.** Textbooks provide *context* to help you convey meaning. Most up-to-date textbooks are well illustrated with photographs and drawings that relate to the new vocabulary.
- ◆ **Additional exercises.** Textbooks usually have accompanying workbooks that give students exercises and material to work on outside of class.
- ◆ **Experienced authors.** Most textbooks are written by

experienced teachers who understand the needs of students and teachers.

◆ **Carefully selected language.** Textbooks offer vocabulary and structures that have been carefully selected and are usually introduced systematically in controlled amounts.

Disadvantages of using textbooks

◆ **Reliance.** Relying on textbooks too much tends to weigh the lessons heavily on presentation of new material. If you spend a lot of time introducing the situations, topics, and vocabulary in the book, you tend to leave too little time for language practice and communicative interaction. The students begin to feel that as a teacher you are "bookbound" (see *Students' views* in Chapter 1, page 10).

◆ **Uniformity.** The format and layout in textbooks can seem stiff and boring. Each unit or chapter in a book is usually carefully planned and set out in the same way and deals with material in the same order. This unvarying format may be helpful for reference and clarity, but the predictability can make the book seem routine after extended use. You can liven up the lesson by changing the order of activities, etc.

◆ **Not a perfect match.** No textbook was written specifically for your class or your students. Each group of learners is different and only you can really cater to your students' individual tastes and needs. On the other hand, not being perfect for your class doesn't mean the book is useless or should be abandoned. It means that you have to decide how to teach with the book (see *Using a textbook,* page 305).

Remember that textbooks are *aids* to teaching. Like a lesson plan, textbooks provide a framework; a framework shouldn't become a straitjacket!

Choosing a textbook

Because there are many textbook series available on the market today, choosing a textbook can be a long and overwhelming process. To start, it may be most helpful to ask the opinions of experienced teachers and consult with other colleagues. Once you have a few textbooks in mind, consider how they will meet your needs. Following are tips and questions to consider when choosing a textbook. These considerations are outlined in the mind map illustration. If your program has already selected a textbook, don't worry that you might not like it. Remember that a big part of a textbook's success is *how* you decide to use it.

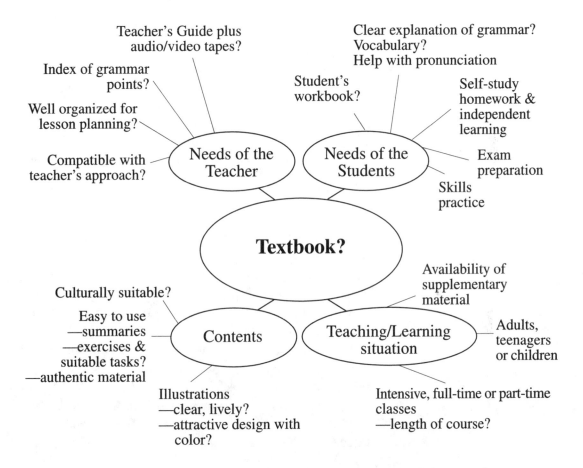

- ◆ **The teacher's guide.** Look at the teacher's guide and read the introduction to find out the stated objectives of the authors of the textbook. Check whether the aims of the textbook match your aims, which should be related to the needs of your students. Note that there is a difference between teacher's guides, manuals, and teacher's editions—some teacher's guides are more thorough than others. Generally, *teacher's editions* combine the student book with the teacher's guide (so that you have both in one). Often a *manual* means a few tips and the answers, whereas a *guide* gives step-by-step instructions.

♦ **Appearance and layout.** Is the textbook attractive and lively in appearance? Is it well illustrated? Are the illustrations culturally loaded or neutral (does it have an international appeal)? Does the book appear to be user-friendly?

♦ **Age level.** Is the book appropriate for the age level of the students? Are the topics of interest to students at that age?

♦ **Language level.** Does the level of language fit your class in terms of both language and skills work?

♦ **Vocabulary.** Is the vocabulary useful and relevant? How many vocabulary words are presented in each unit? Will the vocabulary be easy or difficult for your students? (You should limit new words to 7-10 at a time.)

♦ **Balance of skills.** Is there a sufficient number and variety of activities to help you give practice in all four language skills? Is there a balance of skills practice and opportunities to integrate skills (listening and speaking, reading and writing, speaking and writing, and reading and speaking)? Is there a good balance of communicative functions, structures, vocabulary, and pronunciation features in each unit?

♦ **Cultural awareness.** Is the writer of the book culturally aware? Does the book represent a variety of people? (No stereotyping, racism, etc.) Is the book likely to offend the sensitivities of students being taught in their own countries because the contexts and situations are centered on foreign values? One teacher tried to use a well-known textbook (published in the UK and USA) in Vietnam. This book was very successful with multilingual classes in England and in the USA. It did not work in Vietnam—the students found it too Euro-centered with references to people and things they had no experience of. Keep in mind that students may tend to resent overt attempts to teach European or American culture.

◆ **Price and availability.** Make sure the book is available. What components are available? (Some series come with cassettes, videos, flashcards, photocopiable resource packs, etc.) Is it affordable?

◆ **Useful for planning.** Look again at the teacher's book and consider how useful it will be in lesson planning and in giving you suggestions for presentation and practice. Is the syllabus appropriate? Do the units progress in difficulty?

◆ **Useful outside of class.** Will the textbook and/or workbook help the student with homework and learning outside of the class?

Using a textbook

Remember that a textbook is a resource and a tool, *not* a substitute for your teaching. *You* are responsible for the teaching and cannot depend wholly on any textbook. If possible, you might want to *pilot* the textbook (try it out) first in a few class lessons. The following are steps to take when using a textbook:

◆ **Select.** Look at the book critically, and *select* from it what is relevant to the needs of your students.

◆ **Omit.** Skip units or parts of books that are not necessary, interesting, or relevant to the goals of your lesson.

◆ **Adapt.** Adapt the material in each unit to fit your teaching style, priorities, and the interests of your students.

◆ **Supplement.** Supplement the material in the book with tasks that will give additional practice to the exercises in the book. Use authentic, lively material that is relevant and appropriate for your students.

◆ **Use the teacher's guide.** Consult the teacher's guide that accompanies the textbook. It can help you plan the lesson, get ideas on using context, and think of discussion topics.

Task 1: Choosing a textbook

For this task, use the beginning level of a well-known core textbook (for example, *Headway, Vistas,* or *Reward)* and examine the student's book and the teacher's book. Evaluate the textbook by answering the following questions:

1. Is the textbook visually attractive?

2. How is new material presented? Is the emphasis on teaching grammar and structure, or is it mainly through communicative functions? Does it combine both?

3. Does each unit provide opportunities for the students to practice the four language skills?

4. Is the vocabulary relevant to most students' needs? Is there enough new vocabulary, or too little, or too much? Will the context and the visuals help you to convey the meaning of the vocabulary?

5. Are the points of grammar or function reviewed at intervals through the book?

6. Is there any authentic material, like texts from newspapers or magazines, in the book? Would such material interest the age group of your students?

7. Are audio tapes available with the book? Are there other components with the book?

8. Is the teacher's guide helpful and clear in its advice? Will it help you to plan your lessons? Does it give detailed instructions about presenting and practicing the points in each unit?

Task 2: Using a textbook

Now look at another textbook and answer the following questions:

1. What are the main points of grammar, function, vocabulary, and pronunciation in some of the units?

2. In some of the reading activities, what are students asked to read? Are they asked to read and indicate positive or negative impressions? Would you begin the lesson with such an activity?

3. How would you help students to cope with an exercise that asks them to underline the adjectives in sentences or in a list? Are there such exercises in the book you are examining?

4. What difficulties would you anticipate for the students in a grammar and functions section? Find one and examine it for difficult parts.

5. Can you articulate all of the purposes for the exercises? State the reasons for including some of the exercises (*what* is being practiced and *how*).

6. Do you think a lesson using this textbook would involve you in a lot of presenting and talking? Why or why not?

7. Are there enough activities for the students? Is there a variety? Are there good ideas for discussions?

8. What vocabulary will the students be learning in some of the units?

9. What value are the illustrations in the text?

10. Is there a passage you could use for a dictation?

11. How could you use a theme or exercise from this textbook for further writing practice?

Review questions

1. What are the advantages of using a textbook? The disadvantages?

2. What are ways that you can make a textbook more suitable for your students and your lessons?

3. When teaching in a monolingual class abroad, what cultural aspect(s) of a textbook might cause negative reactions?

Further reading

Grant, N. *Making the Most of Your Textbook*. Addison Wesley Longman, 1987.

Chapter 19

PLANNING LESSONS

How to plan lessons

Lesson planning do's and don'ts

Planning strategies

- Presentation, Practice, and Production (PPP)

- Authentic use, Restricted use, and Clarification and Focus (ARC)

- Test—Teach—Test

Sample lesson plans

- Example 1: Lesson plan for speaking skills practice

- Example 2: Lesson plan for reading skills practice

- Example 3: Lesson plan (in a series of lessons) for listening and speaking skills practice

- Lesson plan format

Review questions

Further reading

PLANNING LESSONS

WHETHER YOU'RE AN EXPERIENCED OR INEXPERIENCED language teacher, it's essential to *plan* your lessons. A plan gives structure and shape to your lessons. It clarifies what you can do in the time available and gives a means of stating the *learning objectives* of the lesson to your students. Students want to know what you expect them to be able to do by the end of the lesson, and by knowing the purpose and objectives of what you're doing, students will feel that you are a well-prepared teacher. Planning also enables you to formulate a *personal teaching objective,* something you want to improve in your teaching style, such as your sense of timing or a reduction in your own talking time. A good lesson plan helps you to prepare appropriate techniques, materials, and procedures for the achievement of the lesson's aims; it helps you work out and organize the *staging* and *timing* of the activities and anticipate students' problems so that you can prepare ways for overcoming them.

Your lesson plan can serve as a reminder to refer to during the actual lesson, which helps keep you on track. Remember, however, that a lesson plan is not as important as responding to the needs of your students. If you must go outside of your plan when problems arise, don't hesitate to do so. As with a textbook, a plan is a framework, not a straitjacket!

How to plan lessons

There is no fixed formula for planning a lesson. We all have our own ways of organizing and working things out; perhaps the best way to go about answering the question of *how* to plan lessons is to ask yourself the following fundamental questions when planning:

- ◆ **Purpose.** Does your plan have a purpose? Learning and teaching objectives? Will the lesson be *useful* in achieving short-term objectives or long-term goals?
- ◆ **Interest and motivation.** Will the learners be *interested* in the

subject matter and thus be *motivated* to participate? Make sure the plan fits the level and age of your students, as well as the content of the class.

♦ **Enjoyment.** Will the learners *enjoy* the activities? Is there a *variety* in the activities? (Too much of the same thing can decrease enjoyment.)

♦ **Practicality.** Is the lesson *practical?* To answer this, consider the following:

  • **Classroom environment.** Can the furniture and seating be suitably arranged?

  • **Materials.** Do you have the appropriate materials? What will you need for the number of students in the class? Do you need to prepare photocopies? Role-play cards? Find pictures or recordings?

  • **Timing and staging.** Is there enough class time for the activities? What is the sequence of the stages and the activities?

Lesson planning do's and don'ts

♦ **Be specific.** The main reason for making lesson plans is that it obliges you, the teacher to decide on specific learning and teaching objectives. Your objectives should therefore be specific and accomplishable. Avoid vague general objectives like "practice listening skills." Rather, specify which sub-skills of listening your students need to practice, such as listening for key facts in a news report. Be very specific about what you want your students to achieve by the end of the lesson. If your objectives are specific and clear, the rest of your plan will be easier to follow, and the procedures will become more obvious and more natural.

♦ **Anticipate problems.** A lesson plan should help you anticipate learning problems. A lesson plan that ignores the predictable difficulties of the learners is not much use. A well-prepared teacher has thought out what problems his or her students are likely to have with concepts, forms, functions, and pronunciation features. Once you have possible problems in mind, you will be able to include means of tackling the problems in your plan. The same form of a word that has quite different meanings or functions, for example, may cause concept problems. The present perfect tense is difficult to use correctly because of its different meanings and uses. Separate these facets of the present perfect in your plan and preferably teach and practice one concept at a time.

◆ **Decide timing.** Timing and change in activities are part of a lesson plan. Divide your lesson into different activities first; then decide approximately how much time will be needed for you to give instructions and for the students to complete each activity. For example, assume the lesson lasts 60 minutes. Divide the hour roughly into four parts—not necessarily equal parts, but approximately 15 minutes each. The presentation or introductory activity may only need 10 minutes, while a role-play may take 20 minutes. Your plan should enable you to be flexible and to adapt to change in circumstances as well as change in activity. Everyone benefits from change and a variety of activities within a learning session. Most importantly, changes in activities allow for the differences of learning styles within a group.

◆ **Have materials ready.** Plan and prepare your learning aids, teaching aids, and materials ahead of time. Make a list and check it before you go into the classroom. It's embarrassing and a waste of time not to have the audio tape cued to the right point or not to have enough role-play cards.

◆ **Avoid too many details.** Avoid writing too many details into your lesson plan. Rather, have your plan consist of general notes. You won't have time during the lesson to read detailed notes and such notes often only clutter up the plan. Make your lesson plan easy to read at a glance.

◆ **File your plans for the future.** Make a copy of your lesson plans and file them for future reference. An inexperienced teacher will naturally take longer to prepare lessons and make plans than an experienced teacher. It's useful and economical to make use of a well-thought out plan again in the future. After each lesson, make notes on your plan to record what went well and what did not. Lesson plans are useful records of what has been taught or not completed.

Planning strategies

There are several planning strategies that you should keep in mind when creating your lessons. These strategies are briefly outlined in this section.

Presentation, Practice, and Production (PPP)

This conventional approach to planning lessons organizes the lesson into three main sections:

♦ **Presentation.** After having selected the target structure, the pronunciation features, and the new vocabulary, present the new language situations or context and try to convey meaning. This phase usually includes some controlled practice or eliciting of the new language. The interaction is mostly teacher to students.

♦ **Practice.** In this phase, make intensive use of the key items already presented. Use mostly controlled practice but do it in pairs, groups, or as a whole class. The interaction is teacher to students and student to student.

♦ **Production.** This phase emphasizes communication between students using the target structures and vocabulary. Unlike the practice phase, it is done freely with less control. Use problem-solving tasks like information gap, role-play, and written exercises. The interactions occur between one student and another student and between two groups of students.

Authentic use, Restricted use, and Clarification and Focus (ARC)

In recent years, teachers have been trying to use more flexible, less formulaic approaches to lesson planning. One of the most interesting strategies is known as ARC, whose three main sections are outlined here:

♦ **Authentic use.** Start with *authentic* uses of the language. Set tasks or state problems that can be solved with the information in the authentic material. This phase might require students to listen to a tape for specific information or to speak freely.

♦ **Restricted use.** Relate the authentic uses (introduced in the first phase) to practice in using the new language. This phase is a guided or directed part of the lesson. If, for example, in the authentic phase the students tried to do tasks involving functional language like agreeing or disagreeing, they now have to use the language in controlled (restricted) practice.

◆ **Clarification and focus.** After having noted student errors or the need for more work on target structures or functions, *clarify* and *focus* on the points that have arisen. Decide to direct or guide students in discovering what they need to focus on by encouraging the use of dictionaries or grammar exercises from their textbooks.

Test—Teach—Test

This is another variation of the ARC approach. In this strategy, the three elements of ARC are really being used in a different order: Restricted use, Clarification and Focus, and Restricted use. Although there isn't overtly an authentic use stage, it can be included in the first restricted use phase. A lesson of this type would be planned along these lines:

◆ **Test.** Choose a communicative activity that requires the use of the target structure or functions. Ask students to do the activity. During the activity, listen and note errors and difficulties.

◆ **Teach.** Clarify and focus on the problems and errors noted during the students' activity. Be prepared to present useful language that was not used by the students.

◆ **Test.** Ask students to do another communicative activity similar to the one in the first stage. The students should be more successful this time as they have had focused teaching and more practice in using the language needed.

Sample lesson plans

As mentioned before, there is no fixed formula for a good lesson. The following sample lesson plans, from both experienced and newly trained teachers, show you different and valid ways of preparing to teach. Whatever your teaching style and whatever teaching situation you are in, it is always good to plan. Try a number of techniques and strategies; find out what suits your students and your own approach. At the end of these plans is a blank format that you may choose to use in planning your own lessons.

Example 1: Lesson plan for speaking skills practice

Name: Faye Kelly (student teacher) *Date:* May 24th

Level: Beginning *Time:* 40 minutes

Learning objective(s): Through a (communicative) information gap activity, students will be practicing physical descriptions using the target structures "s/he's _____" and "s/he has _____." They should be able to produce these structures with a high degree of accuracy and fluency by the end of lesson; also to be reviewed and practiced is the expression, "What's _____ look like?"

Personal teaching objective(s): An efficient set-up to guarantee high accuracy during the activity and sufficient correction of target language structures.

Vocabulary and pronunciation (including phonological highlighting):

straight	/streyt/	a mustache	/ə/ /mʌstæš/
curly	/kərliy/	a beard	/ə/ /bɪərd/
heavy-set	/hɛvɪ sɛt/	a bun	/ə/ /bʌn/

Anticipated knowledge and problems: Possible problem with word order of more than one adjective. I expect students to have some or all the language of physical description already, but I will check it nevertheless.

Solutions: Highlight examples of common adjectives and their word order early on.

Materials: Photocopies of information-gap activity, *Family Portraits,* from *Elementary Communication Games* by Jill Hadfield (cut copies in half to make a "card" for each student).

From *Communication Games* by Jill Hadfield.

Procedures	Timing	Interaction	Purpose of the procedure
Warm-up/Personalization 1. Produce photo of my mother and show to one student; others must ask questions about her physical appearance. 2. Elicit, "What does she look like?" Drill quickly if necessary, but ensure pronunciation is natural. 3. Monitor carefully for target structures of physical description. Students, in pairs, turn to their partners and ask each other about their fathers or mothers.	10 minutes	student to student	1. I can address the target structures in a personalized setting. 2. This question is a key part of the structure I am teaching, and it needs to be accurate. Allows me to find out how much the students actually remember. 3. A trial run for later activity.

Review of Word Order
1. Use examples from the above activity to highlight order of adjectives:
    long, blond hair
    short, brown hair
2. Highlight on board:
size + color (Avoid three-word combinations, but if asked about them, explain.)
	8 minutes	teacher to students	1. Word order is sometimes a problem and students need review.
			2. Students can keep record.
			Danger of overload of information.

Set-up Activity 1. Divide students into groups of four. Assign roles (A, B, C, D), and give out corresponding cards. Check roles. Go over cards, and explain goal of activity. (The object of the game is to find out which family group belongs to each player, and which face belongs to each silhouette. Students do this by describing their families and asking questions.) 2. Get one group to demonstrate to others; monitor closely and correct target structures.	8 minutes	teacher to student	1. Familiarize students with materials. 2. Give then more time to assimilate instructions.

Procedures	Timing	Interaction	Purpose of the procedure
Activity 1. Give time frames. Monitor carefully for "cheating." Correct and encourage correct use of target structures, take notes of any other significant language problems. 2. Give feedback, and let students check in their groups to see if they were correct.	10 minutes	students to students	1. Students work more efficiently. Keep them on track. 2. Self-correction is more meaningful and more efficient.
Wrap-up 1. Quick review of any glaring language problems. 2. Congratulate students on a job well done.	5 minutes	teacher to students	1. Validates purpose of activity. 2. They usually deserve it!

Example 2: Lesson plan for reading skills practice

Name: Joe Duffy (student teacher) *Date:* September 2nd

Level: Low-intermediate *Time:* 45 minutes

Learning objective(s): Students will be developing the sub-skills of reading for gist and reading for details; they will practice formulating questions on a reading text to review question form order, and they will discuss and make cultural comparisons on the topic of tipping as a way of developing their fluency.

Personal teaching objective(s): To use my visuals and the reading material, exploiting both.

Vocabulary and pronunciation (including phonological highlighting):
   to tip/a tip /tɪp/
   a salary /ə/ /sæləriy/
   a hotel bellhop /ə/ /howtɛl/ /bɛlhap/
   a parking valet /ə/ /parkɪŋ/ /væley/
   to bill/a bill /bɪl/
   a service charge /ə/ /sərvɪs/ /čarǰ/

Anticipated knowledge and problems: No problems anticipated; language forms shouldn't present any difficulties. Topic may turn out to be a controversial one because of nationalities of students involved.

319

Materials: Handouts of word-matching exercise. Students will use the reading on page 85 of their textbooks, *To Tip or Not to Tip?* (Level one of *New Interchange* by Jack C. Richards).

To Tip or Not to Tip?

Do you tip for services in your country? When?

Canadians and Americans usually tip in places like restaurants, airports, hotels, and hair salons because many people who work in these places get low salaries. A tip shows that the customer is pleased with the service.

At airports, porters usually get a dollar tip for each bag. Hotel bellhops usually get a dollar for carrying one or two suitcases. A hotel door attendant or parking valet also gets about a dollar for getting a taxi or for parking a car. Many people also tip hotel room attendants, especially when they stay in a hotel for several days. They usually leave a dollar for each day.

The usual tip for other kinds of services — for example, for taxi drivers, barbers, hairdressers, waiters, and waitresses — is between 10 and 20 percent of the bill. The size of the tip depends on how pleased the customer is. In most restaurants, the check does not include a service charge. If the group is large, however, there may be an added service charge. There is no tipping in cafeterias or fast-food restaurants.

From *New Interchange* by Jack C. Richards.

Procedures	Timing	Interaction	Purpose of the procedure
Lead-in/personalization . . . eating out, hotels/motels, favorite food/restaurant	5 minutes	teacher to students, students to teacher	Creating relevance and getting students thinking and making associations.
Pre-teach essential vocabulary 1. Distribute handout with key vocabulary words and their definitions. Students work in pairs to match words with definitions (three-minute timeframe). 2. Meanwhile, write focus question for following step on board. 3. Brisk feedback, but deal with pronunciation difficulties on key words.	5 minutes	students to students, student to student	1. Allow for greater autonomy and assimilation of lexis. More student-centered. 2. Facilitate next step. 3. Validate exercise and because students want pronunciation work.
First reading Set focus task: "Find names of nine professions." Students scan text. In feedback, go over pronunciation of professions.	3 minutes	students	Simple question to give students an opportunity to see text without anxiety.
Second reading 1. Set comprehension task (true/false statements). 2. Check exercise for any difficulty students have with contents. 3. Check instructions. 4. Have students work in pairs. 5. Monitor how they are doing. 6. Quick feedback. Students must justify answers.	2 minutes	teacher to students, students to students	1. More in depth reading for greater understanding. 2. To ensure success of exercise. 3. Less tedious, lower anxiety. 4. Ensures participation of all students. 5. To know when to cut short exercise. 6. Get more student speaking time.

Procedures	Timing	Interaction	Purpose of the procedure
Third reading 1. Set grammar task. Divide students into two groups; each group prepares three *wh-* questions and three *yes/no* questions for the other group. (Group A forms questions from paragraphs 1 and 2; Group B forms questions from paragraph 3.) 2. Check instructions. 3. Monitor carefully for accuracy. 4. When finished, groups individually ask/answer questions. 5. Feedback on errors.	2 minutes, 10 minutes	teacher to students, student to student	1. Further exploit material. Reinforcement of question forms through maximum use of student talking time. 2. Instructions are complex. Safety in numbers! 3. Because students will be using this language and they prefer to be accurate. 4. Active participation. 5. Reinforce pronunciation or forms.
Follow-up 1. Discussion and personalization. Students tell one another about tipping in their countries and how they feel about it (see questions at end of reading). 2. Monitor for outstanding errors; note errors for wrap-up.	10 minutes	student to student	1. Bringing topic once again to the "real" world. 2. To avoid interrupting flow of exercise, but still validating the exercise in eyes of students through later follow-up.
Wrap-up 1. Write errors on board and elicit problem or correction. 2. "That's it. Well done, and have a good day!"			1. Validates exercise. 2. It's nice to say good-bye with a word of encouragement.

Example 3: Lesson plan (in a series of lessons) for listening and speaking skills practice

Name: Chris Macrae (experienced teacher) *Date:* October 4th

Level: Intermediate *Time:* 50 minutes

Learning objective(s):

1. Listening for specific information (news broadcast)
2. Speaking in interviews (role-play)
3. Grammar/structure: Past continuous and simple past practice to check whether students can use what has been previously taught.

Personal teaching objective(s): To use more authentic material in the classroom.

Vocabulary: Essential vocabulary in news reports.

Anticipated problems: Cultural unfamiliarity with some items in recording.

Solution: Avoid using these items in student tasks.

Materials: Recording of radio news broadcast (5 minutes in length); worksheets.

Procedures	Timing	Interaction
Prepare students for the listening task		
Brainstorm in pairs: What's been in the news lately?	3 minutes	student to student
Pairs report back. Write on board what's relevant or needed.	3 minutes	teacher to students
Elicit items that will be needed but not included.	3 minutes	students to teacher
Listening tasks and feedback		
Show worksheet and give instructions, then check understanding.	2 minutes	students to teacher
Student study task (check).	2 minutes	student to student
Allocate tasks (student A does odd numbers; student B does even numbers).	2 minutes	students to teacher
Play tape.	5 minutes	students listen
A's and B's pool information to compete worksheets. Monitor.	2 minutes	student to student
If necessary, play recording again. Repeat above step if needed.	7 minutes	tape to students
Confirm students' answers.	2 minutes	students to teacher
Preparation for role-play		
Divide class into two groups. Group A prepares interview questions for plane crash survivors. Group B prepares questions for money scandal politician.	5 minutes	students to students
Group A prepares to act as money scandal characters. Group B prepares to act as plane crash survivors.	5 minutes	students to students
Role-play		
Pair students from each group (A + B, A+ B . . .).	1 minute	students to teacher
Students A interview students B re: plane crash.	3 minutes	student to student
Students B interview students A re: money scandal.	3 minutes	student to student
Feedback		
Make any necessary correction of errors heard.	3 minutes	teacher to students
Time permitting . . .		
Discuss actual current topics in the media and what media students use.	7 minutes?	

Lesson Plan Format

Name: *Date*:

Level: *Time*:

Learning objective(s):

Personal teaching objectives:

Vocabulary and pronunciation:

Anticipated knowledge and problems:

Solutions:

Materials:

Procedures	Timing	Interaction	Purpose of the procedure

Task 1: Planning a lesson

Now it's your turn to plan a lesson! To help you, answer these questions as you plan:

1. Are the objectives clear? Are there learning *and* teaching objectives?
2. Do you know what you want the students to achieve by the end of the lesson?
3. Have you highlighted pronunciation features? (Use phonemic symbols, stress marks on new words, linking lines for elision, and arrows for intonation.)
4. Is there a warm-up or an anticipation section to give the main context of the lesson?
5. Will there be handouts? If so, are they easy to read and to understand?
6. Have you done the exercises that you expect the students to do? Have you anticipated any weak points? Is there an answer key?
7. Are the exercises or tasks at the right level for the students?
8. Is there a variety of activities?
9. If the lesson introduces new language, have you prepared and written down *concept checking questions* and appropriate answers?
10. Also, for new language items, is there enough *teacher-to-student* practice and *student-to-student* oral practice?
11. If you plan to use the board, have you included a board plan for the lesson plan (especially useful if you are introducing new words and structures)?

Review questions

1. What should you consider in making sure that your lesson plan is practical?

2. What things should you do to plan a successful lesson? Name at least three.

3. What are the three planning strategies? Which one do you like the most? Why?

Further reading

Woodward, T. and Lindstromberg, S. *Planning from Lesson to Lesson.* Addison Wesley Longman.

TEACHING MONOLINGUAL CLASSES

TEACHING MONOLINGUAL CLASSES

MANY TEACHERS GET THEIR FIRST JOBS in schools abroad where the classes are *monolingual*—meaning they have a common language and culture which is usually different from the teacher's. This contrasts with most teacher-training courses, which are held in English-speaking countries where teachers usually practice with *multilingual* classes, with groups of students of *mixed* languages and cultures. Furthermore, the teaching medium in multilingual classes is almost always English because translation into many languages is not possible. The multilingual teaching situation therefore favors the English through English approach and the Direct Method (see Chapter 21, page 340); two approaches which aren't as easy to use in monolingual classes.

The purpose of this chapter is to explore the teaching of monolingual classes. It offers suggestions and advice that may not be focused on in a teacher-training course in which teachers practice with multilingual classes, but that you will need if your first teaching job is abroad.

Monolingual versus multilingual

It is sometimes a shock to many new teachers to find themselves in the *monolingual* English as a foreign language (EFL) teaching situation, especially if they don't know the native language or the cultural background of their students. However, by comparing the two teaching situations, the *mono-* and the *multi-*lingual, we see that the advantages are by no means entirely on the side of the teacher in the multilingual class.

Multilingual	Monolingual
Learners in an English-speaking environment have lots of opportunities to practice English inside and outside of the classroom.	Learners in a non-English speaking environment lack opportunities for practice outside and tend to resort to their native language in the classroom.
The teacher has to deal with common areas of difficulty but can't help with specific problems of particular nationalities.	The teacher can identify and anticipate common problems of all students in the class (error consistency).
Translation is not possible.	Translation is possible—thus a "short-cut" to understanding is available.
Cultural and national mixture is stimulating and provides a resource to be exploited.	Common social/cultural background may result in lack of interest/stimulus in communicating with one another.
Instructions must be given in English.	Instructions can be given in the first language of the students.
Motivation is usually strong and students are willing to study intensively (10-30 hours weekly).	Motivation varies and needs to be maintained. Adults study only about two hours weekly.

Adapting to a monolingual environment

Teaching in a monolingual situation is easier if you know the language and understand the cultural background of the students. If you don't have these advantages, you can help yourself to overcome the difficulties by keeping in mind the following do's and don'ts (also see the task at the end of this chapter):

◆ **Don't be too strict and rigid about the 100% use of English.** Allow students short breaks in which they can use their first language, especially if they want to help fellow students with difficulties relevant to the lesson.

◆ **Do try to learn the language of the students.** Attend a class or arrange a conversation exchange with one or two students (preferably not beginners). At the very least, study the language from books or tapes before you go to the country, and try to find out the linguistic problems that students are likely to have with English. Let students know that you are trying to learn their language. They will usually appreciate your effort; it shows respect for their language and their culture. Also, trying to learn their language will remind you of what it's like to be a student and how frustrating it can be.

◆ **Do meet local people outside of school.** If you spend all your free time with your compatriots, you are missing valuable opportunities to learn about the culture of your students. Get involved in local activities.

◆ **Don't impose your cultural attitudes on students.** Students want to learn English because English is an international language; they don't necessarily want to learn the *culture* of English-speaking peoples.

◆ **Do respect the culture of the students.** It follows from the previous point that you should respect the customs and norms of behavior of the students' culture. You may not like their attitudes, but avoid upsetting them with your beliefs and opinions.

How to teach monolingual classes

One of the main disadvantages of learning English in a non-English speaking country is that students lack opportunities to listen to and speak English outside of the classroom. Moreover, most learners attend classes part-time (usually one evening a week for about two hours) and therefore their progress tends to be slow. In order to help to overcome this double problem, you should encourage the students to learn, study, and practice English outside of the classroom. Keep a checklist of suggestions for out-of-class activities. Your checklist should include the following:

◆ **Assign homework and mini-projects.** As it is very easy to forget what you learned say, six days ago, it is important that you assign—and the students carry out—some work between lessons. After every lesson, give students short exercises to practice what they have learned on their own. You could also assign homework in the form of simple projects (tasks), preferably involving students in pairs. For example, ask students to go to a travel agency and find out what it costs to travel by the cheapest means to an English-speaking country. Also ask them to get information on the costs of different kinds of accommodation (student residences, homestays, etc.) for a month's stay.

◆ **Watch TV and videos.** Programs in English are available in many parts of the world, even if they are mainly news broadcasts. If possible, ask students to watch a particular program outside of class. Give them questions to answer, and have them write about what they've seen. If videotape players are available, select suitable films on video to be watched in students' free time.

◆ **Use movies.** If there's a local movie theater that shows movies in English (not dubbed), it's a good idea to recommend a visit and then discuss the movie in class. Another suggestion is to have "movie night." Show a video tape of a movie and discuss the ideas in it.

◆ **Use newspapers and magazines.** English-language newspapers are available in most countries. There are also magazines that are written especially for English language learners, like *BBC Worldwide Publications.*

◆ **Make radio, cassettes, and CDs available.** The *World Service radio* of the BBC and the *Voice of America* broadcasts bring regular daily news programs and talks. Many ESL/EFL publishers produce audio tapes to supplement textbooks and other texts. Encourage students who have their own tape players to do some listening in their free time. Check (not test) what they are listening to.

◆ **Make reading books and cartoon or comic books available.** Suitable books are graded readers (see *Graded readers,* Chapter 9, page 169). More advanced students should try to read authentic books within their linguistic ability. Choose or suggest books that are not very long and are likely to be enjoyable. Comic books in English can be useful reading practice and especially appeal to younger students.

◆ **Encourage use of self-access centers.** Self-access centers are especially useful for part-time students. They can visit the center at times convenient for them. See Chapter 16, *Learning with Self-Access.*

The non-native teachers and you

When teaching English abroad, you are likely to meet teachers who are natives of the country in which you are teaching. These non-native English-speaking teachers may specialize in translation classes, or they may be there because some students prefer to be taught by teachers who speak the language of the country. Especially if you don't speak the language of the country, you should get to know these teachers. They can give you invaluable help and advice on the learning difficulties of the students. It's worth considering the differences between a native English-speaking teacher (NST) and a non-native English-speaking teacher (NNT).

Native English-speaking teacher (NST)	Non-native English-speaking teacher (NNT)
An NST has native speaker's intuition and knowledge; students feel confident in NST's knowledge and accept his or her authority on the subject.	NNT's knowledge of English is imperfect and incomplete, especially of idiom and pronunciation. However, having studied English, many NNTs have sophisticated knowledge of English grammar and structure.
Not having learned English as a foreign language, NSTs have difficulty in understanding or sympathizing with learners' difficulties and errors.	Because they've had to study and learn English as a foreign language, NNTs have experienced similar problems as the students. They can understand and sympathize with the learners; they are more able to anticipate the difficulties.
NSTs usually do not have much knowledge of the students' language or the ability to communicate in the first language easily.	Not only do they know the first language as well as (or better than) the students, but NNTs also understand the culture and its association with the language.
NSTs have little knowledge of the students' society and culture.	NNTs have native knowledge and awareness of the students' environment and culture.
NSTs can insist on the use of English in the classroom. Students know they can only communicate with the teacher by using English.	Both the NNT and students are aware that they need not use English all the time; temptation to resort to the first language is very strong.

It is clear from the comparison that the NNT has many advantages over the NST, and therefore the NST has much to learn and much to gain from the NNT. If you feel somewhat disadvantaged by the comparison, keep in mind that most learners throughout the world want native English speaking teachers and greatly value the opportunity to listen to you, talk to you, and learn from you. After all, many students have been taught English by NNTs as children at school. The methodology in this teaching tends to be grammar learning and translation, concentrating heavily on grammatical knowledge, reading, and writing and thus neglecting practice of the oral and aural skills.

Task 1: Getting to know the students' culture

In trying to learn about your students' educational and cultural background, you will find many topics to talk about if the students' level of English makes it possible. Perhaps the best thing about trying to get to know your students' culture is that most students like talking about themselves and telling the teacher what they know. Arrange a conversation exchange with some of your students and do the following:

1. Find out about what the students expect you to do as a teacher. How do they expect to learn?

2. Try, without testing, to find out what the students know and don't know about the world (for example, do a game or quiz on general knowledge).

3. Find out what is considered polite and impolite behavior in the street, in a restaurant, in the home (as a visitor), and at a party. Can both males and females go out for entertainment? What are the social rules?

4. Make comparisons, noting similarities and differences between the culture of the students and the cultures of English-speaking people.

5. Ask the students what they like or dislike in music, especially songs. For example, do they like classical music or only pop songs?

<table>
<tr><td>

Review questions

</td><td>

1. What are some of the main differences between teaching in a multilingual class and a monolingual class?

2. Should you insist that students use English all the time in a monolingual class in their own country? Can the use of translation be completely avoided?

4. How are TV and radio broadcasts in English useful to learners? Are they beneficial to learners of all levels?

5. In what ways could the knowledge of English of non-native teachers (NNTs) be useful for native English-speaking teachers (NSTs)?

</td></tr>
</table>

Further reading

Atkinson, D. *Teaching Monolingual Classes.* Addison Wesley Longman, 1993.

Hinkel, E. *Culture in Second Language Teaching and Learning.* Oxford University Press, 1999.

McKay, S. *Teaching English Overseas.* Oxford University Press, 1992. (focus on social, political, and economical factors)

Chapter 21

KEY CONCEPTS IN LANGUAGE TEACHING

Acquisition versus learning

Error analysis versus contrastive analysis

Over-generalization

Direct method

Inductive and deductive approaches

Prescriptive and descriptive approaches

Functional approach

Communicative approach

Humanistic approaches

Some humanistic methods

    - The Silent Way

    - Suggestopedia

    - Counseling Learning and Community Language Learning

    - Total Physical Response (TPR)

Learner-centered and teacher-centered approaches

Review questions

Further reading

KEY CONCEPTS IN LANGUAGE TEACHING

This chapter is intended to clarify terms both used and misused in general language teaching, with a particular focus on English language teaching. In cases where there is a close connection between terms, the terms are compared and contrasted. This is a brief overview of key concepts; it is not intended to fully define the terms, but rather to lead to further reading and discussion.

Acquisition versus learning

Strictly speaking, as children, people *acquire* their first language; they do not normally have to *learn* it. *Acquisition* is therefore a process of unconsciously developing the knowledge and skills of the language. *Learning* a language involves conscious application and monitoring of the output. Language teaching methods that try to simulate the conditions in which a first language is acquired are said to be *natural*. Recently, emphasis on the development of *fluency* is in line with the priority given to acquisition. Language teachers who place *accuracy* first, on the other hand, tend to give priority to more formal learning.

Error analysis versus contrastive analysis

Attitudes towards the significance of learners' errors have changed greatly during the past several decades. It was once argued that linguistics, especially through *contrastive* language studies (comparing native language and target language features), could contribute to language teaching by providing material for syllabus design based on those areas where the native language is likely to interfere and thus cause errors in the output of the target language. More recently, a greater awareness of native language (L1) acquisition and second language learning (L2) processes has led to more tolerance towards errors which are more likely to be seen as evidence of language development.

Over-generalization

This term is used to describe the cause of errors that result from the learner creating analogous forms on the basis of patterns or rules whose restrictions he or she has not learned to apply. For example, a learner becomes aware that to form a plural noun in English, an *-s* or *-es* is added to the unmarked, singular form (changing *book* to *books);* he or she then generalizes this rule to produce *childs** instead of *children.* Similarly, native-speaking children may acquire the rule for the formation of simple past tense verb forms (add *-ed* to the unmarked verb, changing *ask* to *asked*). They often over-generalize and regularize verbs like *go* (forming *goed** instead of *went).*

Direct method

The *direct method* was originally called *direct* because its founder (Gouin) used direct association with the spoken forms of the target language through the senses—mainly visual and auditory. Learners were to be taught French through French, English through English, etc. and translation was to be avoided. In the last century, the term has been used so widely that it has lost any acceptable meaning as a distinct method and takes its meaning from the absence of a mediating language of instruction. It is important because it rejects the traditional writing-focused grammar/translation methods and emphasizes the spoken language.

Inductive and deductive approaches

An *inductive approach* claims that the best way to learn the rules and structural patterns of a new language is through experience, practice, and observation (in effect, an empirical approach). Thus, the learner acquires the structure and rules of a language through drills or patterned practice without overt explanation of grammatical rules.

In a *deductive approach,* on the other hand, the rule and/or model is presented before the examples. It is often assumed that the learners will be able to construct the sentence types or structures from the rule or model. Grammatical forms and structures are thus made explicit and the language practice is to be derived consciously from the models.

Prescriptive and descriptive approaches

A *prescriptive approach* assumes a given (or *received*) standard of correctness in language forms and usage. It is the duty of the teacher to provide this standard. Prescriptive attitudes are often derived from the accepted standards of the written language which are then applied to the spoken language.

A *descriptive approach* tends to be based on observation of how the language is actually used by the majority of native speakers (it is more like descriptive linguistics). Descriptive teaching involves an attempt to be more objective about acceptable language forms and not to impose a particular model as the widely accepted form.

Functional approach

An approach to syllabus design, introduced by the Council of Europe in the 1970s, was originally called the *notional/functional syllabus.* Now this approach is widely known as the *functional approach.* It focuses on common communicative functions (such as how to greet someone, how to ask for directions, and how to extend an invitation). These language functions or uses form the primary categories in a language teaching program. The *exponents* or realizations of the functions are the structures and the vocabulary.

In practical terms, for teaching spoken English (or any other language) using the functional approach, these are the priorities:
1. Decide on the function. (For example, the function is *offering.*)
2. Choose an appropriate structure. *(Would you like something or would you like to do something?)*
3. Choose appropriate vocabulary. (For example, *to have a cup of coffee.)*

The functional approach had a great effect on textbooks and on language teaching; now most courses and curricula have been changed to include more emphasis on communicative functions and how to do things with language. The functional approach largely formed the theoretical basis of communicative language teaching.

Communicative approach

Also known as *communicative language teaching,* this approach aims primarily to enable the learner to become competent in the processes of communication. It is a further development of the functional approach and similarly places great emphasis on teaching basic communicative functions such as requesting, describing, and expressing likes and dislikes.

The *communicative approach* stresses the importance of using language appropriately in social contexts. It is also focuses on placing the learner in situations where real information is needed (where there is a so-called "information gap"). The learner needs to use language to gain knowledge for a particular purpose and not merely as an exercise in linguistic manipulation. Communicative language teaching uses problem-solving and the setting of tasks that actively involve the learner. This approach, like the acquisition model, emphasizes the need for the development of fluency and is less concerned with accuracy or the teaching of grammatical structures.

Humanistic approaches

Humanistic teaching is based on the proposition that learners bring their feelings as well as their reasoning to the task of language learning. This is what is meant by the emphasis on "wholeness" in the literature of psycho-therapists like Carl Rogers, from which ideas for humanistic methods have been drawn. Through humanistic methods, teachers pay serious attention to "affective variables" and to the importance of reducing stress and anxiety in the learning situation. Humanistic teachers are sensitive to the basic need to create an atmosphere that is conducive to learning in a group. They are aware that learners cannot learn well when feeling threatened or isolated.

Another fundamental feature of a humanistic approach is its concern for the individual learner. Humanistic teaching aims to enable the learner to achieve independence. A humanistic teacher is aware that too much direction or too much organized teaching can interfere with the self-development of the learner. The influence of humanistic approaches has made teachers more aware of the need to develop fluency and to be less concerned with accuracy. The correction of errors is therefore not a priority in humanistic approaches. In the *Counseling Language Learning* method of Charles Curran, the teacher keeps a low profile; he or she is a resource person or a facilitator only to be used when the learners indicate that they want help (see *Role-play,* Chapter 14, page 247). Stephen Krashen, in his approach, *Second Language Acquisition and Monitor Theory,* stresses the importance of providing the learner with a rich exposure to L2 (the second or target language) with plenty of "comprehensible input" in a relaxed atmosphere. This input is intended to be intake for acquisition, not for conscious learning.

Some humanistic methods

The best known humanistic methods are *The Silent Way, Suggestopedia,* and *Counseling Learning/Community Language Learning.* The gurus of these humanistic ways—Gattegno, Lozanov, and Charles Curran, all made great claims for their methods and expected their "disciples" to accept the whole package. They expected humanistic teachers to be dedicated to the method they had chosen.

Humanistic methods vary greatly in their content and the techniques they recommend. Following are brief descriptions of some of the methods:

The Silent Way

In this method, the teacher uses mime, gesture, and aids like Cuisenaire rods with a minimum of teacher-to-student presentation. The students do most of the teaching and most of the speaking—hence the name, *The Silent Way.*

Suggestopedia

The main idea of *Suggestopedia* is the inducement of optimal learning conditions. For example, music at 60 beats per minute is used to aid relaxation and to accompany the presentation of texts for comprehension, and role-play through assumed prestigious personalities helps students become less inhibited. Lozanov claims that this approach enables the learner to learn hundreds of new words in a short intensive course. It is claimed that students who are prepared to be *infantilized,* that is to say, become as open and suggestible as children to the new language, might have good results from this presentation. Note that *Suggestopedia* is not a method for the skeptical or eclectic teacher. It has, however, been influential and has appeared in many guises (like *Accelerated Learning).*

Counseling Learning and Community Language Learning

This method was originally designed for monolingual groups with a bilingual teacher. It claimed that ideas and techniques developed in group counseling sessions, designed to help people with emotional and psychological problems, can also be used in teaching language. Through this method, each learning group (ideally 8 learners) is supposed to become a supportive community. The learners decide (in their native language) what they want to express or talk about while the teacher (known as the *facilitator)* moves around the group and translates the learner's phrases into the target language. The learner repeats the words to the other members of the group. A recording is made of the utterances so that they can be played back later, written down for study, and analyzed.

An important feature of Counseling Learning/Community Language Learning is the emphasis placed on the *reflection phase* of a lesson, when the learners are expected to think about and reflect on the value of the activities and the content of the lesson. The method encourages students to be responsible for planning the future of the course and expressing what they want to do in subsequent learning sessions. Counseling Learning is an interesting attempt to be learner-centered by focusing on the work and development of an individual within a group.

Total Physical Response (TPR)

TPR is a language teaching method developed in the later 1970's by James Asher, a psychology professor at San Jose State University, California. Using this method, the teacher teaches language through physical activity. For example, to convey the meaning of *quickly,* the teacher gives simple instructions like "Stand up and walk *quickly* to the door. Go back and sit down *quickly."* The students have to respond to the instructions with the appropriate action. It is claimed that by interpreting meaning through movement and appropriate action, rather than through the abstract study of language forms, the learner is less subjected to stressful, test-like classroom situations and thus learns more effectively.

However, Asher has admitted that TPR procedures are not enough on their own and should be used along with other methods. Furthermore, it is not easy to see how learners at levels higher than beginners would benefit much from this type of activity learning.

TPR has become popular partly because it fits with the emphasis on the role of comprehension in second language acquisition (as in Stephen Krashen's theories).

Whatever their differences, humanistic methods are all based on the same basic principles:

- a sensitivity to individual human emotions,
- the need to focus on the full development of individuals in groups,
- and the need for active learner participation in the learning process.

Learner-centered and teacher-centered approaches

The learner-centered emphasis of recent years owes a great deal to the ideas of the humanistic methods. David Nunan, in his book, *The Learner-Centred Curriculum,* states that "Learner-centeredness is a process of acquiring skills as opposed to a subject-centered approach, which views language as a body of knowledge to be learned." In a *teacher-centered* classroom, the teacher mediates between student and material. In a *learner-centered* classroom, the student and the material are in direct contact; the teacher makes the learning more efficient through orchestration of the variables. Learner-centered practices have grown out of humanistic approaches and communicative language learning aims. Learner-centered teaching in the learner-centered classroom has become the model for good teaching. Unfortunately, those who want to jump on this particular "bandwagon" do not always know what they are supposed to be doing or what they are supposed to be rejecting. It is not always clear that it is not enough to avoid being teacher-centered. There are two main issues to be clear about in learner-centered teaching: the learner-centered curriculum and the learner-centered classroom.

- ◆ **The learner-centered curriculum.** The traditional curriculum-centered approach focused on the teacher's role of getting through the subject matter (the body of knowledge to be learned) prescribed by the curriculum. The learner-centered curriculum, on the other hand, is developed with the learners' needs, interests, and objectives as the focus of the teaching. The teacher is needed to analyze the learners' needs, to set goals that will achieve the learners' aims, and to choose materials that are suitable for the learners' levels. The teacher has certain traditional roles in learner-centered programs, such as testing and checking on learning. The learner-centered curriculum does not achieve its objectives without the organization, skills, and knowledge of the teacher.

◆ **The learner-centered classroom.** The traditional classroom is more teacher-centered in the way decisions are made about the curriculum and the organization of classroom learning. Traditional teacher-centered teaching usually means that the curriculum is set before the beginning of the course; the learners' needs and objectives are not always taken into consideration. Traditional teaching does not necessarily mean bad teaching or neglect of the learners' needs, but these issues are dealt with as they arise and by means of correction and remedial work. The learner-centered classroom differs from a teacher-centered classroom in that:

- learners are more active and participate more,
- learners are closely involved in making decisions about the content of the curriculum and how it is taught,
- learners are encouraged to develop their learning skills and efficient learning strategies,
- and learners are encouraged to set their own objectives and to adopt realistic goals.

Review questions

1. What is the main difference between *acquiring* versus *learning* a language? How is this relevant to language teaching?

2. How have teaching attitudes towards learners' errors changed in recent years?

3. Does the Communicative approach give greater emphasis to fluency or to accuracy? Why?

4. What basic principles do Humanistic methods have in common?

5. In what ways does a learner-centered classroom differ from a teacher-centered classroom?

Further reading

Curran, C. *Counseling Learning.* Apple River Press, 1972.

Gattegno, C. *The Silent Way.* Educational Solutions Inc., 1972.

Krashen, S. *Second Language Acquisition and Second Language Learning.* Prentice Hall, 1988.

Lozanov, G. *Suggestopedia.* Gordon and Breach, 1979.

Nunan, D. *The Learner-Centred Curriculum.* Cambridge University Press, 1991.

Richards, J. C. and Rodgers, T. S. *Approaches and Methods in Language Teaching.* Cambridge University Press, 1986.

Rogers, C. R. *Client-Centered Therapy.* Houghton Miflin, 1951.

Seely, C. and Romijn, E. *TPR is More Than Commands—At All Levels.* Command Performance Language Institute, 1995.

GENERAL DESCRIPTION OF LEVELS

This nine-point scale is commonly used by English Language teaching organizations to determine the levels of learners.

0   **Zero beginner.** Cannot produce either spoken or written language. Cannot understand the language in either spoken or written form.

1   **False beginner.** Can produce isolated words and phrases in spoken and written form. May understand isolated words and phrases in spoken and written form. Not yet able to function socially or carry out any transactions in the language.

2   **Beginning.** Can produce intermittent spoken and written language of a very limited nature in familiar situations and obvious role sets. Can give basic personal information in spoken language, can exchange greetings, ask for simple information and carry out simple transactions necessary to daily life. Can provide basic written information about personal identity for official purposes.

3   **High-beginning.** Can consistently produce spoken and written language in familiar situations. Can convey general meaning in spoken language where topic is familiar but experiences frequent breakdowns in communication beyond the familiar. Can formulate questions necessary to daily life and can provide written personal details in note form.

4   **Low-intermediate.** Has basic competence in spoken English in familiar situations and role sets. Is able to negotiate the transactions needed for daily life and to function adequately in

basic social situations. Can produce written English required for form filling, notes, and simple tasks. Beyond the range of familiar situation, has frequent breakdowns in communication but has some strategies for requesting clarification. Cannot use or understand complex language.

5   **Intermediate.** Has a general knowledge of basic structures and can use these appropriately in most everyday situations. Has acquired some of the language appropriate to personal and/or professional interests. Although likely to make many mistakes, is able to communicate effectively in both spoken and written English and to operate coping strategies in difficult situations.

6   **High-intermediate.** Can operate effectively in spoken and written language. Has comprehensive knowledge of basic language structures and can use them appropriately in most situations. Can understand the gist of passages of spoken and written languages in most general fields and in fields of personal and/or professional interest. Can use and understand complex and idiomatic language in familiar situations. Has some inaccuracies but can often correct them and does not normally make mistakes which hinder communication.

7   **Advanced.** Has operational command of all the basic structures of the language. Can recognize different registers and can operative effectively in registers appropriate to personal and/or professional situations. Can infer meaning and detect nuance in both spoken and written language. Can produce accurate written language for variety of text types. Occasional errors and misunderstandings still occur but these are usually limited to unfamiliar situations.

8   **Professional user.** Has sufficient command of spoken and written language to be effective in the appropriate occupational environment as well as in daily life. Can handle complex language and follow complex passages in spoken and written form. Occasional errors and misunderstandings may occur but has strategies for repair and for handling any difficult situations that hinge on linguistic problems.

9   **Expert user.** Has full command of the language in all its forms, understands its structures, and has strategies for keeping up-to-date with linguistic change. Is aware of varieties of English used and is unlikely to be involved in misunderstandings arising from such variations.

Many language schools use six main levels in general English classes:

Level 1	Zero and false beginners	(0-1 on the above scale)
Level 2	Beginning	(2-3 on the above scale)
Level 3	Low-intermediate	(4 on the above scale)
Level 4	Intermediate	(5 on the above scale)
Level 5	High-intermediate	(6 on the above scale)
Level 6	Advanced	(7 and over on the above scale)

PERFORMANCE OBJECTIVES

Specimen outline for beginning level

By the end of the beginning level, students should be able to demonstrate the following:

- a simple means of talking about the present, the past, the future, and habits or routines
- a sound grasp of the basic pronoun system
- an understanding of the use of simple adverbs of manner, place, time, and frequency
- an understanding of the use of simple attributive adjectives and nouns used as adjectives
- the ability to talk about possession
- a sound grasp of the basic prepositions of place and time
- the ability to form simple questions
- the ability to give and follow instructions
- the ability to use the modal verbs *may* (for future possibility), *must* (for obligation), and *can* (for ability and permission)
- the basic means of talking about quantity *(some, any, much, many, how much, how many, a lot of, lots of)* and size (including *too* and *enough)*
- the ability to give reasons using *because* and *so*
- the ability to make and use the comparative and superlative forms of adjectives
- an understanding of basic classroom metalanguage (verb tenses or "structure")
- the ability to understand basic functional language (both written and spoken)
- the ability to make greetings, introduce themselves and others, and seek similar information about second and third parties
- the ability to make and respond to simple apologies

- the ability to make polite compliments concerning food and dress
- the ability to ask for and give locations and simple directions
- the ability to function in situations like a bus/train station, an airport, or a store
- the ability to make a collect call (ask the operator for assistance) and answer the phone
- the ability to describe simple problems (such as with a bicycle)
- the ability to socialize in a simple way
- the ability to write simple sentences and very basic compound sentences linked by the conjunctions *and, but, because,* and *so*
- the ability to write and understand simple postcards and personal letters
- the ability to understand and fill in simple forms and questionnaires
- familiarity with the phonemic alphabet (if appropriate) and grammatical terminology
- the ability to understand simple informational texts
- an understanding of simple signs, notices, and instructions
- an understanding of simple bus/train station and airport announcements
- the ability to understand bus/train timetables and airport arrival/departure displays

A FIRST LESSON TO ZERO BEGINNERS

How do you start a course if your students don't know any English at all? Use this outline of a 50-minute lesson for quick reference. It assumes that the students are zero beginners and the teaching has to be entirely in English.

Teacher: Good morning! *(Gesture students to reply.)*

Teacher: *(Gesture students to listen by cupping hand to ear.)* I'm John. *(Repeat; gesture students to introduce themselves round the group.)*

                   Time: 5 minutes

Teacher: *(Gesture students to listen—sketch a question mark in the air.)* What's your name? *(Repeat; elicit from students.)*

Students: *(Individually to teacher.)* What's your name?

Teacher: I'm John. What's your name?

Students: *(Individually to teacher.)* I'm _____.

Pairwork to practice.
Open class pairs to reinforce.

                  Time: 10 minutes

Teacher: *(Show map or draw a sketch of the country in which you are teaching. If the country were the United States, for example, point to, elicit, and drill the city names New York, Chicago, Denver, etc.)*

      I'm from Dallas.

Teacher:	*(Model and use the map to substitution drill, pointing to self.)* I'm from Dallas. *(Pointing to student.)* And you?
Student:	I'm from _____.

Pairwork to practice.
Open class pairs to reinforce.

Time: 5 minutes

Teacher:	*(Gesture students to listen—sketch a question mark in the air.)* Where are you from? *(Repeat.)*
Students:	Where are you from? I'm from _____. *(Students give individual answers.)*
Teacher:	Where are you from?
Students:	*(Individually to teacher.)* I'm from _____. And you?
Teacher:	*(Responding to each student.)* I'm from Dallas.

Pairwork to practice.
Change pairs to reinforce.

Time: 10 minutes

Teacher:	*(With gestures/body language to help convey meaning.)* When two people meet, the first one says "Hello."
Students:	Hello.
Teacher:	And the second one says "Hi."
Students:	Hi.

Pairwork/open class to practice.

Teacher:	*(With gestures.)* We're at a party. At the party there are two people: Sue from Chicago *(stick picture of a woman on board, plus her name and the city she is from)* and Mark from Washington *(stick picture of a man on the board, etc.)* Mark thinks Sue is beautiful, so he says? "Hello." *(Drill.)*

Teacher:	And she says? "Hi" (*Continue eliciting. Write the following dialogue on the board and drill. Assign half the class to be Sue and half the class to be Mark; when finished, reverse the roles.*)
Mark:	I'm Mark. What's your name?
Sue:	I'm Sue.
Mark:	Where are you from?
Sue:	I'm from Chicago, and you?
Mark:	I'm from _____.

Pairs practice as Mark and Sue.

Time: 15 minutes

Have pairs change and substitute their own names, etc. into the dialogue.

Get all students on their feet and mingling. Have students practice their dialogues with each other as if they were at a party. Gradually erase sections of the dialogue on the board until there is nothing left for the students to refer to.

Time: 5 minutes

A PLACEMENT TEST

Name: _____

Date: _____

There are four possible choices to complete each sentence. Find the one that best completes the sentence and circle it. For example:

A: Where should we meet?
B: We should meet _____ the bus stop opposite the school.
   a. in   c. (at)
   b. on   d. of

1. A: Would you like a cup of tea?
   B: Yes, I _____.
      a. do   c. would
      b. like   d. wall

2. Please don't talk to me now. I _____ to finish my test.
      a. will try   c. have tried
      b. try   d. am trying

3. A: Does he smoke?
   B: Yes, he _____ twenty a day.
      a. smokes   c. smoke
      b. is smoking   d. has smoked

4. A: Can I help you?
   B: Yes, I'd like _____.
      a. the information   c. any information
      b. to inform   d. some information

5. A: I'd like some coffee.
   B: I'm afraid there isn't _____.
      a. more   c. any
      b. anything   d. some

6. A: Where is your book?
   B. I _____ it last week.
      a. have lost   c. losing
      b. lose   d. lost

7. A: Is John _____ Paul?
   B: No, I don't think so.
      a. more taller than   c. taller than
      b. so tall as   d. taller like

8. A: Can I help you?
   B: Yes, I am looking _____ Mr. Smith's office.
      a. for   c. after
      b. at   d. to

9. A: Why are you running?
   B: There isn't _____ time. The movie's going to start soon.
      a. many   c. much
      b. any   d. some

10. A: Where are you staying?
    B: I'm living _____ Mrs. Smith and her family.
       a. by   c. with
       b. at   d. among

11. A: Has he written to his brother?
    B: Yes, he _____ him a letter last night.
       a. has written   c. had written
       b. was writing   d. wrote

12. She likes living in a warm climate, _____?
       a. wouldn't she   c. won't she
       b. doesn't she   d. isn't she

13. A: Do you smoke?
    B: Not now, but I _____.
       a. use to   c. was used to
       b. am used to   d. used to

14. A: This is my first visit to the doctor.
    B: Who _____ to before?
       a. are you going   c. you went
       b. went you   d. did you go

15. A: Did you do any homework?
    B: Yes, but only _____.
       a. any   c. a few
       b. not much   d. a little

16. Could you lend me some money? I'm very _____ of cash
    at the moment.
       a. down   c. low
       b. scarce   d. short

17. A: Do you know who she is?
    B: No, she didn't _____ her name.
       a. say me   c. tell me
       b. say to me   d. tell to me

18. Everyone understood. The teacher _____ to explain again.
       a. may not   c. didn't need
       b. mustn't   d. needn't

19. That house is in a terrible state. You can see it _____ for
    years.
       a. hasn't been repaired   c. isn't repaired
       b. wasn't repaired   d. hadn't been repaired

20. My watch is broken, but it's not worth _____.
       a. repairing   c. to repair
       b. to repair   d. to be repaired

21. A: I'm terribly tired.
    B: Well, I suggest _____ to bed.
       a. you go   c. you going
       b. you to go   d. you went

22. A: Why didn't you tell me?
    B: You _____ angry if I had.
       a. were   c. had been
       b. were to be   d. would have been

23. A: Here is your five dollars back.
    B: Thanks, but I don't remember _____ it to you.
       a. to lend   c. my lend
       b. lending   d. me to lend

24. A: Is he coming to the meeting?
    B: Well, I asked him _____.
       a. if he will come   c. if he was coming
       b. will he come   d. would he come

25. A: I'm fine; it's only a little cut.
    B: _____ you better see a doctor?
       a. Wouldn't   c. Won't
       b. Shouldn't   d. Hadn't

26. A: Do I have to get ready now?
    B: Yes, it's time we _____.
       a. went   c. will go
       b. would go   d. go

27. A: Do you like your new apartment?
    B: Yes, it's small but it _____ my needs perfectly.
       a. settles   c. supplies
       b. meets   d. fills

28. I suppose tomorrow's bus strike means _____ the start of class.
       a. have delayed   c. to delay
       b. delay   d. delaying

Scoring

29. I wrote to the manager _____ getting my money refunded.
    a. in the hope of   c. with the aim to
    b. on the question to   d. about to

30. A: Did you know everybody at the party?
    B: No, nobody _____ the host.
    a. except   c. other
    b. apart   d. rather

This test is designed for use as a grading assessment that enables the school or program to roughly assess the student's level before he or she arrives to begin a course. The scale below shows how the results of this test can be used to place a student in a class at a suitable level.

Score	Class level
0-5	Zero beginner
6-10	Beginning
11-15	High-beginning
15-20	Intermediate
21-25	High-intermediate
25-30	Advanced

PHONEMIC SYMBOLS: STANDARD AMERICAN ENGLISH

iy	ɪ	ʌ	a	ɔ	ow
b<u>ea</u>t	b<u>i</u>t	b<u>u</u>d	b<u>o</u>b	b<u>ou</u>ght	b<u>oa</u>t
	ɛ	æ	ʊ	uw	ə
	b<u>e</u>t	b<u>a</u>t	b<u>oo</u>k	b<u>oo</u>t	<u>a</u>bout
ey	ay	aw	oy		
b<u>ay</u>	b<u>i</u>ke	c<u>ow</u>	b<u>oy</u>		
p	b	t	d	k	g
pen	Ben	tip	dip	cat	gun
l	r	m	n	ŋ	h
lip	red	me	neat	si<u>ng</u>	hat
f	v	θ	ð	s	z
fish	vest	<u>th</u>in	<u>th</u>e	see	zoo
š	ž	č	ǰ	y	w
ship	leisure	chew	judge	yes	win

PHONEMIC SYMBOLS: STANDARD BRITISH ENGLISH

ɪ bit	iː beat	ʌ bud	ɒ bob	ʊ book	uː boot
ə about	ɜː bird	e bed	æ bad	ɔː board	ɑː bard
ei bay	ai bike	iə beer	eə bare	ɔi box	
ʊə cure	əʊ boat	aʊ cow			
p pen	b ben	t tip	d dip	k cat	g gun
f fish	v vest	h hat	l lip	r red	w wed
m me	n neat	ŋ sing	j yes	θ thin	ð this
ʃ ship	tʃ chew	ʒ leisure	dʒ judge	s see	z zoo

Note that many of the tasks in this book have more than one possible answer. In these cases, only examples or the most common answers are featured in this key.

Chapter 2: Managing Your Classroom

Task 1: Giving instructions (page 21)

A. 1. What's this?
   2. Would you like to go to a restaurant with me?
   3. May I have a different one, please? This one is broken.
   4. Where was the man going?
   5. Write a conversation like this one, but use your own ideas. Help your partner.

B. 1. d, c, a, b
   2. c, b, a, d
   3. c, d, b, a

Task 2: Organizing learning relationships (page 24)

1. B1
2. B1/B2
3. B1
4. B2
5. B3

Chapter 3: Presenting Meaning and Context

Task 1: Teaching meaning (page 30)

to stroll (mime)
weary (facial expression)
a duck (mimic sounds)
in front of (use things in the classroom)
a can opener (objects/realia)
a truck (pictures/photographs)
a disaster (use an appropriate text such as a news report on a flood)

elbow (use yourself and the students)
miserable (facial expression)
to creep (mime)
a mountain (draw)
gaze (facial expression)

Task 2: Choosing contexts (page 32)
1. Your friend has just inherited a lot of money and wants to go buy a very expensive car.
2. Your friend is sick and doesn't know what to do.
3. Your roommate's parents are visiting your hometown. You want to entertain them.
4. What are you going to do after school is over?
5. A friend of a friend is going to stay at your apartment for the weekend and wants to know the rules.

Task 3: Checking lexical concepts (page 36)
More examples (the word that doesn't fit is underlined):

1.	baseball	tennis	<u>chess</u>	football	cricket
2.	car	<u>boat</u>	truck	bus	van
3.	jacket	vest	shirt	<u>jeans</u>	raincoat
4.	wool	linen	cotton	silk	<u>cloth</u>
5.	sister	mother	<u>uncle</u>	aunt	grandmother

Task 4: Checking structural concepts (page 37)
Sample concept questions for each structure:
1. Am I talking about the future, the past, or the present? *(the past)*
   Did she come? *(no)*
   Am I happy or sad about this situation? *(sad)*
2. Are they here? *(no)*
   Are you sure? *(yes)*
   Did you see them go out? *(no)*
3. Did I hurt you? *(yes)*
   Did I want to hurt you? *(no)*
   How do I feel now? *(sorry/apologetic)*
4. Do you smoke? *(yes)*
   Do I think it's a good idea? *(no)*
   Do I want you to smoke? *(no)*

5. Did we miss the plane? *(yes)*
   Did we get a taxi? *(no)*
   Why did we miss the plane? *(Because we didn't get a taxi.)*

Task 5: Checking functional concepts (page 37)
Sample questions:
1. Is this the first time I've seen you today? *(yes)*
   Am I being friendly? *(yes)*
   Do I want a long story about your day? *(no)*
2. Is something wrong? *(yes)*
   Have you seen a doctor? *(no)*
   Do you want to see a doctor? *(no)*
   Am I commanding or advising you to see a doctor? *(advising)*
3. Are you a friend or a stranger? *(a friend)*
   Do I believe you? *(yes)*
   Am I surprised? *(yes)*
4. Do I want to go? *(yes)*
   Do I want you to call me right away? *(no)*
5. Is it a good idea? *(no)*
   Do I want you to do it? *(no)*
   Am I commanding you not to do it? *(no)*

Chapter 4:
Teaching
Vocabulary

Task 1: Using antonyms (page 48)
1. John *bought* a sporty convertible from the automobile salesman.
2. The bank *lent* him $10,000.
3. Margaret is Bill's *aunt*.

Task 2: Understanding word meanings through affixation (page 50)
Check answers with a dictionary.

Task 3: Forming words (page xx)
A.   Chart

	Adjective	Adverb	Noun	Verb	Negative
a.	happy	happily	happiness	(no verb)	unhappy
b.	different	differently	difference	differentiate	indifferent[1]
c.	equal	equally	equality	equalize	unequal
d.	visible	visibly	visibility	(no verb)	invisible
e.	emphatic	emphatically	emphasis	emphasize	unemphatic
f.	sweet	sweetly	sweetness	sweeten	unsweetened
g.	economic[2] economical	economically	economy	economize	uneconomic uneconomical
h.	obedient	obediently	obedience	obey	disobedient
i.	false[3]	falsely	falsehood falsification	falsify	(no negative)
j.	attractive[4]	attractively	attraction attractiveness	attract	unattractive

[1] Note the meaning of the negative form *indifferent*. It does not mean *not different;* you will need to explain this meaning to students or have them look it up.

[2] Where there are two possible adjectives, there is a difference in meaning. *Economic* is used for large scale situations, as in "The country's *economic* growth is accelerating," and *economical* is used for smaller ones, as in "My car is very *economical.*"

[3] *Falsehood* is close in meaning to the concept of untruthfulness, but *falsification* denotes the act of *falsifying* or causing something to become untrue.

[4] *Attraction* is often used to describe an emotional feeling: "They felt a *mutual* attraction." *Attractiveness* refers to the abstract concept of being attractive.

B. Questions
1. Adverbs appear to be the easiest class of words to generalize. For regular adverbs (adverbs of manner) the suffix is almost always –ly.
2. There are four common verb endings used in the chart: -ate, -ize, -en, and –ify.
3. Adjectives show the greatest variety of form or lack of pattern.

Task 4: Teaching vocabulary (page 56)

A. taxi—cab, toilet—the john, residence—home, employer—boss, policeman—cop
B. a. Both can describe people, but the first is usually used for men, the second for women.
    b. Both can describe size, but the second is more often used to express a positive opinion, such as *a great man, a great idea,* or *a great party.*
    c. The difference between *tall* and *high* is that *tall* things are connected to the ground, whereas *high* things are not *(tall trees, high clouds).*
    d. Both are used to say that people or things are well known, but the first is used positively and the second negatively *(Al Pacino is a famous actor, but Al Capone was a notorious gangster).*
    e. Both describe jobs or positions in education, but a professor has a top job—usually the head of a department at a university.
C. All the words describe ways of walking (or moving, in the case of *crawl).* Their meanings are best illustrated by acting out the kind of movement (march like a soldier, limp across the classroom as if wounded, etc.).
D. The word *vehicle* is a cover term for all the other words.
E. c
F. Relationships between words:
    a. reciprocal/converse terms
    b. antonyms
    c. synonyms
    d. collocation
    e. derivative forms
    f. inclusive term with example
    g. reciprocal/converse terms

Chapter 5: Understanding Basic Grammar

Task 1: Understanding structural and lexical words (page 62)

☐   ☐

Twas <u>brillig</u>, and the <u>slithy</u> <u>toves</u>

      ☐

Did <u>gyre</u> and <u>gimble</u> in the <u>wabe</u>:

      ☐

All <u>mimsy</u> were the <u>borogroves</u>,

      ☐

And the <u>mome</u> <u>raths</u> <u>outgrabe</u>.

2. *Note:* Because *toves, gyre, wabe, mome,* and *raths* are words of only one syllable, syllable stress is irrelevant.

4. Carroll followed the normal syntactic or word order patterns of English because only by using the structural norms of English could he offer the reader the delight of making imaginary sense out of his nonsense. It is largely this syntactical element that distinguishes nonsense verse from meaningless gibberish.

Task 2: Understanding word classes (page 63)

A. Grammatical terms

               1   9 1

  a. They're sitting on the <u>grass</u> in <u>the</u> <u>park</u>.

          2   11

  b. He didn't <u>mean</u> <u>to hurt</u> you.

             10   3   1

  c. She was taken to <u>a</u> hospital in <u>critical</u> <u>condition</u>.

        8   5   4

  d. Take <u>my</u> car <u>but</u> drive <u>carefully</u>.

        4   4

  e. She works <u>hard</u> but doesn't earn <u>very</u> much.

           12   5   12

  f. There'll be dancing <u>in</u> the streets <u>and</u> singing <u>at</u> the bus stops!

  6   7

  g. <u>She</u> wanted to take a photograph of <u>him</u>.

           11

  h. They stopped <u>to have</u> a drink.

B. Word class identification

brillig: adjective or noun	toves: noun
slithy: adjective	gyre: verb

gimble: verb

mome: adjective

wabe: noun

raths: noun

mimsy: adjective

outgrabe: adjective or verb

borogroves: noun

The clues are in the common syntactical patterns, or word order (determiner + adjective + noun) and in the spelling and sounds of the individual words themselves. Thus it would be reasonable to interpret *the slithy toves* as, for example, *the slimy toads.*

Task 3: Understanding function (page 65)

1. request
2. greeting
3. request
4. introduction
5. signaling an intention to leave or indicating disbelief
6. questioning or expressing surprise
7. polite invitation
8. offer
9. request
10. seeking an explanation for a refusal to a request

Structures for the function *giving advice:*

Why don't you … ?

Why not … ?

How/What about … ?

You should …

You'd better …

If I were you, I'd …

Have you thought of … ?

It might be an idea to …

Task 4: Understanding modals and their meanings (page 68)

A. Modal meanings

   1 a. *Should* is used for giving advice.

   1 b. *Should* is used to express probability.

   2 a. *Can* is used to ask for and to give permission in informal situations.

   2 b. *Can* is used to talk about ability.

3 a. *May* is used to express probability.

3 b. *May* is used to ask for or to give permission in formal situations.

4 a. *Must* is used to express strong personal obligation.

4 b. *Must* is used to express certainty or inference.

5 a. *Could* is used to ask for permission politely (similar to *may* in 3b above).

5 b. *Could* is used to talk about ability in the past.

B. Modals and functions (example sentences)

Can

ability: *Can* you swim?

permission: *Can* I leave early today?

request or polite order: *Can* you open the window?

possibility: That dog *can* be dangerous! (The dog is sometimes dangerous.)

prohibition: You can't smoke in here.

Could

request: *Could* you open the window?

suggestion: You *could* see a doctor.

possibility: It *could* rain this afternoon.

past ability: I *could* swim when I was five.

permission in the past: You *could* have used my car. I didn't need it.

Must/mustn't

obligation: You *must* arrive on time for lessons.

deduction or inference: She *must* be rich.

prohibition: You *mustn't* eat in the classroom.

Needn't

absence of obligation: You *needn't* apologize.

Ought to

advice: You *ought to* see a doctor.

probability: She *ought to* be here soon.

May

probability/possibility (future): It *may* rain this afternoon.

permission (formal, very polite): You *may* sit down.

Might

permission (very polite): *Might* I sit here?

possibility: It *might* rain this afternoon.

suggestion: You *might* try seeing a doctor.

Should

advice: You *should* see a doctor.

moral obligation: You *should* be kind to your parents.

probability: She *should* be here soon.

attributing blame or criticism: You *should* have told me!

Would

request: *Would* you open the window?

habit/characteristic behavior (past): When I was a child, my father *would* read to me at bedtime.

complaining: I wish it *would* stop raining!

conditional use: If I had enough time and money, I *would* travel around the world.

Task 5: Understanding the simple present (page 71)

1. c
2. d
3. e
4. b
5. h
6. a
7. f
8. g

Task 6: Understanding the present continuous (page 71)

A. All three present continuous forms describe actions (or weather) that are going on at the moment of speaking.

B. 1. *enjoy* (simple present)/*am not enjoying* (present continuous)

2. *am learning/is teaching* (present continuous in both cases)

3. *smokes* (simple present)/*isn't smoking* (present continuous)

Task 7: Understanding the present perfect and present perfect continuous (page 73)

A. *For* is followed by a word or phrase which indicates a period of time: "They have lived there *for* ages (six months, ten years, etc.); I was there *for* five minutes." *Since* is followed by a word or phrase that indicates a point in time: They have lived there *since* 1997 (June, I was born, etc.).

B. Differences in meaning
   1. a. The continuous form is used here because the focus is on a recent activity which is probably unfinished. In this example, there are still some chocolates left in the box.
      b. The simple form is used here because the focus is on a recently completed activity. In this example, there are no chocolates left in the box.
   2. a. The continuous form is used here to indicate an unfinished activity. In this example, it started snowing an hour ago and it is still snowing now.
      b. The continuous form is used here to indicate a recently finished activity for which there is present evidence. In this example, the person can see snow on the ground, so he or she draws a conclusion about the recent past.
   3. a. The simple form is used here to indicate a completed past action with no specific time reference.
      b. In this example, the boss started speaking to Pat over an hour ago and is still speaking to her now. See 2a above.

Task 8: Adverbs and the present perfect tenses (page 74)

A. Questions
   1. Yes, I have been twice recently./No, I haven't gone recently.
   2. Yes, I have./No, I never have.
   3. Yes, I have just gotten out of the tub./No, I haven't. I took one this morning.
B. The simple past tense is used with expressions like *ago, yesterday*, and *last week*.
   1. We *saw* that film a month ago.
   2. I *went* to the beach last weekend.

Task 9: Use of the simple past (page 75)

The following sentence numbers refer to past time: 1, 2, 4, 7, and 8.

Task 10: Simple past contrasted with present perfect (page 75)

1. a. The problem still exists.
   b. The problem has been solved.
2. a. I'm still waiting, or you've just arrived.
   b. I stopped waiting and went elsewhere.

3. a. The exhibit is still on; you have the opportunity to see it.

   b. The exhibit is over; you no longer have the opportunity to see it.

4. a. This question is asking if you've been to Yosemite at any time in your life.

   b. This question assumes that you went to Yosemite for an understood period of time.

Task 11: Using the past continuous (page 76)

Possible questions:

1. What were you doing at 8:00 o'clock yesterday evening?
2. What was Joan doing while you were fixing the car?
3. Where were you living when you got married?
4. What were you doing between 7:00 and 8:00 yesterday evening?
5. What were you doing when you first met David?

Task 12: Using the past perfect continuous (page 77)

1. When the firemen got there, the fire had been burning for two hours.
2. After she had been working there for ten years, they gave her a raise.
3. When the car broke down, they had been traveling for eight hours./After they had been traveling for eight hours, the car broke down.
4. Although the child star of *The Piano* had only been acting for six months, she won an Oscar.
5. When we got to the party, they had been dancing for hours.

Task 13: Using the past tenses (page 78)

1. Acceptable, but only in a context where there is a regularly occurring annoyance: "My boss never tells me in advance when an important client is coming. I wish I knew about it in time!" However, to make a wish about the past, use *wish* + past perfect as in the sentence, "I wish I had known about it in time."
2. Unacceptable. The present perfect tense is not used with *last week*. This sentence should be: "They were here last week."
3. Unacceptable. To indicate the period before Giovanni took the TOEFL exam, use the past perfect tense: "Giovanni had been in America for several months when he took the TOEFL exam."

4. Acceptable, but only as the introductory background to a continuing story. As a statement on its own, it sounds odd because *when I was a child* is not an interruption. "I lived in the country when I was a child" is the more usual form.

5. Acceptable, but only if she is a masochist! To show that the cut to her finger was a single (and, in this case, accidental) event, we use the simple form: "She had (already) cut her finger when I arrived."

6. Unacceptable. Use *used to* + infinitive when the precise time period is unknown and/or unstated. In the case of this sentence, use the simple past: "He lived here for four years."

7. Unacceptable. Use the form *was going to do* to indicate an intended action that didn't actually happen, which doesn't make sense here. In this case, use the simple past: "I went to see my teacher yesterday, and he was satisfied with my work."

8. Unacceptable. Don't state a specific time period with an interrupted past activity. The correct statement should be: "She was watching TV when the phone rang."

9. Unacceptable. There is a logical time problem here, so this is better expressed as "Sharon was going into the bar when I last saw her."

10. Acceptable, but like number 4 above, it should only be used as introductory background to a continuing story. Otherwise, it sounds odd on its own because there is no interruption. In this case, "As I drove to work, I listened to the radio" is the more usual form.

Task 14: *Understanding the passive (page 79)*

A. Questions

1. The other languages are expressed in the impersonal active form: "One speaks English." The English sentence is in the passive.

2. The passive is used in scientific reports because the agent or performer of the action is irrelevant (for example, "The water was heated to the boiling point"). The passive is used in newspaper headlines because the subject is often more important than the agent, and the meaning can be conveyed

more succinctly in the passive form. For example, *President Assassinated* is shorter than *Someone has assassinated the President.* The passive form is used by diplomats and politicians because it is more formal. Also see the answer to question number 4 below.

3. The passive is less common in colloquial speech because people do not want to sound too formal and stuffy.

4. When people want to avoid explicitly admitting responsibility, they use the passive. For example, "Income tax has been increased" is safer for a politician to declare than "I have increased income tax." A person who doesn't want to be blamed for a mistake will say, "A mistake has been made." As a general guideline, the active form is used in informal situations and the passive form in more formal ones.

B. Matching
   1. b
   2. c
   3. d
   4. e
   5. a

C. Passive sentences
   1. This is an acceptable passive sentence and does not present a problem in transforming from the active.
   2. This sentence is not well chosen for passive transformation because it could be transformed into more than one passive sentence: "The house was shown to us," or "We were shown the house."
   3. This sentence is not well chosen for passive transformation because it contains a *prepositional verb (break into)* and the word order is tricky for students. A better sentence is: "Our apartment was broken into last night."
   4. This one was well chosen. The passive transformation, "That mountain has never been climbed," presents few problems.
   5. This sentence is not well chosen for passive transformation. You wouldn't naturally say, "The vacation is being looked

forward to by us."

6. This sentence is not well chosen for passive transformation. You wouldn't naturally say, "The moon was jumped over by the cow."

D. The text

Malcolm X Widow Badly Burned in Fire
'Started by Grandson'

Dr. Betty Shabazz, the widow of civil rights leader, Malcolm X, was in critical condition in a hospital in the Bronx last night. Most of her skin <u>had been burned</u> in a fire at her apartment which police say <u>was started</u> by her grandson. Shortly after the fire <u>was reported</u>, the 12-year-old boy <u>was found</u> wandering the streets nearby in a daze, his clothes smelling strongly of gasoline. The boy, Malcolm, who had been in his grandmother's care, was missing from her apartment when the firefighters arrived. According to the police, the boy seemed angry because he <u>had been forced</u> to live with his grandmother.

Malcolm is the son of Qubilah, Malcolm X's daughter, who <u>was indicted</u> on charges of plotting to kill Louis Farrakhan, the leader of the Nation of Islam, in January, 1995. Farrakhan <u>had been accused</u> by Betty Shabazz of taking part in the assassination of Malcolm X in 1965. Qubilah saw her father <u>being killed</u> in a ballroom in Washington Heights when she was only four years old. When her indictment <u>was dismissed</u> last month, she moved to Texas, but her son, Malcolm, <u>was sent</u> to live with his grandmother in New York.

Detectives said yesterday that the boy <u>had been taken</u> into custody and <u>will be tried</u> as a juvenile in Family Court. According to police reports, Malcolm drenched the hallway of his grandmother's three-bedroom apartment with gasoline and waited until she arrived before setting fire to it. Firefighters found Dr. Shabazz lying outside her apartment on the hallway floor. "She <u>had been</u> severely <u>burned</u>, but was conscious enough to tell us that someone else had been in the apartment with her."

It <u>was announced</u> today that Betty Shabazz had died of her burns. The news left friends of the family shocked and unable to believe what has happened. President Clinton said, "Dr. Betty Shabazz devoted a long career to education and helping deprived women and children."

had been burned *(past perfect)*

was started *(simple past)*

was reported *(simple past)*

was found *(simple past)*

had been forced *(past perfect)*

was indicted *(simple past)*

had been accused *(past perfect)*

being killed *(past continuous)*

was dismissed *(simple past)*

was sent *(simple past)*

had been taken *(past perfect)*

will be tried *(simple future)*

had been burned *(past perfect)*

was announced *(simple past)*

Task 15: Verbs followed by an infinitive or the verb + –ing (page 83)

A. Sentence differences

1. The first question is general. The second question is an invitation to do it now.

2. The first sentence means "I gave up smoking." The second sentence means "I stopped some other activity in order to smoke a cigarette." The verb *stop* is normally followed by the *-ing* form.

3. The first sentence means "I now recall doing the action (leaving) in the past." The second sentence means "I didn't forget to perform the action. I remembered, and then I did it."

4. No difference in meaning.

5. The first sentence is a formal way of telling someone now that his or her application has been rejected. The second sentence is an apology for misinforming someone in a previous letter that he or she had been unsuccessful.

B. Sentence corrections
1. "I'm not *used to eating* such a large breakfast." *Be used to* is followed by the *verb + ing* because *to* is a preposition here.
2. "I'm looking forward *to meeting* you." *To* is a preposition (not part of an infinitive) so it must be followed by *verb + ing* form.
3. "I enjoyed *seeing it very much*." *Enjoy* is always followed by a noun or, as in the sentence, *verb + ing* form.
4. "I'm not interested *in going* to baseball games." *In* is a preposition and is followed by a noun or *verb + ing*.
5. "I object *to having* to work so late." *To* after *object* is a preposition and therefore has to be followed by the *verb + ing (having)*, not by the infinitive *(to have)*.

C. Verb forms
1. doing
2. doing
3. spending
4. watching
5. to meet
6. to send
7. going
8. to eat

Task 16: Understanding future expressions (page 85)

A. Charts

Situation number	Form	Function
1.	should	make a suggestion
2.	will	make a decision at the time of speaking
3.	are going to	planned future
4 a.	will need (or simple present)	first conditional
4 b.	will (or simple present)	scheduled future time
5.	no verb needed (we need)	urgency
6 a.	present continuous	arranged future
6 b.	will (is going to be)	future based on current evidence

7.	will be flying (future continuous)	event occurring around a future point in time
8 a.	won't	negative promise
8 b.	will	positive promise

B. Correcting sentences
1. I feel awful. I think *I'm going* to faint.
2. I don't like the idea, but *I'll give* him the keys if you insist.
3. She hasn't studied very much, but I expect *she'll pass* the exam.
4. I listened to the weather forecast today. They say *it'll rain* (or *it's going to rain*) tomorrow.
5. I'm sorry but I won't *be coming* to class tomorrow.
6. 'Bye, *I'll see* you tomorrow.
7. I have an appointment at the dentist's. *I'm going* this afternoon.
8. My plane leaves San Francisco for Denver at 7:00 a.m., so at about 8:30 a.m., *I'll be flying* over the Rockies.
9. I'm sorry I can't go to the movies because *I'm having* a party tonight.
10. Don't be late! The train *leaves* at 6:30 a.m.

Task 17: Understanding conditional sentences (page 89)

A. In sentence 1, the speaker thinks it's likely you'll come in July and meet his or her sister. In sentence 2, the speaker does not think you'll come and so you're not likely to meet his or her sister.
B. The first sentence
C. The second sentence
D. Matching

1. l	5. h	9. j	
2. f	6. e	10. b	
3. i	7. k	11. g	
4. c	8. d	12. a	

E. Reversing the order of the clauses does not affect the meaning significantly, although there may be some change in emphasis.

F. Grouping
    Group 1: Sentence numbers 1, 2, 3, 4, and 11 are first conditionals
    (future conditionals).
    Group 2: Sentence numbers 5, 6, 7, and 8 are second conditionals
    (would conditionals).
    Group 3: Sentence numbers 9, 10, and 12 are third conditionals
    (would have conditionals).

G. Functions
    Threatening or warning: 3, 4, 11
    Expressing regret: 9, 12
    Giving advice: 4, 6
    Blaming: 10
    Offering: 1, 2
    Imagining: 7, 8

H. Functions
    1. predicting
    2. asking for permission
    3. requesting
    4. expressing regret
    5. requesting

Task 18: Understanding other conditional sentence patterns (page 91)

A. The chart
    1. Making a bargain or deal
    2. Giving formal advice or a warning
    3. Past perfect/would + infinitive
    4. If you want the bread to keep, put it in the freezer. (example
    sentence)

B. Verb forms
    1. have finished or finish
    2. calls or should call
    3. invited
    4. you'll peel/I'll slice or you peel/I'll slice
    5. did or would do
    6. you've filled in
    7. it'll taste or it tastes
    8. had won

9. will be/come or would be/came or would be/would come
10. it'll look

Chapter 6: Teaching Pronunciation

Task 1: Practicing phonemic transcription (page 102)

A. Matching

1. Thomas /t/
2. jump /ǰ/
3. sugar /š/
4. those /ð/
5. contract /k/
6. united /y/
7. physique /f/
8. pneumonia /n/
9. enough /ɪ/
10. thank /θ/

B. Matching

1. cowboy /oy/
2. thumb /m/
3. watched /t/
4. wealth /θ/
5. bags /z/
6. weigh /ey/

C. Matching

1. puff /pʌf/
2. pole /powl/
3. palm /pam/
4. put /pʊt/
5. pool /puwl/

Task 2: Transcribing vowel sounds (page 103)

1. /æ/
2. /ɛ/
3. /ɪ/
4. /a/
5. /ʌ/
6. /ər/
7. /ar/
8. /ɔr/
9. /ʊ/
10. /uw/

Task 3: Transcribing diphthongs (page 103)

1. /neym/
2. /taym/
3. /nowt/
4. /noyz/
5. /naw/

Task 4: Working with vowel sounds and diphthongs (page 104)
1. red /ɛ/
2. blue /uw/
3. white /ay/
4. grey /ey/
5. green /iy/
6. gold /ow/

Task 5: Practicing pronunciation of vowel sounds (page 104)
For all three questions, the vowel is pronounced with the schwa sound, /ə/.

Task 6: Understanding the sounds of the past tense –ed (page 104)
A. Chart
1. asked /t/
2. skated /ɪd/
3. watched /t/
4. posted /ɪd/
5. laughed /t/
6. refused /d/
7. missed /t/
8. stayed /d/
9. bored /d/
10. mended /ɪd/

B. The rules
1. /ɪd/
2. /t/
3. /d/

Task 7: Awareness of stress (page 110)
A. Stressed syllables
1. inter<u>na</u>tional
2. re<u>vi</u>sion
3. edu<u>ca</u>tion
4. examin<u>a</u>tion
5. consti<u>tu</u>tion
6. revo<u>lu</u>tion
7. computeriz<u>a</u>tion

B. Stressed vowels

1. dem<u>o</u>crat	demo<u>cra</u>tic	dem<u>o</u>cracy
2. <u>pho</u>tograph	photo<u>gra</u>phic	pho<u>to</u>graphy
3. <u>e</u>ducate	edu<u>ca</u>tion	edu<u>ca</u>tional
4. <u>te</u>legram	tele<u>gra</u>phic	te<u>le</u>graphy
5. <u>in</u>tellect	in<u>te</u>lligence	intel<u>lec</u>tual

C. Change in stress

1. a <u>di</u>gest	to di<u>gest</u>
2. an <u>ac</u>cent	to ac<u>cent</u>
3. a <u>con</u>tract	to con<u>tract</u>
4. a <u>per</u>mit	to per<u>mit</u>
5. the <u>pro</u>duce	to pro<u>duce</u>
6. the <u>de</u>sert	to de<u>sert</u>

Pattern: the nouns have the *first* syllable stressed; the verbs have the stress on the *second* syllable.

Task 8: Noticing stress: words in sentences (page 111)
No answers needed.

Task 9: Practicing contrastive stress (page 111)
1. North
2. red
3. two

Task 10: Understanding rhythm and intonation (page 114)

A. Fine

Yes

Oh

B. Who

When

Where

Task 11: Understanding catenation (page 116)
1. want to = /wɔnə/
2. did you = /dɪǰə/
3. did you = /diǰə/
4. did they = /dɪðey/
5. can't you = /kænčə/
6. did he = /dɪdiy/

Chapter 7: Teaching Listening

Task 1: Staging a listening skills lesson (page 126)
The correct order of the stages is as follows:
b, d, i, a, e, h, g, j, c, e, h, g, f

Task 2: Understanding the purposes of the stages (page 127)

1. i	3. d	5. e	7. h
2. f	4. b	6. g	8. j

Chapter 8: Teaching Speaking

Task 1: Ways of eliciting (page 140)
A. Vocabulary
1. to jog *(mime)*
2. to feed someone *(picture of a mother feeding a baby; ask questions like "What is the mother doing?")*
3. jealous *(show a movie/TV clip of someone seeing their boy/girlfriend kissing someone else; ask students how they would feel)*
4. a refund *(describe a situation: for example, "I buy a jacket from a clothing store. When I get home I find a hole in it. I go back to the store because I want my money back. What do I ask for?")*
5. above and below *(demonstrate with objects in the classroom; give instructions like "Hold your hand above your head.")*
6. bald *(definition: "What do we call a person with no hair?")*
7. a banana *(realia/picture)*
8. depressed *(use synonyms: sad, not happy, etc.)*
9. a costume *(use realia or visual aids like Halloween pictures)*
10. a lion *(mime/gestures: roar like a lion!)*

B. Functions
   1. an apology (*I'm late for class. What do I say?*)
   2. a warning (*I smoke sixty cigarettes a day. What do you say to me?*)
   3. congratulating someone (*I'm getting married tomorrow! What do you say?*)

Chapter 10:
Teaching
Writing

Scrambled sequences (page 184)
Unscrambled version of the story:
It was a bitterly cold day in Chicago. Detectives Ryan and Schwarz were outside the Lake Motel. They were watching a man getting out of a black Mercedes. The man was carrying an overnight bag that seemed unusually heavy. Was the murder weapon in the bag? The two detectives looked at each other. Schwarz said, "Could this be the guy we have been looking for?"

Chapter 11:
Correcting
Errors

Task 1: False cognates (page 200)
A. Translations
   French
   passer un examen (to take an exam)
   librairie (bookshop)
   furieux (furious)
   sensible (sensitive)
   histoire (story)
   eventuellement (possibly)
   German
   singen (to sing)
   sympatisch (likeable/nice)
   aktuell (current/topical)
   menu (selection on a computer)
   werk (factory or work of an artist)
   bekommen (to get/obtain)

Italian

    coincidenza (link/connection)

    sensibile (sensitive)

    controllare (to check/verify)

    straniero (foreigner)

    assistare (attend)

    di fronte a (opposite)

Spanish

    embarazada (pregnant)

    professor (teacher)

    constipado (to have a cold)

    contenta (pleased)

    padres (parents)

    avisar (to inform/tell)

B. Sentences

1. We don't know because *great* is often misused to mean large.
2. The speaker stopped traffic! (In French, *circulation* refers to the movement of traffic.)
3. No, the speaker shouted. (In French *crier* means to shout.)
4. The speaker thinks that *suburbs* are slums or poor districts on the outskirts of big cities. (In Spanish, *suburbi* means slums.)
5. The speaker wanted to ask, "Can I use your toilet?" (This is a Japanese mis-translation of *borrow* for *use.)*
6. No, the speaker should have used *diary* or *appointment book.*

Task 2: Correcting various errors (page 202)

1. She <u>lives in</u> Boston in a small apartment.
2. I <u>saw</u> that film yesterday.
3. I <u>want to</u> be a <u>teacher</u> in a school.
4. I have stopped <u>playing</u> football because of the injury to my leg.
5. I'd like you <u>to help</u> me.
6. They are very <u>excited</u> about seeing Switzerland.
7. Student: I <u>come</u> from Germany.
8. He was a man who <u>robbed</u> (or <u>stole from</u>) old ladies.
9. My mother is a good <u>cook</u>.
10. She's beautiful, isn't <u>she</u>?

Task 3: Making corrections in writing (page 206)
Version with correction marks:

> Dear Alan,
>
> Thank you for your invitation that I <u>have received</u> ᵀ today.
>
> I <u>enjoy myself</u> **ww** and accept the invitation, but I'm <u>afraid</u> **ww**
>
> because I don't know <u>very well</u> **wo** the people who are invited
>
> to the party. I would like to know if <u>I have the possibility</u> **!**
>
> of bringing a friend, he is ˄very <u>kindly</u> **ww**, charming boy. I
>
> <u>know</u> ᵀ him <u>since</u> **prep.** ten years. My problem is that I don't
>
> know if I must put on a <u>dress</u> **ww** could you tell me? At what
>
> time the <u>party starts</u> **G**? <u>Please not too late</u> **!** because I must
>
> come on <u>feet</u> **ww** and the party is so far ˄the house. I'm looking
>
> forward to <u>see</u> **G** you Saturday night.
>
> <u>Bye Bye,</u> **ww**
>
> Mario

Corrected Version:

> Dear Alan,
>
> Thank you for your invitation, which I received today. I am happy to accept the invitation, but I'm a bit nervous because I don't know the people who are invited to the party very well.
>
> I'd like to know if I could bring a friend. He is a very nice, charming boy. I have known him for ten years.
>
> My problem is that I don't know if I should wear a suit. Could you let me know?
>
> At what time does the party start? I hope it isn't too late because I must come on foot and the party is so far from my house.
>
> I'm looking forward to seeing you on Saturday night.
>
> Yours,
>
> Mario

Task 4: Making corrections (page 207)

Suggestions (there are other ways):

1. Indicate that *tennis table* should be *table tennis* with a gesture to change the words around.
2. Use your fingers to indicate that there should be six words, but that the third word (*to*) should be removed, and a word (*the* or *a*) must be inserted between *to* and *dentist*.
3. Put up four fingers and indicate a problem with the second word, *talk*.
4. Put up five fingers, bend the middle finger to show removal of *the*, and then cross fingers to show a change in word order from *hair blond* to *blond hair*.
5. Use arrows to indicate that the second word (*see*) is wrong and should be *saw*.

Chapter 12:
Teaching with
Visual Aids

Task 1: Using the board (page 215)

A. Answers vary.

B. 1.

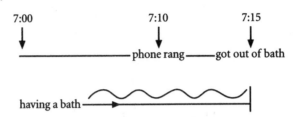

2.

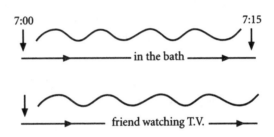

Task 2: Using visual aids (page 216)

A. Matching
    1. i, j
    2. c, d
    3. a, f, g
    4. e
    5. b, f, h
    6. i, j

B. Visual types
    1. A photo of someone smoking a cigarette (He *used to* smoke.)
    2. Cans of different soft drinks, etc.
    3. A video clip of a situation showing someone complaining (such as an angry customer speaking to the manager of a restaurant)
    4. Pictures of sick people/a photo of a doctor and patient
    5. Objects like cups and glasses/quantities of liquid in bottles or jars/containers of salt or sugar

Chapter 15:
Teaching with
Songs

Task 1: Choosing and using songs (page 263)
The number of each song is followed by the level and letter of language activity it could be used for. These are only suggestions!

1. I, c	6. E, f
2. I, e	7. HI, a
3. E, h	8. I, j
4. E, b	9. I, i
5. I, g	10. I, d

Song 2: My Way (page 267)
The real words to each verse (these replace the words in bold in the text):
First verse: near, final, that's full, each and every highway
Second verse: Regrets, mention, saw it through, careful
Third verse: times, through, faced

Song 3: You are Not Alone (page 268)
The correct words are **in bold:**

Another day has **gone.**
I am still all **alone.**
How could this be?
You're not **here** with me?

You never said **good-bye.**
Someone tell me **why.**
Did you have to **go?**
And leave my world so **cold?**

Chorus
Everyday I sit and **ask** myself,
How did it slip away?
Something whispers in my **ear** and says . . .

You are not alone.
I am **here** with you.
Though you're **far** away,
I am here to **stay.**

You are not alone.
I am **here** with you.
Though we're **far** apart,
You're always in my **heart.**

Just the other **night,**
I thought I heard you **cry,**
Asking me to go,
And hold you in my **arms.**

I can **hear** your prayers,
Your burdens I will bear,
But first I **need** you here,
Then forever can begin.

Repeated chorus
Whisper **three** words then I'll come **running.**
And girl you **know** that I'll be there.

Chapter 17:
Testing

Answers to the cloze text, Inventor of the Future, *pages 290–291.*

1.	to	15.	was
2.	age	16.	it
3.	not	17.	the
4.	many	18.	so
5.	modern	19.	use
6.	for	20.	inventions
7.	today	21.	been
8.	that	22.	was
9.	99%	23.	by
10.	for	24.	when
11.	time	25.	the
12.	had	26.	who
13.	own	27.	electric
14.	made